MODERN MAN

IN SEARCH OF

A SOUL

BY

C. G. JUNG

AUTHOR OF

"PSYCHOLOGICAL TYPES", "THE PSYCHOLOGY OF THE UNCONSCIOUS"
"CONTRIBUTIONS TO ANALYTICAL PSYCHOLOGY", ETC.

ROUTLEDGE & KEGAN PAUL LTD
BROADWAY HOUSE: 68–74 CARTER LANE
LONDON, EC4V 5EL

First published 1933
Reprinted twelve times
Published as a Routledge paperback 1961
by Routledge & Kegan Paul Ltd
Broadway House, 68–74 Carter Lane
London, EC4V 5EL

Printed in Great Britain by
Redwood Press Limited
Trowbridge, Wiltshire

Reprinted 1962
Reprinted 1966
Reprinted 1970
Reprinted 1973

Translated by
W. S. DELL
AND
CARY F. BAYNES

ISBN 0 7100 1629 8 (c)
ISBN 0 7100 4614 6 (p)

CONTENTS

TRANSLATORS' PREFACE

WITHIN the last decade there have been many references from varied sources to the fact that the western world stands on the verge of a spiritual rebirth, that is, a fundamental change of attitude toward the values of life. After a long period of outward expansion, we are beginning to look within ourselves once more. There is very general agreement as to the phenomena surrounding this increasing shift of interest from facts as such to their meaning and value to us as individuals, but as soon as we begin to analyse the anticipations nursed by the various groups in our world with respect to the change that is to be hoped for, agreement is at an end and a sharp conflict of forces makes itself felt.

By those who uphold revealed religion, the rebirth that seems imminent is thought of as a renaissance of Catholicism or Protestantism, as the case may be. They see mankind streaming by the million back to the bosom of the Church, there to be comforted for the disillusionments and disasters of our post-war world, there to be taught the paths that will lead out of chaos. Renewal of faith in Christianity, they say, will bring us back to a sure way of life and restore the inspiration the world has lost.

Another great group of people think that the new attitude is to be attained by the total destruction of religion as it has up to now been understood. Religion is, they say, a relic of superstitious barbarism, and in its place must come a new and lasting period of "enlightenment". Let man but apply his knowledge in the right way, especially his knowledge of economics and technology, and all the great bogies of poverty, ignorance, greed, etc., will vanish into thin air and man will be restored to his lost paradise. To them the rebirth is to be in the realm of reason alone, and the intellect becomes the arbiter of man's fate.

Between these two extremes of traditional faith and militant rationalism, every conceivable shade of opinion about this great problem of humanity's next step in psychic evolution is to be found. It may be said that the middle position is held by those people who know that they have outgrown the Church as exemplified in Christianity, but who have not therefore been brought to deny the fact that a religious attitude to life is as essential to them as a belief in the authenticity of science. These people have experienced the soul as vividly as the body, the body as vividly as the soul. And the soul has manifested itself to them in ways not to be explained in terms either of traditional theology or of materialism. They do not wish to sever the real piety they feel within themselves from the body of scientific fact to which reason gives its sanction. They are convinced that if they can attain to more knowledge of the inner workings of their own minds, more information about the subtle but none the less perfectly definite laws that govern the psyche, they can achieve the new attitude that is demanded without having on the one hand to regress to what is but a thinly veiled mediæval theology, or on the other, to fall victims to the illusions of nineteenth-century ideology.

It is to this last group of people that Jung speaks in convincing terms. He does not evade the difficult task of synthesizing his knowledge of the soul, gained in his many years of practice as psychiatrist and analyst, into a fund of information available and applicable to everyone. He gives those clues to the nature and functioning of the psyche for which the modern man is painfully groping. The point of view he lays before us is a challenge to the spirit, and evokes an active response in everyone who has felt within himself an urge to grow beyond his inheritance.

.   .   .   .   .

With one exception,[1] all the essays which make up this volume have been delivered as lectures. The German texts of four of them have been brought out in separate publications [2] and the others are to be found in a volume [3] together with several other essays which have already appeared in English.

We are indebted to Mrs. Violet de Laszlo for many helpful suggestions in regard to the essay, *Psychotherapists or the Clergy*. Both Dr. Jung and Mrs. Jung have been kind enough to read and criticize the translations in part.

CARY F. BAYNES.

ZÜRICH, *March* 1933.

---

[1] *Freud and Jung—Contrasts*, was written at the special request of a German editor.

[2] (a) For the German text of *Psychology and Literature* (*Psychologie und die Literaturwissenschaft*) see *Die Philosophie der Literaturwissenschaft*, by Professor Emil Ermatinger, Junker und Dünnhaut, Berlin, 1929. An English translation by Eugene Jolas appeared in *Transition*, 1930.

(b) *Psychotherapists or the Clergy—A Dilemma* is in German entitled : *Die Beziehungen der Psychotherapie zur Seelsorge*, Rascher & Cie, Zürich, 1932.

(c) *The Basic Postulates of Analytical Psychology* appeared in the *Europäische Revue* for July 1931, under the title, *Die Entschleierung der Seele*.

(d) *Dream Analysis In Its Practical Application* appears in the *Bericht über den VI Allgemeinen ärtzlichen Kongress für Psychotherapie*, Dresden, April 1930.

[3] *Seelenprobleme der Gegenwart*, Rascher & Cie, Zürich, 1931.

MODERN MAN
IN SEARCH OF A SOUL

I

DREAM-ANALYSIS IN ITS PRACTICAL
APPLICATION

THE use of dream-analysis in psychotherapy is still a
much-debated question. Many practitioners find it indispensable in the treatment of neuroses, and ascribe as much
importance to the psychic activity manifested in dreams
as to consciousness itself. Others, on the contrary, dispute
the value of dream-analysis, and regard dreams as a negligible
by-product of the psyche.

Obviously, if a person holds the view that the unconscious
plays a leading rôle in the formation of neuroses, he will
attribute practical significance to dreams as direct expressions of the unconscious. If, on the other hand, he
denies the unconscious or thinks that it has no part in the
development of neuroses, he will minimize the importance
of dream-analysis. It is regrettable that in this year of
grace 1931, more than half a century since Carus formulated
the concept of the unconscious, over a century since Kant
spoke of the " immeasurable . . . field of obscure ideas ",
and nearly two hundred years since Leibniz postulated an

I

unconscious psychic activity, not to mention the achievements of Janet, Flournoy and Freud—that after all this, the actuality of the unconscious should still be a matter for controversy. Since it is my intention to deal exclusively with questions of practical treatment, I will not attempt in this place a defence of the hypothesis of the unconscious, though it is obvious enough that dream-analysis stands or falls with this hypothesis. Without it the dream appears to be merely a freak of nature, a meaningless conglomerate of memory-fragments left over from the happenings of the day. Were the dream nothing more than this, there would be no excuse for the present discussion. We must recognize the unconscious if we are to treat of dream-analysis at all, for we do not resort to it as a mere exercise of the wits, but as a method for uncovering hitherto unconscious psychic contents which are causally related to the neurosis and therefore of importance in its treatment. Anyone who deems this hypothesis unacceptable must simply rule out the question of the practicability of dream-analysis.

But since, according to our hypothesis, the unconscious plays a causal part in the neurosis, and since dreams are the direct expression of unconscious psychic activity, the attempt to analyse and interpret dreams is entirely justified from a scientific standpoint. Quite apart from therapeutic results, we may expect this line of endeavour to give us scientific insight into psychic causality. For the practitioner, however, scientific discoveries can at most be a gratifying by-product of his efforts in the field of therapy. He will not feel called upon to apply dream-analysis to his patients on the chance that it may throw light upon the problem of psychic causality. He may believe, of course, that the insight so gained is of therapeutic value—in which case he will regard dream-analysis as one of his professional duties. It is well known that the Freudian school is of the opinion that important therapeutic effects are achieved by throwing light upon the unconscious causal factors— that is, by explaining them to the patient and thus making him conscious of the sources of his trouble.

If we assume, for the time being, that this expectation is borne out by the facts, we can restrict ourselves to the questions whether or not dream-analysis enables us to discover the unconscious causes of the neurosis, and whether it can do this unaided, or must be used in conjunction with other methods. The Freudian answer, I may assume, is common knowledge. My own experience confirms this view inasmuch as I have found that dreams not infrequently bring to light in an unmistakable way the unconscious contents that are causal factors in a neurosis. Most often it is the initial dreams that do this—-I mean, those dreams that a patient reports at the very outset of a treatment. An illustration will perhaps be helpful.

I was consulted by a man who held a prominent position in the world. He was afflicted with a sense of anxiety and insecurity, and complained of dizziness sometimes resulting in nausea, of a heavy head and difficulty in breathing—this being an exact description of the symptoms of mountain-sickness. He had had an unusually successful career, and had risen, with the help of ambition, industry and native talent, from a humble origin as the son of a poor peasant. Step by step he had climbed, attaining at last an important post that offered him every opportunity for further social advancement. He had actually reached a place in life from which he could have begun his ascent into the upper regions, when suddenly his neurosis intervened. At this

point of his story the patient could not refrain from that
stereotyped exclamation which begins with the familiar
words : " And just now, when I . . ." The fact that he
had all the symptoms of mountain-sickness was highly
appropriate to the peculiar situation in which he found
himself. He had brought with him to the consultation two
dreams of the preceding night.

The first dream was as follows : " I am once more in
the small village where I was born. Some peasant boys
who went to school with me are standing together in the
street. I walk past them, pretending not to know them. I
hear one of them, who is pointing at me, say : ' He doesn't
often come back to our village.' " No tricks of interpretation
are needed to recognize and to understand the allusion to
the humble beginnings of the dreamer's career. The dream
says quite clearly : " You forget how far down you
began."

Here is the second dream : " I am in a great hurry
because I am going on a journey. I hunt up my baggage,
but cannot find it. Time flies, and the train will soon be
leaving. Finally I succeed in getting all my things together.
I hurry along the street, discover that I have forgotten
a brief-case containing important papers, dash breathlessly
back again, find it at last, and then run towards the station,
but make hardly any headway. With a final effort I rush
on to the platform only to find the train steaming out into
the yards. It is very long, and runs in a curious S-shaped
curve. It occurs to me that if the driver is not careful, and
puts on full steam when he comes to the straight stretch,
the rear coaches will still be on the curve and will be thrown
over by the speed of the train. As a matter of fact the
driver opens the throttle as I try to shout. The rear coaches

rock frightfully, and are actually thrown off the rails. There is a terrible catastrophe. I awake in terror."

Here, too, we can understand without much difficulty the situation represented by the dream. It pictures the patient's frantic haste to advance himself still further. Since the driver at the front of the train goes thoughtlessly ahead, the coaches behind him rock and finally overturn— that is, a neurosis is developed. It is clear that, at this period of life, the patient had reached the highest point of his career—that the effort of the long ascent from his lowly origin had exhausted his strength. He should have contented himself with his achievements, but instead he is driven by his ambition to attempt to scale heights of success for which he is not fitted. The neurosis came upon him as a warning. Circumstances prevented my treating the patient, and my view of his case did not satisfy him. The upshot was that events ran their course in the way indicated by the dream. He tried to exploit the professional openings that tempted his ambition and ran so violently off the track that the train-wreck was realized in actual life. The patient's anamnesis permitted the inference that the mountain-sickness pointed to his inability to climb any further. The inference is confirmed by his dreams which present this inability as a fact.

We here come upon a characteristic of dreams that must take first place in any discussion of the applicability of dream-analysis to the treatment of neuroses. The dream gives a true picture of the subjective state, while the conscious mind denies that this state exists, or recognizes it only grudgingly. The patient's conscious ego could see no reason why he should not go steadily forward ; he continued his struggle for advancement, refusing to admit the fact which subsequent events made all too plain—that he was actually at the end of his tether. When, in such cases, we listen to the dictates of the conscious mind, we are always in doubt. We can draw opposite conclusions from the patient's anamnesis. After all, the private soldier may carry a marshal's baton in his knapsack, and many a son of poor parents has achieved the highest success. Why should it not be so in my patient's case ? Since my judgement is fallible, why should my own conjecture be more dependable than his ? At this point the dream comes in as the expression of an involuntary psychic process not controlled by the conscious outlook. It presents the subjective state as it really is. It has no respect for my conjectures or for the patient's views as to how things should be, but simply tells how the matter stands. I have therefore made it a rule to put dreams on a plane with physiological fact. If sugar appears in the urine, then the urine contains sugar, and not albumen or urobilin or something else that I may have been led to expect. This is to say that I take dreams as facts that are invaluable for diagnosis.

It is the way of dreams to give us more than we ask, and this is true of those I have just cited as illustrations. They not only allowed us an insight into the causes of the neurosis, but afforded a prognosis as well. What is more, they showed us at what point the treatment should begin. The patient must be prevented from going full steam ahead. This is precisely what he tells himself in the dream.

For the time being we will content ourselves with this hint, and return to the question whether dreams enable us to explain the causes of a neurosis. I have cited two dreams that actually do this. But I could equally well cite any number of initial dreams which do nothing of the kind, although they are perfectly transparent. I do not wish for the present to consider dreams which call for searching analysis and interpretation.

The point is that there are neuroses whose actual origins we discover only at the very end of an analysis, and there are also cases in which it is of no benefit to have discovered the origin of the neurosis. This brings me back to the Freudian view, mentioned above, that for the purposes of therapy it is necessary for the patient to become conscious of the causal factors in his disturbance—a view that is little more than a survival of the old theory of the trauma. I do not, of course, deny that many neuroses have a traumatic origin ; I simply contest the notion that all neuroses are of this nature and arise without exception from some crucial experience of childhood. This view of the question results in a causalistic approach. The doctor must give his whole attention to the patient's past ; he must always ask : " Why ? " and neglect the equally pertinent question : " What for ? " This is frequently very harmful to the patient, for he is forced to search in his memory—perhaps over a course of years—for a hypothetical event in his childhood, while things of immediate importance are grossly neglected. A purely causalistic approach is too narrow to do justice to the true significance, either of the dream, or of the neurosis. A person is biassed who turns to dreams for the sole purpose of discovering the hidden cause of the neurosis, for he leaves aside the larger part of the dream's actual contribution. The dreams I have cited unmistakably present the ætiological factors in the neurosis ; but it is clear that they also offer a prognosis or anticipation of the future and a suggestion as to the course of treatment as well. We must furthermore bear in mind that a great many dreams do not touch upon the causes of the neurosis, but treat of quite different matters—among others, of the patient's attitude to the doctor. I should like to illustrate this by recounting three dreams of the same patient. She consulted three different analysts in turn, and at the beginning of each treatment she had one of these dreams.

Here is the first: " I must cross the frontier into the next country, but no one can tell me where the boundary lies, and I cannot find it." The treatment which followed this dream was unsuccessful, and was soon broken off.

The second dream is as follows: " I must cross the frontier. It is a black night, and I cannot find the custom-house. After a long search I notice a small light far away and suppose that the frontier lies over there. But in order to reach it, I must cross a valley and pass through a dark wood, in which I lose my sense of direction. Then I notice that someone is with me. This person suddenly clings to me like a madman and I awake in terror." That treatment also was discontinued after a few weeks, the reason being that the patient was completely disoriented by the analyst's unconscious identification with her.

The third dream took place when the patient came into my hands. It runs: " I must cross a frontier, or rather, I have already crossed it, and find myself in a Swiss custom-house. I have only a handbag with me, and believe that I have nothing to declare. But the customs official dives into my bag and, to my astonishment, pulls out two full-sized mattresses." The patient married during the course of her treatment with me, but not without a violent resistance to this step. The cause of her neurotic resistance came to light only after many months, and there is not a hint of it anywhere in these dreams. They are without exception anticipations of the difficulties she is to have with the analysts to whom she has come for treatment.

I could cite many other dreams to the same effect, but these may suffice to show that dreams can be anticipatory and, in that case, must lose their particular meaning if they are treated in a purely causalistic way. These three dreams give clear information about the analytical situation, and it is extremely important for the purposes of therapy that this be rightly understood. The first doctor understood the situation and sent the patient to the second. Here she drew her own conclusions from her dream, and decided to leave. My interpretation of her third dream disappointed her greatly, but she was distinctly encouraged to go on in spite of all difficulties by the fact that it reported the frontier already crossed.

Initial dreams are often amazingly transparent and clear-cut. But as the work of analysis progresses, the dreams in a little while cease to be clear. If they should prove exceptional, and keep their clarity, we can be sure that the analysis has as yet not touched some important part of the personality. As a rule, the dreams become less transparent, and more blurred, shortly after the beginning of the treatment. It becomes increasingly difficult to interpret them, a further reason for this being that a point may soon be reached where the doctor is unable, if the truth be told, to understand the situation as a whole. This is how the matter really stands, for to say that the dreams are unintelligible is a mere reflection of the doctor's subjective opinion. Nothing is unclear to the understanding; it is only when we fail to understand that things appear unintelligible and confused. In themselves, dreams are clear—that is, they are just as they must be under the given conditions. If we look back at these " unintelligible " dreams from a later stage of the treatment or from a distance of some years, we are often astounded at our own blindness. It is a fact that, as an analysis progresses, we come upon dreams that are strikingly obscure in comparison with the initial dreams. But the doctor should not be too sure that these later dreams are really confused, or be too hasty in accusing the patient of deliberate resistance. He would do better to take the fact as an indication of his own growing inability to understand the situation. The psychiatrist likewise is prone to call a patient " confused " when he would do well to recognize the projection and admit his own confusion, for it is really his understanding that grows confused in face of the patient's strange behaviour. For the purposes of therapy, moreover, it is highly important for the analyst to admit his lack of understanding from time to time, for nothing is more unbearable for the patient than to be always understood. The latter in any case relies too much upon the mysterious insight of the doctor, and, by appealing to his professional vanity, lays a dangerous trap for him. By taking refuge in the doctor's self-confidence and " profound " understanding, the patient loses all sense of reality, falls into a stubborn transference, and retards the cure.

Understanding is clearly a subjective process. It may be very one-sided, in that the physician understands while the patient does not. In such a case the doctor sometimes feels it his duty to convince the patient, and if the latter will not allow himself to be convinced, the doctor accuses him of resistance. When the understanding is all on my side, I find it advisable to stress my lack of understanding. It is relatively unimportant whether the doctor understands or not, but everything hangs on the patient's doing so. What is really needed is a mutual agreement which is the fruit of joint reflection. It is one-sided, and therefore dangerous, understanding for the doctor to prejudge the dream from the standpoint of a certain doctrine and to make a pronouncement which may be theoretically sound, but does not win the patient's assent. In so far as the pronouncement fails in this respect, it is incorrect in the practical sense; and it may also be incorrect in the sense that it anticipates and thereby cripples the actual development of the patient. We appeal only to the patient's brain if we try to inculcate a truth; but if we help him to grow up to this truth in the course of his own development, we have reached his heart, and this appeal goes deeper and acts with greater force.

When the doctor's interpretation is based merely upon a one-sided theory or a preconceived opinion, his chances of convincing the patient or of achieving any therapeutic results depend chiefly upon suggestion. And let no one deceive himself as to the effects of suggestion. In itself suggestion is not to be despised, but it has serious limitations, and reacts upon the patient's independence of character in a very undesirable way. A practising analyst may be supposed to believe in the significance and value of the widening of consciousness—I mean by this the procedure of bringing to light the parts of the personality which were previously unconscious and subjecting them to conscious discrimination and criticism. It is an undertaking which requires the patient to face his problems, and taxes his powers of conscious judgement and decision. It is nothing less than a challenge to the ethical sense, a call to arms that must be answered by the whole personality. Therefore, with respect to personal development, the analytical approach is of a higher order than methods of treatment based upon suggestion. This is a kind of magic that works in the dark and makes no ethical demands upon the personality. Methods of treatment based upon suggestion are deceptive makeshifts ; they are incompatible with the principles of analytical therapy, and should be avoided. But suggestion can of course be avoided only when the doctor is aware of the many doors through which it can enter. There remains in the best of circumstances enough—and more than enough—unconscious suggestion.

The analyst who wishes to rule out conscious suggestion must consider any dream interpretation invalid that does not win the assent of the patient, and he must search until he finds a formulation that does. This is a rule which, I believe, must always be observed, especially in dealing with those dreams whose obscurity is evidence of lack of understanding on the part of the doctor as well as of the patient. The doctor should regard every dream as a new departure—as a source of information about unknown conditions concerning which he has as much to learn as the patient. It goes without saying that he should hold no preconceived opinions based upon a particular theory, but stand ready in every single case to construct a totally new theory of dreams. There is still a boundless opportunity for pioneer-work in this field.

The view that dreams are merely imaginary fulfilments of suppressed wishes has long ago been superseded. It is certainly true that there are dreams which embody suppressed wishes and fears, but what is there which the dream cannot on occasion embody ? Dreams may give expression to ineluctable truths, to philosophical pronouncements, illusions, wild fantasies, memories, plans, anticipations, irrational experiences, even telepathic visions, and heaven knows what besides. One thing we ought never to forget : almost the half of our lives is passed in a more or less unconscious state. The dream is specifically the utterance of the unconscious. We may call consciousness the daylight realm of the human psyche, and contrast it with the nocturnal realm of unconscious psychic activity which we apprehend as dreamlike fantasy. It is certain that consciousness consists not only of wishes and fears, but of vastly more than these, and it is highly probable that the unconscious psyche contains a wealth of contents and living forms equal to or even greater than does consciousness, which is characterized by concentration, limitation and exclusion.

This being the state of affairs, it is imperative that we should not pare down the meaning of a dream to fit some narrow doctrine. We must remember that there are not a few patients who imitate the technical or theoretical jargon of the doctor, and do this even in their dreams. No language exists that cannot be misused. It is hard to realize how badly we are fooled by the abuse of ideas ; it even seems as if the unconscious had a way of strangling the physician in the coils of his own theory. All this being so, I leave theory aside as much as possible in analysing dreams. We cannot, of course, dispense with theory entirely, for it is needed to make things intelligible. It is on the basis of theory, for instance, that I expect dreams to have a meaning. I cannot prove in every case that dreams are meaningful, for there are dreams that neither doctor nor patient understands. But I must regard them as hypothetically meaningful in order to find courage to deal with them at all. To say that dreams contribute in an important way to conscious knowledge, and that a dream which fails to do so is a dream which has not been properly interpreted—this, too, is a theoretical statement. But I must adopt this hypothesis in order to make it clear to myself why I analyse dreams. On the other hand, every hypothesis about the nature of the dream, its function and structure, is merely a rule of thumb and must be subject to constant modifications. We must never forget in dream-analysis, even for a moment, that we move on treacherous ground where nothing is certain but uncertainty. A suitable warning to the dream-interpreter—if only it were not so paradoxical—would be : " Do anything you like, only don't try to understand ! "

When we take up an obscure dream, our first task is not to understand and interpret it, but to establish the context with minute care. What I have in mind is not a boundless sweep of " free associations " starting from any and every image in the dream, but a careful and conscious illumination of those chains of association that are directly connected with particular images. Many patients have first to be educated to this task, for they resemble the doctor in their urgent desire to understand and to interpret offhand. This is particularly the case when they have already been educated—or rather, miseducated—by their reading or by a previous analysis that went wrong. They give associations in accordance with a theory ; that is, they try to understand and interpret, and thus they nearly always get stuck. Like the doctor, they wish at once to get behind the dream in the false belief that it is a mere façade concealing the true meaning. Perhaps we may call the dream a façade, but we must remember that the fronts of most houses by no means trick or deceive us, but, on the contrary, follow the plan of the building and often betray its inner arrangement. The " manifest " dream-picture is the dream itself, and contains the " latent " meaning. If I find sugar in the urine, it is sugar, and not a façade that conceals albumen. When Freud speaks of the " dream-façade ", he is really speaking, not of the dream itself, but of its obscurity, and in so doing is projecting upon the dream his own lack of understanding. We say that the dream has a false front only because we fail to see into it. We would do better to say that we are dealing with something like a text that is unintelligible, not because it has a façade, but simply because we cannot read it. We do not have to get behind such a text in the first place, but must learn to read it.

We shall best succeed in reading dreams by establishing their context, as already remarked. We shall not succeed with the help of free associations, any more than we could use that means to decipher a Hittite inscription. Free associations will help me to uncover all my own complexes, but for this purpose I need not start from the dream—I might as well take a sentence in a newspaper or a " Keep out " sign. If we associate freely to a dream, our complexes will turn up right enough, but we shall hardly ever discover the meaning of the dream. To do this, we must keep as close as possible to the dream-images themselves. When a person has dreamed of a deal table, little is accomplished by his associating it with his writing-desk which is not made of deal. The dream refers expressly to a deal table. If at this point nothing occurs to the dreamer, his hesitation signifies that a particular darkness surrounds the dream-image, and this is suspicious. We would expect him to have dozens of associations to a deal table, and when he

cannot find a single one, this must have a meaning. In such cases we should return again and again to the image. I say to my patients : " Suppose I had no idea what the words ' deal table ' mean. Describe this object and give me its history in such a way that I cannot fail to understand what sort of thing it is." We succeed in this way in establishing a good part of the context of that particular dream-image. When we have done this for all the images in the dream, we are ready for the venture of interpretation.

Every interpretation is hypothetical, for it is a mere attempt to read an unfamiliar text. An obscure dream, taken by itself, can rarely be interpreted with any certainty, so that I attach little importance to the interpretation of single dreams. With a series of dreams we can have more confidence in our interpretations, for the later dreams correct the mistakes we have made in handling those that went before. We are also better able, in a dream series, to recognize the important contents and basic themes, and I therefore urge my patients to make a careful record of their dreams and the interpretations given them. I also show them how to work up their dreams in the way I have just indicated, so that they can bring me in writing the dream and the material that forms the context of the dream. In later stages of analysis I let them work out the interpretations as well. The patient learns in this way how to consult the unconscious without the doctor's help.

If dreams did nothing more than inform us about the causal factors in a neurosis, we could safely let the doctor handle them alone. My way of dealing with them, moreover, would be quite superfluous if all that we could expect of them were a collection of hints and insights helpful to the doctor. But since it is probable, as I have shown in a few examples, that dreams contain more than practical helps for the doctor, dream-analysis deserves very special consideration. Sometimes, indeed, it is a matter of life and death.

Among many cases of this sort, I have been especially impressed with one that concerned a colleague of mine in Zürich. He was a man somewhat older than myself whom I saw from time to time, and who always teased me on these occasions about my interest in dream-interpretation. I met him one day in the street, and he called out to me: "How are things going? Are you still interpreting dreams? By the way, I've had another idiotic dream. Does it mean something too?" He had dreamed as follows: "I am climbing a high mountain over steep, snow-covered slopes. I mount higher and higher—it is marvellous weather. The higher I climb, the better I feel. I think: 'If only I could go on climbing like this for ever!' When I reach the summit, my happiness and elation are so strong that I feel I could mount right up into space. And I discover that I actually can do this. I go on climbing on empty air. I awake in a real ecstasy." When he had told me his dream, I said: "My dear. man, I know you can't give up mountaineering, but let me implore you not to go alone from now on. When you go, take two guides, and you must promise on your word of honour to follow their directions." "Incorrigible!" he replied laughing, and said good-bye. I never saw him again. Two months later came the first blow. When out alone, he was buried by an avalanche, but was dug out in the nick of time by a military patrol which happened to come along. Three months after this the end came. He went on a climb accompanied by a younger friend, but without guides. An alpinist standing below saw him literally step out into the air as he was letting himself down a rock wall. He fell on to the head of his friend, who was waiting beneath him, and both were dashed to pieces far below. That was *ecstasis* in the full meaning of the word.

No amount of scepticism and critical reserve has ever enabled me to regard dreams as negligible occurrences. Often enough they appear senseless, but it is obviously we who lack the sense and the ingenuity to read the enigmatical message from the nocturnal realm of the psyche. When we see that at least a half of man's life is passed in this realm, that consciousness has its roots there, and that the unconscious operates in and out of waking existence, it would seem incumbent upon medical psychology to sharpen its perceptions by a systematic study of dreams. No one doubts the importance of conscious experience ; why then should we question the importance of unconscious happenings ? They also belong to human life, and they are sometimes more truly a part of it for weal or woe than any events of the day.

Dreams give information about the secrets of the inner life and reveal to the dreamer hidden factors of his personality. As long as these are undiscovered, they disturb his waking life and betray themselves only in the form of symptoms. This means that we cannot effectively treat the patient from the side of consciousness alone, but must bring about a change in and through the unconscious. As far as present knowledge goes, there is only one way of doing this : there must be a thorough-going, conscious assimilation of unconscious contents. By " assimilation ", I mean a mutual interpenetration of conscious and unconscious contents, and not—as is too commonly thought—a one-sided valuation, interpretation and deformation of unconscious contents by the conscious mind. As to the value and significance of unconscious contents in general, very mistaken views are abroad. It is well known that the Freudian school presents the unconscious in a thoroughly depreciatory light, just as also it looks on primitive man as little better than a wild beast. Its nursery-tales about the terrible old man of the tribe and its teachings about the " infantile-perverse-criminal " unconscious have led people to make a dangerous monster out of the unconscious, that really very natural thing. As if all that is good, reasonable, beautiful and worth living for had taken up its abode in consciousness ! Have the horrors of the World War really not opened our eyes ? Are we still unable to see that man's conscious mind is even more devilish and perverse than the unconscious ?

I was recently reproached with the charge that my teaching about the assimilation of the unconscious, were it accepted, would undermine culture and exalt primitivity at the cost of our highest values. Such an opinion can have no foundation other than the erroneous belief that the unconscious is a monster. Such a view arises from fear of nature and of life as it actually is. Freud has invented the idea of sublimation to save us from the imaginary claws of the unconscious. But what actually exists cannot be alchemistically sublimated, and if anything is apparently sublimated, it never was what a false interpretation took it to be.

The unconscious is not a demonic monster, but a thing of nature that is perfectly neutral as far as moral sense, æsthetic taste and intellectual judgement go. It is dangerous only when our conscious attitude towards it becomes hopelessly false. And this danger grows in the measure that we practise repressions. But as soon as the patient begins to assimilate the contents that were previously unconscious, the danger from the side of the unconscious diminishes. As the process of assimilation goes on, it puts an end to the dissociation of the personality and to the anxiety that attends and inspires the separation of the two realms of the psyche. That which my critic feared—I mean the overwhelming of consciousness by the unconscious —is most likely to occur when the unconscious is excluded from life by repressions, or is misunderstood and depreciated.

A fundamental mistake, and one which is commonly made, is this : it is supposed that the contents of the unconscious are unequivocal and are marked with plus or minus signs that are immutable. As I see the question, this view is too naïve. The psyche is a self-regulating system that maintains itself in equilibrium as the body does. Every process that goes too far immediately and inevitably calls forth a compensatory activity. Without such adjustments a normal metabolism would not exist, nor would the normal psyche. We can take the idea of compensation, so understood, as a law of psychic happening. Too little on one side results in too much on the other. The relation between conscious and unconscious is compensatory. This fact, which is easily verifiable, affords a rule for dream interpretation. It is always helpful, when we set out to interpret a dream, to ask : What conscious attitude does it compensate ?

Although compensation may take the form of imaginary wish-fulfilment, it generally presents itself as an actuality which becomes the more strikingly actual the more we try to repress it. We know that we do not conquer thirst by repressing it. The dream-content is to be taken in all seriousness as something that has actually happened to us ; it should be treated as a contributory factor in framing our conscious outlook. If we do not do this, we shall keep that one-sided, conscious attitude which evoked the unconscious compensation in the first place. But this way holds little hope of our ever judging ourselves correctly or finding any balance in life.

If anyone should set out to replace his conscious outlook by the dictates of the unconscious—and this is the prospect which my critics find so alarming—he would only succeed in repressing the former, and it would reappear as an unconscious compensation. The unconscious would thus have changed its face and completely reversed its position. It would have become timidly reasonable, in striking contrast to its former tone. It is not generally believed that the unconscious operates in this way, yet such reversals constantly take place and constitute its essential function. This is why every dream is a source of information and a means of self-regulation, and why dreams are our most effective aids in the task of building up the personality.

The unconscious itself does not harbour explosive materials, but it may become explosive owing to the repressions exercised by a self-sufficient, or cowardly, conscious outlook. All the more reason, then, for giving heed to that side ! It should now be clear why I have made it a practical rule always to ask, before trying to interpret a dream : What conscious attitude does it compensate ? As may be seen, I thus bring the dream into the closest possible connection with the conscious state. I even maintain that it is impossible to interpret a dream with any degree of certainty unless we know what the conscious situation is. For it is only in the light of this knowledge that we can make out whether the unconscious content carries a plus or minus sign. The dream is not an isolated psychic event completely cut off from daily life. If it seems so to us, that is only an illusion that arises from our lack of understanding. In reality, the relation between consciousness and the dream is strictly causal, and they interact in the subtlest of ways.

I should like to show with the help of an illustration how important it is to find the true value of unconscious contents. A young man brought me the following dream : " My father is driving away from the house in his new car. He drives very clumsily, and I get very excited about his apparent stupidity. He goes this way and that, forward and backward, repeatedly getting the car into a tight place. Finally he runs into a wall and badly damages the car. I shout at him in a perfect rage, telling him he ought to behave himself. My father only laughs, and then I see that he is dead drunk." There is no foundation in fact for the dream. The dreamer is convinced that his father would never behave in that way, even if he were drunk. The dreamer himself is used to cars ; he is a careful driver, and very moderate in the use of alcohol, especially when he has to drive. Bad driving, and even slight injuries to the car, irritate him greatly. The son's relation to his father is good. He admires him for being an unusually successful man. We can say, without any attempt at interpretation, that the dream presents a very unfavourable picture of the father. What, then, should we take its meaning to be as far as the son is concerned ? Is his relation to his father good only in appearance, and does it really consist of over-compensated resistances ? If this is so we should attribute a plus sign to the dream-content ; we should have to tell the young man : " This is your actual relation to your father." But since I could find nothing equivocal or neurotic in the facts about the son's relation to his father, I had no warrant for disturbing the young man's feelings with such a destructive pronouncement. To do so would have prejudiced the outcome of the treatment.

But if his relation to his father is really excellent, why must the dream manufacture such an improbable story to discredit the father ? The dreamer's unconscious must have a distinct tendency to produce such a dream. Has the young man resistances to his father, after all, which are perhaps fed by jealousy or a certain sense of inferiority ? But before we go out of our way to burden his conscience— and with sensitive young people there is always the risk that we do this too lightly—we had better, for once, drop the question of why he had this dream, and ask ourselves instead : What for ? The answer, in this case, would be that his unconscious clearly tries to depreciate his father. If we take this as a compensation, we are forced to the conclusion that his relation to his father is not only good, but even too good. The young man actually deserves the French sobriquet of *fils à papa*. His father is still too much the guarantor of his existence, and he is still living what I call a provisional life. He runs the risk of failing to realize himself because there is too much " father " on every side. This is why the unconscious manufactures a kind of blasphemy : it seeks to lower the father and to elevate the son. " An immoral business ", we may be tempted to say. Every father who lacks insight would be on his guard here. And yet this compensation is entirely to the point. It forces the son to contrast himself with his

B

father, and that is the only way in which he can become aware of himself.

The interpretation just outlined was apparently the correct one, for it struck home. It won the spontaneous assent of the young man, and did no violence to his feeling for his father, or to the father's feeling for him. But this interpretation was only possible when the father-son relation had been studied in the light of all the facts that were accessible to consciousness Without a knowledge of the conscious situation the true meaning of the dream would have remained in doubt.

It is of the first importance for the assimilation of dream-contents that no violence be done to the real values of the conscious personality. If the conscious personality is destroyed, or even crippled, there is no one left to do the assimilating. When we recognize the importance of the unconscious we are not embarking upon a Bolshevist experiment which puts the lowest on top. This would only bring about a return of the situation we are trying to correct. We must see to it that the conscious personality remains intact, for we can only turn the unconscious compensations to good account when the conscious personality co-operates in the venture. When it comes to the assimilation of a content it is never a question of " this *or* that ", but of " this *and* that ".

Just as the interpretation of dreams requires exact knowledge of the conscious *status quo*, so the treatment of dream symbolism demands that we take into account the dreamer's philosophical, religious and moral convictions. It is far wiser in practice not to regard the dream-symbols as signs or symptoms of a fixed character. We should rather take them as true symbols—that is to say, as expressions of something not yet consciously recognized or conceptually formulated. In addition to this, they must be considered in relation to the dreamer's immediate state of consciousness. I emphasize that this way of treating the dream-symbols is advisable in practice because theoretically there do exist relatively fixed symbols whose meaning must on no account be referred to anything whose content is known, or to anything that can be formulated in concepts. If there were no relatively fixed symbols, it would be impossible to determine the structure of the unconscious. There would be nothing in it which could be in any way laid hold of or described.

It may seem strange that I should attribute an indefinite content to the relatively fixed symbols. But it is the indefinite content that marks the symbol as against the mere sign or symptom. It is well known that the Freudian school operates with hard and fast sexual " symbols " ; but these are just what I should call signs, for they are made to stand for sexuality, and this is supposed to be something definitive. As a matter of fact, Freud's concept of sexuality is thoroughly elastic, and so vague that it can be made to include almost anything. The word itself is familiar, but what it denotes amounts to an indeterminable or variable x that stands for the physiological activity of the glands at one extreme and the highest reaches of the spirit at the other. Instead of taking a dogmatic stand that rests upon the illusion that we know something because we have a familiar word for it, I prefer to regard the symbol as the announcement of something unknown, hard to recognize and not to be fully determined. Take, for instance, the so-called phallic symbols, which are supposed to stand for the *membrum virile* and nothing more. Psychologically speaking, the *membrum* is itself—as Kranefeldt has recently pointed out—a symbolic image whose wider content cannot easily be determined. As was customary throughout antiquity, primitive people today make a free use of phallic symbols, yet it never occurs to them to confuse the phallus, as a ritualistic symbol, with the penis. They always take the phallus to mean the creative *mana*, the power of healing and fertility, " that which is unusually potent ", to use Lehmann's expression. Its equivalents in mythology and in dreams are the bull, the ass, the pomegranate, the *yoni*, the he-goat, the lightning, the horse's hoof, the dance, the magical cohabitation in the furrow, and the menstrual fluid, to mention only a few of many. That which underlies all of these images—and sexuality itself—is an archetypal content that is hard to grasp, and that finds its best psychological expression in the primitive *mana* symbol. In each of the images given above we can see a relatively fixed symbol—*i.e.* the *mana* symbol—but we cannot for all that be certain that when they occur in dreams they have no other meaning.

The practical need may call for quite another interpretation. To be sure, if we had to interpret dreams in an exhaustive way according to scientific principles, we should have to refer every such symbol to an archetype. But, in practice, this kind of interpretation might be a grave blunder, for the patient's psychological state may require anything rather than the giving of attention to a theory of dreams. It is therefore advisable, for the purposes of therapy, to look for the meaning of symbols as they relate to the conscious situation—in other words, to treat them as if they were not fixed. This is as much as to say that we must renounce all preconceived opinions, however knowing they make us feel, and try to discover the meaning of things for the patient. If we do this, our interpretations will obviously not go very far towards satisfying a theory of dreams ; in fact, they may fall very short in this respect. But if the practitioner operates too much with fixed symbols, there is danger of his falling into mere routine and dogmatism, thus failing to meet the patient's need. It is unfortunate that, to illustrate the above, I should have to go into greater detail than space here permits, but I have elsewhere published illustrative material that amply supports my statements.

As already remarked, it frequently happens at the very beginning of a treatment that a dream reveals to the doctor, in a wide perspective, the general direction in which the unconscious is moving. But, for practical reasons, it may not be feasible to make clear to the patient, at this early stage, the deeper meaning of his dream. The demands of therapy are binding upon us in this way also. When the doctor gains such a far-reaching insight, it is thanks to his experience in the matter of relatively fixed symbols. Such insight can be of the very greatest value in diagnosis and in prognosis as well. I was once consulted in the case of a seventeen-year-old girl. One specialist had suggested that she might be in the first stages of progressive atrophy of the muscles, while another thought that she was a hysteric. Because of this second opinion, I was called in. The clinical picture made me suspect an organic disease, but the girl showed traits of hysteria as well. I asked for dreams. The patient answered at once : " Yes, I have terrible dreams. Just recently I dreamed I was coming home at night. Everything is as quiet as death. The door into the living-room is half open, and I see my mother hanging from the chandelier and swinging to and fro in a cold wind that

blows in through the open windows. At another time I
dreamed that a terrible noise breaks out in the house at
night. I go to see what has happened, and find that a
frightened horse is tearing through the rooms. At last it
finds the door into the hall, and jumps through the hall
window from the fourth floor down into the street. I was
terrified to see it lying below, all mangled."

The way in which these dreams allude to death is enough
to give one pause. But many persons have anxiety dreams
now and then. We must therefore look more closely into
the meaning of the outstanding symbols, " mother " and
" horse ". These figures must be equivalent one to the
other, for they both do the same thing : they commit
suicide. The mother symbol is archetypal and refers to
a place of origin, to nature, that which passively creates,
hence to substance and matter, to material nature, the lower
body (womb) and the vegetative functions. It connotes
also the unconscious, natural and instinctive life, the
physiological realm, the body in which we dwell or are
contained, for the " mother " is also a vessel, the hollow
form (*uterus*) that carries and nourishes, and it thus stands
for the foundations of consciousness. Being within something or contained in something suggests darkness, the
nocturnal—a state of anxiety. With these allusions I am
presenting the idea of the mother in many of its mythological
and etymological transformations ; I am also giving an
important part of the *yin* concept of Chinese philosophy.
All this is dream-content, but it is not something which
the seventeen-year-old girl has acquired in her individual
existence ; it is rather a bequest from the past. On the
one hand it has been kept alive by the language, and on
the other hand it is inherited with the structure of the

psyche and is therefore to be found in all times and among all peoples.

The familiar word " mother " refers apparently to the best-known of mothers in particular—to " my mother ". But the mother symbol points to a darker meaning which eludes conceptual formulation and can only be vaguely apprehended as the hidden, nature-bound life of the body. Yet even this expression is too narrow, and excludes too many pertinent side-meanings. The psychic reality which underlies this symbol is so inconceivably complex that we can only discern it from afar off, and then but very dimly. It is such realities that call for symbolic expression.

If we apply our findings to the dream, its meaning will be : the unconscious life destroys itself. That is the dream's message to the conscious mind of the dreamer and to everyone who has ears to hear.

" Horse " is an archetype that is widely current in mythology and folk-lore. As an animal it represents the non-human psyche, the sub-human, animal side, and therefore the unconscious. This is why the horse in folk-lore sometimes sees visions, hears voices, and speaks. As a beast of burden it is closely related to the mother-archetype ; the Valkyries bear the dead hero to Valhalla and the Trojan horse encloses the Greeks. As an animal lower than man it represents the lower part of the body and the animal drives that take their rise from there. The horse is dynamic power and a means of locomotion ; it carries one away like a surge of instinct. It is subject to panics like all instinctive creatures who lack higher consciousness. Also it has to do with sorcery and magical spells—especially the black, night horse which heralds death.

It is evident, then, that " horse " is the equivalent of

" mother " with a slight shift of meaning. The mother
stands for life at its origin, and the horse for the merely
animal life of the body. If we apply this meaning to the
dream, it says : the animal life destroys itself.

The two dreams make nearly the same assertion, but, as
is usually the case, the second is more specific. The peculiar
subtlety of the dream is brought out in both instances :
there is no mention of the death of the individual. It is
notorious that one often dreams of one's own death, but
that is no serious matter. When it is really a question of
death, the dream speaks another language. Both of these
dreams, then, point to a serious, and even fatal, organic
disease. The prognosis was shortly after borne out in fact.

As for the relatively fixed symbols, this example gives a
fair idea of their general nature. There are a great many
of them, and they may differ in individual cases by subtle
shifts of meaning. It is only through comparative studies
in mythology, folk-lore, religion and language that we can
determine these symbols in a scientific way. The evolutionary stages through which the human psyche has passed
are more clearly discernible in the dream than in consciousness. The dream speaks in images, and gives expression
to instincts, that are derived from the most primitive levels
of nature. Consciousness all too easily departs from the
law of nature ; but it can be brought again into harmony
with the latter by the assimilation of unconscious contents.
By fostering this process we lead the patient to the
rediscovery of the law of his own being.

I have not been able, in so short a space, to deal with
anything but the elements of the subject. I could not put
together before your eyes, stone by stone, the edifice that
is reared in every analysis from the materials of the

unconscious and finds its completion in the restoration of
the total personality. The way of successive assimilations
reaches far beyond the curative results that specifically
concern the doctor. It leads in the end to that distant
goal (which may perhaps have been the first urge to life),
the bringing into reality of the whole human being—that is,
individuation. We physicians are without doubt the first
scientific observers of these obscure processes of nature.
As a rule we see only a pathological phase of the development,
and lose sight of the patient as soon as he is cured. But
it is only when the cure has been effected that we are in
a position to study the normal process of change, itself
a matter of years or decades. If we had some knowledge
of the ends towards which unconscious, psychic growth is
tending, and if our psychological insight were not drawn
exclusively from the pathological phase, we should have
a less confused idea of the processes revealed by dreams
and a clearer recognition of what it is that the symbols
point to. In my opinion, every doctor should be aware of
the fact that psychotherapy in general, and analysis in
particular, is a procedure that breaks into a purposeful and
continuous development, now here and now there, and
thus singles out particular phases which may seem to follow
opposing courses. Since every analysis by itself shows only
one part or aspect of the deeper course of development,
nothing but hopeless confusion can result from casuistic
comparisons. For this reason I have preferred to confine
myself to the rudiments of the subject and to practical
considerations. It is only in actual contact with the facts as
they occur that we can come to anything like a satisfactory
agreement.

PROBLEMS OF MODERN PSYCHOTHERAPY

PSYCHOTHERAPY, or the treatment of the mind by psychological methods, is identified in popular thought today with
" psychoanalysis ". This word is now so widely accepted
that everyone who uses it seems at the same time to grasp
its meaning ; yet it is seldom that a layman knows precisely
what it covers.

According to the intention of its creator, Freud, it can
be appropriately applied only to his own particular method
of explaining psychic symptoms in terms of certain repressed
impulses. Inasmuch as this technique is the consequence
of a particular approach to life, the idea of psychoanalysis
includes certain theoretical assumptions, among them the
Freudian theory of sexuality. The founder of psychoanalysis
himself explicitly insists upon this circumscription. But,
Freud notwithstanding, the layman applies the concept of
psychoanalysis to every kind of modern endeavour to
probe the mind by scientific methods. Thus Adler's school
must submit to being labelled " psychoanalytic " despite
the fact that Adler's view-point and method are apparently
in irreconcilable opposition to those of Freud. Because
of this contrast, Adler himself does not call his teaching
" psychoanalysis ", but " individual psychology " ; while I
prefer to call my own approach " analytical psychology ".
I wish the term to stand for a general conception embracing

both " psychoanalysis " and " individual psychology ", as well as other efforts in this field.

Since the mind is common to mankind it may seem to the layman that there can be only one psychology, and he may therefore suppose the divergences between the schools to be either subjective quibbling, or else a commonplace disguise for the efforts of mediocrities who seek to exalt themselves upon a throne. I could easily lengthen the list of " psychologies " by mentioning other systems that are not to be included under the head of " analytical psychology ". There are, in fact, many methods, stand-points, views and convictions which are all at war with one another—the main reason for this being that, since they fail to be mutually comprehensible, none of them can grant the validity of any other. The many-sidedness and variety of psychological opinions in our time is nothing less than astonishing, and it is confusing for the layman that no general survey of them can be made.

When we find the most diverse remedies prescribed in a text-book of pathology for a given disease, we may confidently assume that none of these remedies is particularly efficacious. So, when many different ways of approaching the psyche are recommended, we may rest assured that none of them leads with absolute certainty to the goal, least of all those advocated in a fanatical way. The very number of present-day " psychologies " amounts to a confession of perplexity. The difficulty of gaining access to the mind is gradually borne in upon us, and the mind itself is seen to be, to use Nietzsche's expression, a " horned " problem. It is small wonder therefore that efforts to attack this elusive riddle are multiplied, first from one side and then from another. The variety of contradictory standpoints and opinions of which we have spoken is the inevitable result.

The reader will doubtless agree that in discussing psychoanalysis we should not limit ourselves to its narrower definition, but deal in general with the results and failures of the various contemporary endeavours to solve the problem of the psyche—endeavours which we have agreed shall all be embraced in the concept of analytical psychology.

And moreover, why is there suddenly so much interest in the human psyche as something to be experienced? This has not been the case for thousands of years. I wish merely to raise this apparently irrelevant question, and will not try to answer it. It is in reality not irrelevant, because this interest underlies all such modern movements as theosophy, occultism, astrology and so forth.

All that is embraced today in the layman's idea of "psychoanalysis" originated in medical practice; and consequently most of it is medical psychology. It bears the unmistakable imprint of the physician's consulting-room—a fact which is evident not only in its terminology, but also in its framework of theory. We constantly come upon postulates which the physician has taken over from natural science and in particular from biology. This fact has largely contributed to the hostility between modern psychology and the academic fields of philosophy, history and classical learning. Modern psychology is empirical and close to nature, while these studies are grounded in the intellect. The distance between nature and mind, difficult to bridge at best, is increased by a medical and biological nomenclature which sometimes appears of practical utility, but more often severely taxes our good-will.

In view of the confusion of concepts that exists, I have

felt it necessary to indulge in the foregoing general remarks. I should like now to turn to the task in hand and consider the actual achievements of analytical psychology.   Since the various endeavours embraced by this term are so heterogeneous, it is extremely difficult to take up a generally inclusive standpoint.   If, then, with regard to the aims and results of these endeavours, I try to distinguish certain classes, or rather stages, I do it with some reservation. I regard it as a merely provisional arrangement, and grant that it may seem as arbitrary as a surveyor's triangulation of a country.   Be that as it may, I venture to arrange the sum-total of findings under the four heads of confession, explanation, education, and transformation.   I shall now proceed to discuss the meaning of these somewhat unusual terms.

The first beginnings of all analytical treatment are to be found in its prototype, the confessional.   Since, however, the two practices have no direct causal connection, but rather grow from a common psychic root, it is difficult for an outsider to see at once the relation between the ground-work of psychoanalysis and the religious institution of the confessional.

As soon as man was capable of conceiving the idea of sin, he had recourse to psychic concealment—or, to put it in analytical language, repressions arose.   Anything that is concealed is a secret.   The maintenance of secrets acts like a psychic poison which alienates their possessor from the community.   In small doses, this poison may actually be a priceless remedy, even an essential preliminary to the differentiation of the individual.   This is so much the case that, even on a primitive level, man has felt an irresistible need to invent secrets ;   their possession saves him from dissolving in the unconsciousness of mere community life, and thus from a fatal psychic injury. As is well known, the many ancient mystery cults with their secret rituals served this instinct for differentiation. Even the Christian sacraments were looked upon as mysteries in the early Church, and, as in the case of baptism, were celebrated in private apartments and only referred to under a veil of allegory.

However beneficial a secret shared with several persons may be, a merely private secret has a destructive effect. It resembles a burden of guilt which cuts off the unfortunate possessor from communion with his fellow-beings. Yet if we are conscious of what we conceal, the harm done is decidedly less than if we do not know what we are repressing —or even that we have repressions at all. In the latter case we not merely keep a content consciously private, but we conceal it even from ourselves. It then splits off from consciousness as an independent complex, to lead a separate existence in the unconscious, where it can be neither corrected nor interfered with by the conscious mind. The complex is thus an autonomous portion of the psyche which, as experience has shown, develops a peculiar fantasy-life of its own. What we call fantasy is simply spontaneous psychic activity ; and it wells up whenever the repressive action of the conscious mind relaxes or ceases altogether, as in sleep. In sleep this activity shows itself in the form of dreams. And we continue to dream in waking life beneath the threshold of consciousness, especially when this activity is conditioned by a repressed or otherwise unconscious complex. It should be said in passing that unconscious contents are by no means exclusively such as were once conscious and, by being repressed, have later grown into unconscious complexes. Quite otherwise, the unconscious has contents peculiar to itself which, slowly growing upward from the depths, at last come into consciousness. We should therefore in no wise picture the unconscious psyche to ourselves as a mere receptacle for contents discarded by the conscious mind.

All psychic contents which either approach the threshold of consciousness from below, or have sunk only slightly beneath it, have an effect upon our conscious activities. Since the content itself is not conscious, these effects are necessarily indirect. Most of our lapses of the tongue, of the pen, of memory, and the like, are traceable to these disturbances, as are likewise all neurotic symptoms. These are nearly always of psychic origin, the exceptions being shock effects from shell-explosions and other causes. The mildest forms of neurosis are the " lapses " already referred to—blunders of speech, the sudden forgetting of names and dates, unexpected clumsiness leading to injuries or accidents, misunderstandings of personal motives or of what we have heard or read, and so-called hallucinations of memory which cause us to suppose erroneously that we have said or done this or that. In all these cases a thorough investigation can show the existence of a content which in an indirect and unconscious way has distorted the conscious performance.

In general, therefore, an unconscious secret is more harmful than one that is conscious. I have seen many patients in difficult situations of life which might have driven weaker natures to suicide. These patients had at times a tendency towards suicide, but, on account of their inherent reasonableness, would not allow the suicidal urge to come into consciousness. But it remained active in the unconscious, and brought about all kinds of dangerous accidents—as for instance an attack of faintness or hesitation in front of an advancing motor-car, the swallowing of corrosive sublimate in the belief that it was a cough mixture, a sudden zest for dangerous acrobatics, and so forth. When it was possible to make the suicidal leaning conscious, common-sense could helpfully intervene ; the patients could then recognize and avoid those situations that tempted them to self-destruction.

As we have seen, every personal secret has the effect of a sin or of guilt—whether or not it is, from the standpoint of popular morality, a wrongful secret. Now another form of concealment is the act of " withholding "—it being usually emotions that are withheld. As in the case of secrets, so here also we must make a reservation : self-restraint is healthful and beneficial ; it is even a virtue. This is why we find self-discipline to have been one of man's earliest moral attainments. Among primitive peoples it has its place in the initiation ceremonies, chiefly in the forms of ascetic continence and the stoical endurance of pain and fear. Self-restraint, however, is here practised within the secret society as something undertaken in company with others. But if self-restraint is only a private matter, and perhaps devoid of any religious aspect, then it may be as harmful as the personal secret. From this kind of self-restraint come our well-known ugly moods and the irritability of the over-virtuous. The emotion withheld is also something we conceal—something which we can hide even from ourselves—an art in which men particularly excel, while women, with very few exceptions, are by nature averse to doing such violence to their emotions. When emotion is withheld it tends to isolate and disturb us quite as much as an unconscious secret, and is equally guilt-laden.

Just as nature bears us ill-will, as it were, if we possess a secret to which mankind has not attained, so also has she a grudge against us if we withhold our emotions from our fellow-men. Nature decidedly abhors a vacuum in this respect, in the long run nothing is more unbearable than a tepid harmony in personal relations brought about by withholding emotion. The repressed emotions are often of a kind we wish to keep secret. But more often there is no secret worthy of the name ; there are merely quite avowable emotions which, from being withheld at some important juncture, have become unconscious.

It is probable that one form of neurosis is conditioned by the predominance of secrets, and another by the pre-dominance of restrained emotions. At any rate the hysterical subject, who is very free with his emotions, is most often the possessor of a secret, while the hardened psychasthenic suffers from inability to digest his emotions.

To cherish secrets and to restrain emotions are psychic misdemeanours for which nature finally visits us with sickness—that is, when we do these things in private. But when they are done in communion with others they satisfy nature and may even count as useful virtues. It is only restraint practised in and for oneself that is unwhole-some. It is as if man had an inalienable right to behold all that is dark, imperfect, stupid and guilty in his fellow-beings—for such of course are the things that we keep private to protect ourselves. It seems to be a sin in the eyes of nature to hide our insufficiency—just as much as to live entirely on our inferior side. There appears to be a conscience in mankind which severely punishes the man who does not somehow and at some time, at whatever cost to his pride, cease to defend and assert himself, and instead confess himself fallible and human. Until he can do this, an impenetrable wall shuts him out from the living experience of feeling himself a man among men. Here we find a key to the great significance of true, unstereotyped confession— a significance known in all the initiation and mystery cults of the ancient world, as is shown by a saying from the Greek mysteries : " Give up what thou hast, and then thou wilt receive ".

We may well take this saying as a motto for the first stage in psychotherapeutic treatment. It is a fact that the beginnings of psychoanalysis were fundamentally nothing else than the scientific rediscovery of an ancient truth ; even the name catharsis (or cleansing), which was given to the earliest method of treatment, comes from the Greek initiation rites. The early method of catharsis consisted in putting the patient, with or without hypnotic aid, in touch with the hinterland of his mind—that is to say, into that state which the Eastern *yoga* systems describe as meditation or contemplation. In contrast to the meditation found in *yoga* practice, the psychoanalytic aim is to observe the shadowy presentations—whether in the form of images or of feelings—that are spontaneously evolved in the unconscious psyche and appear without his bidding to the man who looks within. In this way we find once more things that we have repressed or forgotten. Painful though it may be, this is in itself a gain—for what is inferior or even worthless belongs to me as my shadow and gives me substance and mass. How can I be substantial if I fail to cast a shadow ? I must have a dark side also if I am to be whole ; and inasmuch as I become conscious of my shadow I also remember that I am a human being like any other. In any case, when I keep it to myself, this rediscovery of that which makes me whole restores the condition which preceded the neurosis or the splitting off of the complex.   In keeping the matter private I have only attained a partial cure—for I still continue in my state of isolation.   It is only with the help of confession that I am able to throw myself into the arms of humanity freed at last from the burden of moral exile.   The goal of treatment by catharsis is full confession—no merely intellectual acknowledgement of the facts, but their confirmation by the heart and the actual release of the suppressed emotions.

As can easily be imagined, such confessions have a great effect with simple people, and their curative results are often astonishing.   Yet I do not wish to point to the fact that some patients are cured as being the main achievement of psychotherapy at this level ; what I wish to call attention to is the systematic emphasis given to the significance of confession.   It is this which strikes home to all of us.   For we are all in some way or other kept asunder by our secrets ; and instead of seeking through confession to bridge the abysses that separate us from one another, we choose the easy by-way of deceptive opinions and illusions.   In saying this, however, I am far from wishing to enunciate a general maxim.   It would be hard to go too far in condemning the bad taste of a common, mutual confession of sins.   The fact established by psychology is simply this : we are dealing here with a delicate matter.   We cannot handle it directly or by itself, for it offers us a problem with unusually " pointed horns."   A consideration of the next stage—that of explanation—will make this clear.

It is evident enough that the new psychology would have remained at the stage of confession had catharsis proved itself a panacea.   First and foremost, it is not always possible to bring certain patients close enough to the unconscious to enable them to perceive the shadows. Indeed, there are many patients, for the most part complicated, highly conscious persons, who are so firmly anchored in consciousness that nothing can pry them loose. They often develop the most violent resistances whenever an attempt is made to push consciousness aside ; they wish to talk with the physician of things about which they are fully conscious— to make their difficulties intelligible and to discuss them. They already have quite enough to confess, they say ; they do not have to turn to the unconscious for that. For such patients a complete technique for effecting the approach to the unconscious is needed.

This is one fact which at the outset seriously restricts us in applying the method of catharsis. The other limitation is revealed later on, and its discussion at once leads us to the problems of the second stage—the stage of explanation. Let us suppose that in a given case the confession demanded by the method of catharsis has taken place—that the neurosis has disappeared, or that the symptoms at least have vanished. The patient could now be dismissed as cured if it depended on the physician alone. But he—or especially she—cannot get away. The patient seems bound to the physician by the act of confession. If this apparently meaningless attachment is forcibly severed, there is a bad relapse.

It is both curious and significant that there are cases where no attachment develops. The patient goes away apparently cured—but he is now so fascinated by the hinterland of his own mind that he continues to practise catharsis by himself at the expense of his adaptation to life. He is bound to the unconscious—to himself—not to the physician. He has obviously shared the experience of Theseus and his comrade Pirithous in their descent to Hades to bring back the goddess of the underworld. Tiring on the way, they sat down to rest for a while, only to find that they had grown to the rocks and could not rise.

These curious and unexpected occurrences must be explained to the patients, while the first-mentioned cases who were inaccessible to catharsis must also be handled by the method of explanation. In spite of the fact that the two classes of patients are apparently quite different, it is at the same point that explanation is called for—that is, where the problem of fixation arises, as was recognized by Freud. This fixation is evident enough in patients who have undergone catharsis, and it is especially clear in those who remain attached to the physician. Something similar has already been observed as an unpleasant result of hypnotic treatment, but the inner mechanism of such a tie was not understood. It now appears that the questionable bond essentially corresponds to the relation between father and child. The patient falls into a sort of childish dependence from which he cannot protect himself even by reason and insight. The fixation is at times astonishingly strong—so much so that one suspects it of being fed by forces quite out of the common. But since the process of transference is an unconscious one, the patient is unable to give any information about it. We are obviously dealing with a new symptom—a neurotic formation directly induced by the treatment. The question therefore arises : How is this new difficulty to be met ? The unmistakable outward sign of the situation is that the memory-image of the father with its accent of feeling is transferred to the physician. Inasmuch as the latter willy-nilly appears in the rôle of father, the patient slips into a childish relation. He has not, of course, been made childish by this relation ; there was always something childish about him, but it was suppressed. Now it comes to the surface, and—the long-lost father being found again—it tries to reproduce the family situation of childhood. Freud gave to this symptom the appropriate name of " transference ". A certain dependence upon the physician who has helped you is of course normal and understandable enough. What is abnormal and un-expected is the unusual obstinacy of the transference and its inaccessibility to conscious correction.

It is one of Freud's outstanding achievements to have explained the nature of this tie—at least in the light of man's personal history—and so to have cleared the way for an important advance in psychological knowledge. It has today been put beyond a doubt that it is caused by unconscious fantasies. These fantasies have in the main what we may call an " incestuous " character ; and this seems adequately to explain the fact that they remain unconscious and cannot be expected to turn up in the most thorough confession. Although Freud always speaks of incest-fantasies as if they were repressed, further experience shows us that in many cases they have never been conscious or have been sensed only in the vaguest way—for which reason they could not be intentionally repressed. More recent research seems to show that the incest-fantasies are usually unconscious and so remain till they are dragged to light in analytical treatment. By this I do not mean that pulling them up from the unconscious is an interference with nature which we should avoid ; I merely wish to suggest that the procedure is almost as drastic as a surgical operation. But it is wholly unavoidable in that the analytical procedure induces a transference which is abnormal, and can only be dealt with by reaching the incest-fantasies.

While the method of catharsis restores to the ego such contents as are accessible to consciousness and are normally included in it, the process of clearing up the transference brings to light contents which, because of their nature, were almost inaccessible to consciousness. This is the main difference between the stage of confession and the stage of explanation.

We have discussed above two sets of cases : those of such patients as do not lend themselves to the method of catharsis, and those for whom it gives results. We have moreover just treated of those whose fixation takes the form of a transference. Besides these there are those people we have also mentioned who develop no attachment to the physician, but rather one to their own unconscious, in which they become entangled as in a web. In these cases the parental image is not transferred to a human object. It is seen as a fantasy, and yet it exerts the same power of attraction and produces the same attachment as does the transference.

The patients who cannot give themselves without reserve to treatment by catharsis can be understood in the light of Freudian research. We can see that, even before coming to the doctor, they had identified themselves with their parents, and derive from this identification that force of authority, that independence and critical power which enables them to offer a successful resistance to the treatment. These are chiefly cultivated and differentiated persons. While others become the helpless victims of the unconscious parental image, these draw strength from it by unconsciously identifying themselves with their parents.

In the matter of the transference, we can get nowhere

with the help of confession. It was this which drove Freud to a fundamental renovation of Breuer's original technique of catharsis, and to what he himself called the " interpretative method ". This further step necessarily follows, for the relationship produced by the transference especially requires explanation. The layman can hardly appreciate the importance of this ; but the doctor who finds himself suddenly entangled in a web of incomprehensible and fantastic notions sees it all too clearly. He must interpret the transference to the patient—that is, explain to him what it is that he projects upon his doctor. Since the patient himself does not know what it is, the physician is forced to subject what scraps of fantasy he can obtain from the patient to analytical interpretation. It is first and foremost our dreams which furnish this important material. While investigating the suppression of wishes which are incompatible with our conscious standpoint, Freud studied dreams in search of these wishes, and in the process discovered the incestuous contents of which I have spoken. These were of course not the only materials revealed by the investigation ; he discovered all the filth of which human nature is capable—and it is notorious that it would require a lifetime to make even a rough inventory of it.

The end-product of the Freudian method of explanation is a detailed elaboration of man's shadow-side such as had never been carried out before. It is the most effective antidote imaginable to all idealistic illusions about the nature of man ; and it is therefore no wonder that there arose on all sides the most violent opposition to Freud and his school. We could expect nothing else of those who believe in illusions on principle ; but I maintain that there are not a few among the opponents of the method of explanation who have no illusions as to man's shadow-side, and who yet object to a biassed portrayal of man from the shadow-side alone. After all, the essential thing is not the shadow, but the body which casts it.

Freud's method of interpretation rests upon " reductive " explanations which unfailingly lead backward and downward, and it has a destructive effect if it is used in an exaggerated and one-sided way. Nevertheless psychology has profited greatly from Freud's pioneer work ; it has learned that human nature has also a black side, and that not man alone possesses this side, but his works, his institutions, and his convictions as well. Even our purest and holiest beliefs can be traced to the crudest origins. This way of looking at things even has its justification, for the beginning of all living organisms is simple and lowly ; we build our houses from the foundation up. No thoughtful person will deny that Salomon Reinach's explanation of the Last Supper in terms of primitive totemism is fraught with meaning ; nor will he object to the incest-theme being pointed out in the myths of the Greek divinities. It is painful—there is no denying it—to interpret radiant things from the shadow-side, and thus in a measure reduce them to their origins in dreary filth. But it seems to me to be an imperfection in things of beauty, and a weakness in man, if an explanation from the shadow-side has a destructive effect. The horror which we feel for Freudian interpretations is entirely due to our own barbaric or childish naïveté, which believes that there can be heights without corresponding depths, and which blinds us to the really " final " truth that, when carried to extremes, opposites meet. Our mistake would lie in supposing that what is radiant no longer exists because it has been explained from the shadow-side. This is a regrettable error into which Freud himself has fallen. Yet the shadow belongs to the light as the evil belongs to the good, and *vice versa*. Therefore I cannot regret the shock that was felt at the exposure of our occidental illusions and pettiness ; on the contrary, I welcome this exposure and attach to it an almost incalculable significance. It is one of those swings of the pendulum which, as history has so often shown, set matters right again. It forces us to accept a present-day philosophical relativism such as has been formulated by Einstein for mathematical physics, and which is fundamentally a truth of the far East whose ultimate effects upon us we cannot foresee.

Nothing influences our conduct less than do intellectual ideas. But when an idea is the expression of psychic experience which bears fruit in regions as far separated and as free from historical relation as East and West, then we must look into the matter closely. For such ideas represent forces that are beyond logical justification and moral sanction ; they are always stronger than man and his brain. Man believes indeed that he moulds these ideas, but in reality they mould him and make him their unwitting mouthpiece.

To return again to the problem of fixation, I should like now to deal with the effects of the process of explanation. The patient becomes aware of the unsoundness of his position with respect to the doctor when his transference has been traced back to its dark origins ; he cannot avoid seeing how inappropriate and childish his claims are. If he has been inflated by a sense of authority, he will exchange his elevated position for one that is more modest, and will accept an insecurity which may prove very wholesome. If he has not yet renounced his infantile claims upon the doctor, he will now recognize the inescapable truth that to make claims on others is a childish self-indulgence which must be replaced by a greater sense of his own responsibility. The man of insight will draw his own moral conclusions. Convinced of his own deficiencies, he will use this knowledge as a means of protection ; he will plunge into the struggle for existence and consume in progressive work and experience that force of longing which has caused him to cling obstinately to a child's paradise or at least to look back at it over his shoulder. A normal adaptation and patience with his own shortcomings will become his guiding moral principles, and he will try to free himself from sentimentality and illusion. The inevitable result will be that he turns away from the unconscious as from a source of weakness and temptation— the field of moral and social defeat.

The problem which now faces the patient is that of being educated as a social being, and with this we come to the third stage. Mere insight into themselves is sufficient for morally sensitive persons who have enough driving force to carry them forward ; for those with little imagination for moral values, however, it does not suffice. Without the spur of external necessity, self-knowledge is ineffective for them even when they are deeply convinced—to say nothing of those who have been struck by the analyst's interpretation and yet doubt it after all. These last are mentally disciplined people who grasp the truth of a " reductive " explanation, but cannot accept it when it merely invalidates their hopes and ideals. In these cases also mere insight is insufficient. It is a weakness of the method of explanation that it succeeds only with sensitive persons who can draw independent moral conclusions from their understanding of themselves. It is true that we can get further with explanation than with uninterpreted confession alone, for it at least trains the mind, and therefore may awaken sleeping powers which can intervene in a helpful way. But the fact remains that the most thorough explanation leaves the patient in many cases an intelligent but still incapable child. The trouble is that Freudian explanations in terms of pleasure and its satisfaction are one-sided and therefore insufficient, especially when applied to the later stages of development. This viewpoint will not account for everybody; for even if everyone possesses this side, it is not always the most important. A hungry artist prefers bread to a beautiful painting, and a man in love prefers a woman to his public career; yet the painting may be of the greatest importance to the one and public office to the other. On the average, those who easily achieve social adaptation and social position are better accounted for by the pleasure principle than are the unadapted whose social shortcomings leave them with a craving for power and importance. The older brother who follows in the footsteps of his father and attains a commanding position, may be tortured by his desires; but the younger brother who feels repressed and overshadowed by the other two, may be goaded by ambition or the craving for respect. He may even yield so completely to this passion that nothing else is vital to him.

At this point we become aware that Freud's explanation of things falls short, and it is precisely here that his former pupil, Adler, comes forward to fill the gap. Adler has shown convincingly that many cases of neurosis can be more satisfactorily explained on the ground of an urge to power than by the pleasure principle. His interpretation therefore is designed to show the patient that he " arranges " his symptoms and exploits his neurosis to attain a fictitious

importance ; that even his transference and his other
fixations serve his will to power, and thus represent a
" masculine protest " against a fancied subjection. Adler
obviously has his eye on repressed and socially unsuccessful
people whose one passion is for self-assertion. These people
are neurotic because they always imagine themselves
oppressed and tilt at the windmills of their own fancies,
thus putting the goal they most desire quite out of reach.

In essentials, Adler's method begins at the second stage ;
he explains the symptoms in the sense just indicated, and
to this extent appeals to the patient's understanding. Yet
it is characteristic of Adler that he does not expect too
much of understanding, but, taking a further step, has
clearly recognized the need for social education. While
Freud is an investigator and interpreter, Adler is chiefly
an educator. In refusing to leave the patient in a childish
condition, helpless for all his valuable understanding, and
in trying by every device of education to make him a
normally adapted person, Adler modifies Freud's procedure.
He does all this apparently in the conviction that social
adaptation and normalization are indispensable—that they
are even the most desirable goals and the most suitable
fulfilment for a human being. The widespread social
influence of Adler's school is a consequence of this outlook—
as also its neglect of the unconscious, which on occasions, it
seems, amounts to complete denial. This is probably a
swing of the pendulum—an inevitable reaction to Freud's
emphasis on the unconscious, which corresponds to the
natural aversion for it which we have noted in patients
who are struggling for adaptation and health. For if
the unconscious is held to be a mere receptacle for all
the evil shadow-things in human nature, including even

primeval slime-deposits, we really do not see why we should still linger on the edge of this swamp into which we once fell. The investigator may see in the mud-puddle a world full of wonders, but to the ordinary man it is something upon which he prefers to turn his back. Just as early Buddhism recognized no gods because it had to free itself from an inheritance of nearly two million gods, so must psychology, if it is to develop further, renounce so essentially negative an approach to the unconscious as Freud's.

The Adlerian school, with its educational intent, begins at the very point where Freud leaves off, and thus helps the patient who has learned to see into himself to find the way to normal life. It is obviously not enough for him to know how and why he fell ill, for to understand the causes of an evil does very little towards curing it. We must never forget that the crooked paths of a neurosis lead to as many obstinate habits, and that, despite any amount of understanding, these do not disappear until they are replaced by other habits. But habits are only won by exercise, and appropriate education is the sole means to this end. The patient must be, as it were, prodded into other paths, and this always requires an educating will. We can therefore see why it is that Adler's approach has found favour chiefly with clergymen and teachers, while Freud's school has its advocates among physicians and intellectuals, who one and all are bad nurses and educators.

Every stage in our psychic development has something peculiarly final about it. When we have experienced catharsis with its wholesale confession we feel that we have reached our goal at last; all has come out, all is known, every anxiety has been lived through and every tear shed; now things will go as they ought. After the work of explanation we are equally persuaded that we now know how the neurosis arose. The earliest memories have been unearthed, the deepest roots dug up ; the transference was nothing but the wish-fulfilling fantasy of a child's paradise or a regression to the old family situation ; the way to a normally disillusioned life is now open. But then comes the period of education, which makes us realize that no confession and no amount of explaining will make the ill-formed tree grow straight, but that it must be trained with the gardener's art upon the trellis before normal adaptation can be attained.

The curious sense of finality which attends every stage of development accounts for the fact that there are people using catharsis today who have apparently never heard of dream interpretation ; Freudians who do not understand a word of Adler, and Adlerians who do not wish to hear any mention of the unconscious. Each is deceived by the sense of finality peculiar to the stage of development at which he stands, and this gives rise to that confusion of opinions and views which makes it so hard for us to find our bearings.

But what causes this sense of finality which evokes such bigoted obstinacy in all directions ? I can only explain it to myself on the ground that each stage of development is summed up in a basic truth, and that therefore cases frequently recur which demonstrate this truth in a striking way. Our world is so exceedingly rich in delusions that a truth is priceless, and no one will let it slip because of a few exceptions with which it cannot be brought into accord. Whoever doubts this truth is of course looked upon as a faithless reprobate, while a note of fanaticism and intolerance creeps into the discussion on all sides.

And yet each of us can carry the torch of knowledge

but a part of the way, until another takes it from him. Could we but accept this in an impersonal way—could we but grasp the fact that we are not the personal creators of our truths, but only their exponents who thus make articulate the psychic needs of our day—then much of the poison and bitterness might be spared and we should be able to perceive the profound and super-personal continuity of the human mind.

We generally take too little account of the fact that the doctor who uses catharsis as a mode of treatment is something more than the embodiment of an abstract idea which automatically produces nothing but catharsis. He is also a man. His thinking, to be sure, may be limited to his special field, but in his behaviour he exerts the influence of a complete human being. Without being clearly conscious of it or giving it a name, he unwittingly does a great deal in the way of explanation and education ; and other analysts do as much in the way of catharsis without raising it to the level of a principle.

The three stages of analytical psychology so far dealt with are by no means of such a nature that the last can replace the first or the second. All three quite properly co-exist and are salient aspects of one and the same problem ; they no more invalidate each other than do confession and absolution. And the same is true of the fourth—the stage of transformation : it must not claim to be the finally-achieved and only valid truth. Its part is to make up a deficit left by the previous stages ; it comes to meet an additional and still unsatisfied need.

In order to make clear what this fourth stage has in view, and to throw some light on the curious term " transformation ", we must first take account of those psychic needs of man which were not given a place in the other stages. In other words, we must ascertain what could seem more desirable or lead further than the claim to be a normally adapted, social being. Nothing is more useful or fitting than to be a normal human being; but the very notion of a " normal human being " suggests a restriction to the average—as does also the concept of adaptation. It is only a man who, as things stand, already finds it difficult to come to terms with the everyday world who can see in this restriction a desirable improvement: a man, let us say, whose neurosis unfits him for normal life. To be " normal " is a splendid ideal for the unsuccessful, for all those who have not yet found an adaptation. But for people who have far more ability than the average, for whom it was never hard to gain successes and to accomplish their share of the world's work—for them restriction to the normal signifies the bed of Procrustes, unbearable boredom, infernal sterility and hopelessness. As a consequence there are many people who become neurotic because they are only normal, as there are people who are neurotic because they cannot become normal. For the former the very thought that you want to educate them to normality is a nightmare; their deepest need is really to be able to lead " abnormal " lives.

A man can hope for satisfaction and fulfilment only in what he does not yet possess; he cannot find pleasure in something of which he has already had too much. To be a socially adapted being has no charms for one to whom to be so is mere child's play. Always to do what is right becomes a bore for the man who knows how, whereas the eternal bungler cherishes the secret longing to be right for once in some distant future.

The needs and necessities of individuals vary. What sets one free is for another a prison—as for instance normality and adaptation. Although it is a biological dictum that man is a herd animal and is only healthy when he lives as a social being, yet the first case we observe may seem to upset this statement, and to prove that man is only healthy when leading an abnormal and unsocial life. It is a terrible misfortune that practical psychology can offer no generally valid recipes and norms. There are only individual cases whose needs and demands are totally different—so different that we really cannot foresee what course a given case will follow. It is therefore wise of the physician to renounce all premature assumptions. This does not mean that he should throw all his assumptions overboard, but that he should regard them in any given case as hypothetical.

Yet it is not the doctor's whole task to instruct or convince his patient; he must rather show him how the doctor reacts to his particular case. For twist and turn the matter as we may, the relation between physician and patient remains personal within the frame of the impersonal, professional treatment. We cannot by any device bring it about that the treatment is not the outcome of a mutual influence in which the whole being of the patient as well as that of the doctor plays its part. Two primary factors come together in the treatment—that is, two persons, neither of whom is a fixed and determinable magnitude. Their fields of consciousness may be quite clearly defined, but they bring with them besides an indefinitely extended sphere of unconsciousness. For this reason the personalities of the doctor and patient have often more to do with the outcome of the treatment than what the doctor says or thinks—although we must not undervalue this latter factor as a disturbing or healing one. The meeting of two personalities is like the contact of two chemical substances : if there is any reaction, both are transformed. We should expect the doctor to have an influence on the patient in every effective psychic treatment ; but this influence can only take place when he too is affected by the patient. You can exert no influence if you are not susceptible to influence. It is futile for the doctor to shield himself from the influence of the patient and to surround himself with a smoke-screen of fatherly and professional authority. If he does so he merely forbids himself the use of a highly important organ of information, and the patient influences him unconsciously none the less. The unconscious changes in the doctor which the patient thus brings about are well known to many psychotherapists ; they are disturbances, or even injuries, peculiar to the profession, which illustrate in a striking way the patient's almost " chemical " influence. One of the best known of them is the counter-transference which the transference evokes. But the effects are often more subtle, and their nature is best conveyed by the old idea of the demon of sickness. According to this a sufferer transmits his disease to a healthy person whose powers subdue the demon—but not without a negative influence upon the well-being of the healer.

In the relation between doctor and patient we meet with imponderable factors which bring about a mutual transformation. In this exchange, the more stable and the stronger personality will decide the final issue. But I have seen many cases in which the patient has proved stronger than the doctor in defiance of all theory and the doctor's intention ; and where this has happened it has most often, though not always, been to the disadvantage of the doctor.

The fact of mutual influence and all that goes with it underlies the stage of transformation. More than a quarter of a century of wide practical experience was needed for the clear recognition of these manifestations. Freud himself has admitted their importance and has therefore seconded my demand that the analyst himself be analysed.

But what is the wider meaning of this demand? It means nothing less than that the doctor " is just as much in analysis " as the patient. He is as much a part of the psychic process of the treatment as is the patient, and is equally exposed to the transforming influences. Indeed, if the doctor is more or less inaccessible to this influence, he is correspondingly robbed of his influence over the patient ; if he is influenced only unconsciously, he shows a defect of consciousness which prevents him from seeing the patient correctly. In both cases the result of the treatment is compromised.

The physician, then, is called upon himself to face that task which he wishes the patient to face. If it is a question of becoming socially adapted, he himself must become so— or, in the reverse case, appropriately non-adapted. There are of course a thousand different aspects of this requirement in therapy, according to the situation in a given case. One doctor believes in overcoming infantilism—and therefore he must have overcome his own infantilism. Another believes in the abreaction of all emotion—and so he must have abreacted all his own emotions. A third believes in complete consciousness—so that he must have reached an advanced state of consciousness himself. At all events the doctor must consistently try to meet his own therapeutic demands if he wishes to assure himself of a proper influence on his patient. All these guiding principles in therapy confront the doctor with important ethical duties which can be summed up in the single rule : be the man through whom you wish to influence others. Mere talk has always been considered hollow, and there is no trick, however cunning, by which one can evade this simple rule for long. The fact of being convinced, and not the subject-matter of conviction—it is this which has always carried weight.

The fourth stage of analytical psychology, then, demands not only the transformation of the patient, but also the counter-application to himself by the doctor of the system which he prescribes in any given case. And in dealing with himself the doctor must display as much relentlessness, consistency and perseverance as in dealing with his patients. To work upon himself with an equal concentration is truly no small achievement ; for he brings to bear all the attentiveness and critical judgement he can summon in showing his patients their mistaken paths, their false conclusions and infantile subterfuges. No one pays the doctor for his introspective efforts ; and moreover, we are generally not interested enough in ourselves. Again, we so commonly undervalue the deeper aspects of the human psyche that we hold self-examination or preoccupation with ourselves to be almost morbid. We evidently suspect ourselves of harbouring rather unwholesome things all too reminiscent of a sick-room. The physician must overcome these resistances in himself, for who can educate others while himself uneducated ? Who can enlighten his fellows while still in the dark about himself, and who can purify if he is himself unclean ?

The step from educating others to self-education is demanded of the doctor in the stage of transformation. It is the corollary of the demand that the patient transform himself and thus complete the earlier stages of the treatment. This challenge to the doctor to transform himself in order to effect a change in the patient meets with scant popular approval, for three reasons. First of all it seems unpractical; secondly, there is a prejudice against being occupied with ourselves ; and thirdly, it is sometimes very painful to make ourselves live up to everything that we expect of the patient. This last is the strongest reason for the unpopularity of the demand that the doctor examine himself ; for if he conscientiously " doctors " himself he will soon discover things in his nature which are completely opposed to normalization, or which continue to haunt him in the most disturbing way in spite of exhaustive explanations and thorough abreaction. What will he do about these things ? He always knows what the patient should do about them—it is his professional duty to do so. But what will he in all sincerity do about them when they involve himself or perhaps those who stand nearest to him ? If he examines himself he will discover some inferior side which brings him dangerously near to his patient and perhaps even blights his authority. How will he handle this tormenting discovery ? This somewhat " neurotic " question will touch him on the quick, no matter how normal he deems himself to be. He will also discover that the ultimate questions which oppress him as well as his patients cannot be solved by any amount of " treatment ". He will let them see that to expect solutions from others is a way of remaining childish ; and he will see for himself that, if no solutions can be found, these questions must only be repressed again.

I will not discuss further the matter of self-examination and the many problems it raises, because the great obscurity which still surrounds our study of the psyche allows of little interest in them. I would rather emphasize what has already been said: that the newest developments of analytical psychology confront us with the imponderable elements of human personality; that we have learned to place in the foreground the personality of the doctor himself as a curative or harmful factor; and that we have begun to demand his own transformation—the self-education of the educator. Everything that happened to the patient must now happen to the doctor, and he must pass through the stages of confession, explanation and education so that his personality will not react unfavourably on the patient. The physician may no longer slip out of his own difficulties by treating the difficulties of others. He will remember that a man who suffers from a running abscess is not fit to perform a surgical operation.

Just as the discovery of the unconscious shadow-side once forced the school of Freud to deal even with questions of religion, so the latest advance of analytical psychology makes an unavoidable problem of the doctor's ethical attitude. The self-criticism and self-examination demanded of him radically alter our view of the human psyche. This cannot be grasped from the standpoint of natural science; it is not only the sufferer but the physician as well; not only the object but also the subject; not only a function of the brain, but the *sine qua non* of consciousness itself.

What was formerly a method of medical treatment now becomes a method of self-education, and therewith the horizon of our modern psychology is immeasurably widened. The medical diploma is no longer the crucial thing, but human quality instead. This is a significant step. All the implements of psychotherapy developed in clinical practice, refined and systematized, are now put at our service and can be used for our self-education and self-perfectioning. Analytical psychology is no longer bound to the consulting-room of the doctor; its chains have been severed. We might say that it transcends itself, and now advances to fill that void which hitherto has marked the psychic insufficiency of Western culture as compared with that of the East. We Occidentals had learned to tame and subject the psyche, but we knew nothing about its methodical development and its functions. Our civilization is still young, and we therefore required all the devices of the animal-tamer to make the defiant barbarian and the savage in us in some measure tractable. But when we reach a higher cultural level, we must forgo compulsion and turn to self-development. For this we must have knowledge of a way or a method—and so far we have known of none. It seems to me that the findings and experiences of analytical psychology can at least provide a foundation; for as soon as psychotherapy requires the self-perfecting of the doctor, it is freed from its clinical origins and ceases to be a mere method for treating the sick. It is now of service to the healthy as well, or at least to those who have a right to psychic health and whose illness is at most the suffering that tortures us all. For this reason we may hope to see analytical psychology become of general use—more so even than the methods which constitute its preliminary stages and which severally carry a general truth. But between the realization of this hope and the actual present there lies an abyss over which no bridge is to be found. We have yet to build it stone by stone.

III

THE AIMS OF PSYCHOTHERAPY

It is generally agreed today that neuroses are functional psychic disturbances and are to be cured by psychic methods of treatment. But when we come to the questions of the formation of the neurosis and of the basic principles of therapy, all agreement ends, and we have to acknowledge that we have as yet no fully satisfactory conception of the nature of the neurosis nor of the principles of treatment. While it is true that two trends or schools of thought have gained a special hearing, their teachings by no means exhaust the numerous divergent opinions that have come to be expressed in our time. There are also many non-partisans who, amid the general conflict of opinion, have formulated their own views. If, therefore, we sought to paint a comprehensive picture of the situation, we should have to match upon our palette the subtle colour-gradations of the rainbow.

I would gladly paint such a picture if it lay in my power, for I have always felt the need of comparing the numerous viewpoints. I have never succeeded in the long-run in not giving divergent opinions their due. Such opinions could never arise—much less secure a following—if they did not correspond to some special disposition, some special character, some fundamental psychic experience that is more or less prevalent. If we were to exclude such opinions as simply wrong and worthless, we should be rejecting this particular

63

disposition or this particular experience as a misinterpretation
—that is, we should be doing violence to our own empirical
material. The wide approval which greeted Freud's explanation of the neuroses in terms of sexual causation, and
his view that the happenings in the psyche turn essentially
upon infantile pleasure and its satisfaction, should be
instructive to the psychologist. It shows him that this
manner of thinking and feeling coincides with a relatively
widespread tendency or spiritual current which, quite apart
from Freud's theory, has appeared in other places, in other
circumstances, in various minds and in different forms. I
should call it a manifestation of the collective psyche. Let
me point first to the works of Havelock Ellis and Auguste
Forel and the contributors to *Anthropophyteia* ; also to
the attitude to sexuality in Anglo-Saxon countries during
the post-Victorian period, as well as to the widespread
discussion of sexual matters in general literature which had
already set in with the French realists. Freud is one of the
exponents of a present-day psychic predisposition that has
a special history of its own ; but for obvious reasons we
cannot go into that history here.

The approbation which Adler, no less than Freud, has
met with on both sides of the ocean, permits the same
inference. It is undeniable that a great many people find
satisfaction in explaining their troubles in terms of an urge
to power arising from a sense of inferiority. Nor can it be
disputed that this view accounts for actual psychic happenings which are not given their due in the Freudian system.
I need hardly mention in detail the forces of the collective
psyche and the social factors which underlie the Adlerian
view and call for precisely this theoretical formulation.
These matters are sufficiently obvious.

It would be an unpardonable error to overlook the element of truth in both the Freudian and Adlerian viewpoints, but it would be no less unpardonable to take either of them as the sole truth. Both truths correspond to psychic realities. There are actual cases which, in the main, are best described and explained by one or other of the two theories. I can accuse neither of these investigators of error; on the contrary, I try to apply both hypotheses as far as possible, because I fully accept their relative validity. It would certainly never have occurred to me to depart from Freud's path if I had not stumbled upon facts which forced me to modify his theory; and the same is true of my relation to the Adlerian viewpoint. It seems hardly necessary to add that I hold the truth of my own views to be equally relative, and regard myself also as the exponent of a certain pre-disposition.

It is in applied psychology, if anywhere, that today we should be modest and grant validity to a number of apparently contradictory opinions; for we are still far from having anything like a thorough knowledge of the human psyche, that most challenging field of scientific enquiry. For the present we have merely more or less plausible opinions that defy reconciliation. When, therefore, I undertake to present my views in a general way, I hope I shall not be misunderstood. I am not recommending a novel truth; still less am I heralding an ultimate gospel. I can speak only of attempts to throw light upon psychic facts that are obscure to me, or of efforts to overcome therapeutic difficulties.

And it is just with this last question that I should like to begin, since it is here that we find the most pressing need for modifications. As is well known, one can get along for quite a time with an inadequate theory, but not with inadequate therapeutic methods. In my psychotherapeutic practice covering nearly thirty years, I have met with a fair number of failures which were far more impressive to me than my successes. Almost anybody, from the primitive medicine-man and the prayer-healer up, can gain successes in psychotherapy. But the psychotherapist learns little or nothing from his successes. They mainly confirm him in his mistakes, while his failures, on the other hand, are priceless experiences in that they not only open up the way to a deeper truth, but force him to change his views and methods.

I certainly recognize how much my work has been furthered first by Freud and then by Adler ; and whenever possible I apply their standpoints to my practical treatment of patients. Nevertheless I insist upon the fact that I have met with failures which I feel could have been avoided had I taken into consideration those empirical data which later forced me into modifications of their views. It is impossible to describe all the situations with which I was confronted, and I must content myself with singling out a few typical cases. It was with older patients that I had the greatest difficulties—that is, with persons over forty. In handling younger people I generally find the familiar viewpoints of Freud and Adler applicable enough, for they offer a treatment which brings the patient to a certain level of adaptation and normality, apparently without leaving any disturbing after-effects. With older people, according to my experience, this is often not the case. It seems to me that the elements of the psyche undergo in the course of life a very marked change—so much so, that we may distinguish between a psychology of the morning of life and a psychology of its

afternoon. As a rule, the life of a young person is characterized by a general unfolding and a striving toward concrete
ends ; his neurosis, if he develops one, can be traced to his
hesitation or his shrinking back from this necessity. But
the life of an older person is marked by a contraction of
forces, by the affirmation of what has been achieved, and
the curtailment of further growth. His neurosis comes
mainly from his clinging to a youthful attitude which is
now out of season. Just as the youthful neurotic is afraid
of life, so the older one shrinks back from death. What was
a normal goal for the young man, inevitably becomes a
neurotic hindrance to the older person. In the case of the
young neurotic, what was once a normal dependence on his
parents inevitably becomes, through his hesitation to face
the world, an incest-relation which is inimical to life. It
must be remembered that, despite all similarities, resistance,
repression, transference, " guiding fictions " and so forth,
have one meaning when we find them in young people,
while in older persons they have quite another. The aims
of therapy should undoubtedly be modified to meet this
fact. The age of the patient seems to me, therefore, a
most important *indicium*.

But there are also various *indicia* which we should note
within the period of youth itself. Thus, according to my
view, it is a blunder in technique to treat from the Freudian
standpoint a patient of the type to whom the Adlerian
psychology applies, that is, an unsuccessful person with an
infantile need for self-assertion. Conversely, it would be a
gross error to force the Adlerian viewpoint upon a successful
man whose motives can be understood in terms of the
pleasure principle. In doubtful cases the resistances of the
patient may serve as valuable signposts. I am inclined at

the start to take deep-seated resistances seriously, strange as this may sound. For I am convinced that the doctor is not necessarily in a better position to know what is wanted than is the patient's own psychic constitution, which may be quite unconscious to the patient himself. This modesty on the part of the doctor is altogether appropriate in view of the situation today. Not only have we as yet no generally valid psychology, but what is more, the variety of psychic constitutions is untold, and there also exist more or less individual psyches which refuse to fit into any general scheme.

As to this question of psychic constitution, it is well known that I postulate two different basic attitudes in accordance with the typical differences already suspected by many students of human nature—the extraverted and the introverted attitudes. These attitudes also I take to be important *indicia*, as likewise the predominance of a particular psychic function over other functions. The great variability of individual life necessitates constant modifications of theory which are often applied by the doctor quite unconsciously, but which in principle do not at all coincide with his theoretical creed.

While we are on this question of psychic constitution, I must not fail to point out that there are some people whose attitude is essentially spiritual and others whose attitude is essentially materialistic. It must not be assumed that such an attitude is accidentally acquired or springs from some misunderstanding. These attitudes show themselves as ingrained passions which no criticism or persuasion can stamp out ; there are even cases where an apparently outspoken materialism has its source in the denial of a religious disposition. Cases of the reverse type are better known today, although they are not more frequent than the others. These attitudes also are *indicia* which, in my opinion, ought not to be overlooked.

When we use the word *indicium* it might appear to mean, as in medical parlance generally, that this or that treatment is indicated. Perhaps this should be the case, but psychotherapy has assuredly reached no such degree of certainty —for which reason our *indicia* are unfortunately not much more than mere warnings against one-sidedness.

The human psyche is highly equivocal. In every single case we must consider the question whether an attitude or a so-called *habitus* exists in its own right, or is perhaps only a compensation for the opposite. I must confess that I have so often been mistaken in this matter, that in any concrete case I am at pains to avoid all theoretical presuppositions as to the structure of the neurosis and as to what the patient can and ought to do. As far as possible, I let pure experience decide the therapeutic aims. This may perhaps seem strange, because it is usually assumed that the therapist should have an aim. But it seems to me that in psychotherapy especially it is advisable for the physician not to have too fixed a goal. He can scarcely know what is wanted better than do nature and the will-to-live of the sick person. The great decisions of human life have as a rule far more to do with the instincts and other mysterious unconscious factors than with conscious will and well-meaning reasonableness. The shoe that fits one person pinches another ; there is no recipe for living that suits all cases. Each of us carries his own life-form—an indeterminable form which cannot be superseded by any other.

None of these considerations, of course, prevents our

doing everything possible to make the lives of patients normal and reasonable. If this brings about a satisfactory result, then we can let it go at that ; but if it is insufficient, then, for better or for worse, the therapist must be guided by the data presented through the patient's unconscious. Here we must follow nature as a guide, and the course the physician then adopts is less a question of treatment than of developing the creative possibilities that lie in the patient himself.

What I have to say begins with the point where treatment ceases and development sets in. My contribution to psychotherapy is confined to those cases in which rational treatment yields no satisfactory results. The clinical material at my disposal is of a special nature : new cases are decidedly in the minority. Most of my patients have already gone through some form of psychotherapeutic treatment, usually with partial or negative results. About a third of my cases are suffering from no clinically definable neurosis, but from the senselessness and emptiness of their lives. It seems to me, however, that this can well be described as the general neurosis of our time. Fully two-thirds of my patients have passed middle age.

It is difficult to treat patients of this particular kind by rational methods, because they are in the main socially well-adapted individuals of considerable ability, to whom normalization means nothing. As for so-called normal people, I am even worse off in their regard, for I have no ready-made life-philosophy to hand out to them. In the majority of my cases, the resources of consciousness have been exhausted ; the ordinary expression for this situation is : " I am stuck." It is chiefly this fact that forces me to look for hidden possibilities. For I do not know what to say to the patient when he asks me : " What do you advise ? What shall I do ? " I do not know any better than he. I know only one thing : that when to my conscious outlook there is no possible way of going ahead, and I am therefore " stuck ", my unconscious will react to the unbearable standstill.

This coming to a standstill is a psychic occurrence so often repeated in the evolution of mankind, that it has become the theme of many a fairy-tale and myth. We are told of the Open Sesame to the locked door, or of some helpful animal who finds the hidden way. We might put it in this way : " getting stuck " is a typical event which, in the course of time, has evoked typical reactions and compensations. We may therefore expect with a certain degree of probability that something similar will appear in the reactions of the unconscious, as, for example, in dreams.

In such cases, therefore, my attention is directed more particularly to dreams. This is not because I am tied to the notion that dreams must always be called to the rescue, or because I possess a mysterious dream-theory which tells me how everything must shape itself ; but quite simply from perplexity. I do not know where else to go for help, and so I try to find it in dreams ; these at least present us with images pointing to something or other, and that is at any rate better than nothing. I have no theory about dreams ; I do not know how dreams arise. I am altogether in doubt as to whether my way of handling dreams even deserves the name of " method ".

I share all my readers' prejudices against dream inter-pretation as being the quintessence of uncertainty and arbitrariness. But, on the other hand, I know that if we meditate on a dream sufficiently long and thoroughly—if we take it about with us and turn it over and over—something almost always comes of it. This something is of course not of such a kind that we can boast of its scientific nature or rationalize it, but it is a practical and important hint which shows the patient in what direction the unconscious is leading him. I even *may* not give first importance to the question whether our study of the dream gives a scientifically verifiable result ; if I do this, I am following an exclusively personal aim, and one which is therefore auto-erotic. I must content myself with the fact that the result means something to the patient and sets his life into motion again. I may allow myself only *one* criterion for the validity of my interpretation of the dream—and this is that it *works*. As for my scientific hobby—my desire to know why it is that the dream works—this I must reserve for my spare time.

The contents of the initial dreams are infinitely varied— I mean those dreams which the patient relates to me at the beginning of the treatment. In many cases they point directly to the past and bring to mind what is forgotten and lost to the personality. It is from these very losses that one-sidedness results, and this causes the standstill and consequent disorientation. In psychological terms, one-sidedness may lead to a sudden loss of libido. All our previous activities become uninteresting, even senseless, and the goals towards which we strove lose their value. What in one person is merely a passing mood may in another become a chronic condition. In these cases it often happens that other possibilities of development of the personality lie somewhere or other in the past, and no one, not even the patient, knows about them. But the dream may reveal the clue. In other cases the dream points to present facts, as for example marriage or social position, which have never been consciously accepted as sources of problems and conflicts.

These possibilities fall within the scope of rational explanation, and it is not difficult to make such initial dreams plausible. The real difficulty begins when dreams, as is often the case, do not point to anything tangible—especially when they show a kind of foreknowledge of the future. I do not mean that such dreams are necessarily prophetic, but that they anticipate or " reconnoitre ". Such dreams contain inklings of possibilities, and therefore can never be made plausible to an outsider. They are often not plausible even to me, and then I say to my patients : " I don't believe it, but follow up the clue." As I have said, the stimulating effect is the sole criterion, and it is by no means necessary that we should understand why such an effect takes place. This is especially true of dreams containing mythological images which are sometimes incredibly strange and baffling. These dreams contain something like " unconscious metaphysics " ; they are expressions of undifferentiated psychic activity which may often contain the germs of conscious thought.[1]

In a long initial dream of one of my " normal " patients, the illness of his sister's child played an important part. She was a little girl of two. Some time before, this sister really had lost a boy through illness, but otherwise none of her children were ill. The image of the sick child in the dream at first proved baffling to him—undoubtedly because it in no way fitted in with the facts. Since there was no direct and close connection between the dreamer and his sister he

[1] Plato's vision of the cave is an imaginative anticipation of the problem of knowledge which was to occupy philosophers for centuries to come. Dreams and fantasies on occasion show a philosophic insight which is comparable to such a vision. (*Trans.*)

could find in this image little that was personal to him. Then suddenly it occurred to him that two years earlier he had taken up the study of occultism, and that it was this which had led him to psychology. The child was evidently his interest in the things of the psyche, an idea which I should never have hit upon of my own accord. Looked at from the side of theory, this dream-image can mean anything or nothing. For that matter, does a thing or a fact ever mean anything in and of itself ? We can only be sure that it is always the human being who interprets, that is, gives meaning to a fact. And that is the gist of the matter for psychology. It impressed the dreamer as a new and interesting idea that the study of occultism might have something sickly about it. Somehow the thought struck home. And this is the decisive point : the interpretation *works*, however we may elect to account for its working. For the dreamer this thought contained a criticism, and through it a certain change in attitude was brought about. By such slight changes, which one could never think out rationally, things begin to move and the dead point is overcome.

In commenting upon this example I could say in a figure of speech that the dream *meant* that the occult studies of the dreamer had something sickly about them. And in this sense I may also speak of " unconscious metaphysics ", if the dreamer is brought by his dream to this very thought. But I go still further ; I not only give the patient an opportunity to see what occurs to him in connection with his dream, but I allow myself to do the same. I give him the benefit of my guesses and opinions. If, in doing this I should open the door to so-called " suggestion ", I see no occasion for regret ; it is well known that we are susceptible only to those suggestions with which we are already secretly in accord. No harm is done if now and then one goes astray in this riddle-reading. Sooner or later the psyche rejects the mistake, much as an organism does a foreign body. I need not try to prove that my dream interpretation is correct, which would be a somewhat hopeless undertaking, but must simply help the patient to find what it is that activates him—I was almost betrayed into saying what is actual.

It is of especial importance for me to know as much as possible about primitive psychology, mythology, archæology and comparative religion, for the reason that these fields afford me priceless analogies with which I can enrich the associations of my patients. Working together, we are then able to find the apparently irrelevant full of meaning and vastly increase the effectiveness of the dream. Thus to enter a realm of immediate experience is most stimulating for those who have done their utmost in the personal and rational spheres of life and yet have found no meaning and no satisfaction there. In this way, too, the matter-of-fact and the commonplace come to wear an altered countenance, and can even acquire a new glamour. For it all depends on how we look at things, and not on how they are in themselves. The least of things with a meaning is worth more in life than the greatest of things without it.

I do not think that I underestimate the risk of this undertaking. It is as if one began to build a bridge out into space. Indeed, one might even allege—as has often been done—that in following this procedure the doctor and his patient are both together indulging in mere fantasies. And I do not consider this an objection, but quite to the point. I even make an effort to second the patient in his fantasies. Truth to tell, I have a very high opinion of fantasy. To me, it is actually the maternally creative side of the masculine spirit. When all is said and done, we are never proof against fantasy. It is true that there are worthless, inadequate, morbid and unsatisfying fantasies whose sterile nature will be quickly recognized by every person endowed with common-sense ; but this of course proves nothing against the value of creative imagination. All the works of man have their origin in creative fantasy. What right have .we then to depreciate imagination ? In the ordinary course of things, fantasy does not easily go astray ; it is too deep for that, and too closely bound up with the tap-root of human and animal instinct. In surprising ways it always rights itself again. The creative activity of the imagination frees man from his bondage to the " nothing but " and liberates in him the spirit of play. As Schiller says, man is completely human only when he is playing.

My aim is to bring about a psychic state in which my patient begins to experiment with his own nature—a state of fluidity, change and growth, in which there is no longer anything eternally fixed and hopelessly petrified. It is of course only by stating its general principles that I can present my technique here. In handling a dream or a fantasy I make it a rule never to go beyond the meaning which has an effect upon the patient ; I merely strive in each case to make this meaning as conscious to him as possible, so that he can also become aware of its supra-personal connections. This is important, for when something quite universal happens to a man and he supposes it to be an experience peculiar to himself, then his attitude is obviously wrong, that is, too personal, and it tends to exclude him from human society. We require not only a present-day, personal consciousness, but also a supra-personal consciousness which is open to the sense of historical continuity. However far-fetched it may sound, experience shows that many neuroses are caused by the fact that people blind themselves to their own religious promptings because of a childish passion for rational enlightenment. The psychologist of today ought to realize once and for all that we are no longer dealing with questions of dogma and creed. A religious attitude is an element in psychic life whose importance can hardly be overrated. And it is precisely for the religious outlook that the sense of historical continuity is indispensable.

To return to the question of my technique, I ask myself to what extent I am indebted to Freud. In any case I learned it from Freud's method of free association, and I regard my technique as a further development of this method.

As long as I help the patient to discover the effective elements in his dream, and as long as I try to show him the general meaning of his symbols, he is still, psychologically speaking, in a state of childhood. For the time being he depends on his dreams and is always asking himself whether the subsequent dream will give him new light or not. Moreover, he is dependent on my having ideas about his dreams and on my ability to increase his insight through my knowledge. Thus he is still in an undesirably passive condition in which everything is uncertain and questionable ; neither he nor I know the journey's end. Often it is not much more than a groping about in Egyptian darkness. In this condition we must not expect any very marked effects, for the uncertainty is too great. Moreover we constantly run the risk that what we have woven by day, the night will unravel. The danger is that nothing comes to pass ; that nothing keeps its shape. It not infrequently happens in these circumstances that the patient has an especially colourful or curious dream, and says to me : " Do you know, if only I were a painter I would make a picture of it." Or the dreams treat of photographs, of paintings, drawings or illuminated manuscripts, or perhaps of the films.

I have turned these hints to practical account, and I now urge my patients at such times actually to paint what they have seen in dream or fantasy. As a rule, I am met with the objection : " I am not a painter." To this I usually reply that neither are modern painters—for which very reason modern painting is absolutely free—and that it is anyhow not a question of the beautiful, but merely of the trouble one takes with the picture. How little my way of painting has to do with " art " I saw recently in the case of a talented portraitist ; she had to begin all over again with pitiably childish efforts—literally as if she had never had a brush in her hand. To paint what we see before us is a different matter from painting what we see within.

Many of my more advanced patients, then, begin to paint. I can well understand that everyone will consider this as an utterly futile sort of dilettantism. However, it must be remembered that we are speaking not of people who have still to prove their social usefulness, but of those who can no longer find significance in their value to society, and who have come upon the deeper and more dangerous question of the meaning of their individual lives. To be a particle in a mass has meaning and charm only for the man who has not yet advanced to that stage, but none for the man who has experienced it to satiety. The importance of individual life may always be denied by the " educator " whose pride it is to breed mass-men. But any other person will sooner or later be driven to find this meaning for himself.

Although from time to time my patients produce artistically beautiful creations which might very well be shown in modern " art " exhibitions, I nevertheless treat them as wholly worthless according to the tests of serious art. It is even essential that no such value be allowed them, for otherwise my patients might imagine themselves to be artists, and this would spoil the good effects of the exercise. It is not a question of art—or rather it should not be a question of art—but of something more, something other than mere art : namely the living effect upon the patient himself. The meaning of individual life, whose importance from the social standpoint is negligible, is here accorded the highest value, and for its sake the patient struggles to give form, however crude and childish, to the inexpressible.

But why do I encourage patients to express themselves at a certain stage of development by means of brush, pencil or pen ? My purpose is the same here as in my handling of dreams : I wish to produce an effect. In the childish condition described above, the patient remains in a passive state ; but now he begins to play an active part. At first he puts on paper what has come to him in fantasy, and thereby gives it the status of a deliberate act. He not only talks about it, but he is actually *doing* something about it. Psychologically speaking, it is one thing for a person to have an interesting conversation with his doctor twice a week—the results of which hang somewhere or other in mid-air—and quite another thing to struggle for hours at a time with refractory brush and colours, and to produce in the end something which, at its face value, is perfectly senseless. Were his fantasy *really* senseless to him, the effort to paint

it would be so irksome that he could scarcely be brought
to perform this exercise a second time. But since his
fantasy does not seem to him entirely senseless, his busying
himself with it increases its effect upon him. Moreover, the
effort to give visible form to the image enforces a study of it
in all its parts, so that in this way its effects can be completely experienced. The discipline of drawing endows the
fantasy with an element of reality, thus lending it greater
weight and greater driving power. And actually these
crude pictures do produce effects which, I must admit, are
rather difficult to describe. When a patient has seen once
or twice how he is freed from a wretched state of mind by
working at a symbolical picture, he will thenceforward turn
to this means of release whenever things go badly with him.
In this way something invaluable is won, namely a growth
of independence, a step towards psychological maturity. The
patient can make himself creatively independent by this
method—if I may call it such. He is no longer dependent
on his dreams or on his doctor's knowledge, but can give
form to his own inner experience by painting it. For what
he paints are active fantasies—it is that which activates
him. And that which is active within is himself, but not
in the sense of his previous error when he mistook his
personal ego for the self ; it is himself in a new sense, for
his ego now appears as an object actuated by the life-forces
within. He strives to represent as fully as possible in his
picture-series that which works within him, only to discover
in the end that it is the eternally unknown and alien—the
hidden foundations of psychic life.

I cannot possibly picture to you the extent to which these
discoveries change a patient's standpoint and values, and
how they shift the centre of gravity of the personality. It

is as though the ego were the earth, and it suddenly discovered that the sun (or the self) was the centre of the
planetary orbits and of the earth's orbit as well.

But have we not always known all this to be so ? I myself
believe that we have always known it. But I may know
about something with my head which the other man in me
is far from knowing, and I may in fact live as though I did
not know it. Most of my patients knew the deeper truth,
but did not live it. And why did they not live it ? Because
of that bias which makes us all put the ego in the centre of
our lives—and this bias comes from the over-valuation of
consciousness.

It is highly important for a young person who is still
unadapted and has as yet achieved nothing, to shape the
conscious ego as effectively as possible—that is, to educate
the will. Unless he is positively a genius he even may not
believe in anything active within himself that is not identical
with his will. He must feel himself a man of will, and he
may safely depreciate everything else within himself or
suppose it subject to his will—for without this illusion he can
scarcely bring about a social adaptation.

It is otherwise with the patient in the second half of life
who no longer needs to educate his conscious will, but who,
to understand the meaning of his individual life, must learn
to experience his own inner being. Social usefulness is no
longer an aim for him, although he does not question its
desirability. Fully aware as he is of the social unimportance
of his creative activity, he looks upon it as a way of working
out his own development and thus benefiting himself. This
activity likewise frees him progressively from a morbid
dependence, and he thus wins an inner firmness and a new
trust in himself. These last achievements in turn serve to

further the patient in his social existence. For an inwardly sound and self-confident person will be more adequate to his social tasks than one who is not on good terms with his unconscious.

I have purposely avoided weighting down my essay with theory, for which reason many things must remain obscure and unexplained. But in order to make intelligible the pictures produced by my patients, certain theoretical points must at least be mentioned. A feature common to all these pictures is a primitive symbolism which is conspicuous both in the drawing and in the colouring. The colours are usually quite barbaric in their intensity; often, too, an archaic quality is present. These peculiarities point to the nature of the creative forces which have produced the pictures. They are non-rational, symbolistic currents in the evolution of man, and are so archaic that it is easy to draw parallels between them and similar manifestations in the fields of archæology and comparative religion. We may therefore readily assume that these pictures originate chiefly in that realm of psychic life which I have called the collective unconscious. By this term I designate an unconscious psychic activity present in all human beings which not only gives rise to symbolical pictures today, but was the source of all similar products of the past. Such pictures spring from—and satisfy—a natural need. It is as if, through these pictures, we bring to expression that part of the psyche which reaches back into the primitive past and reconcile it with present-day consciousness, thus mitigating its disturbing effects upon the latter.

It is true, I must add, that the mere execution of the pictures is not all that is required. It is necessary besides to have an intellectual and emotional understanding of them;

they must be consciously integrated, made intelligible, and morally assimilated. We must subject them to a process of interpretation. But despite the fact that I have so often travelled this path with individual patients, I have not yet succeeded in making the process clear to a wider circle and in working it up in a form suitable for publication. This has so far been accomplished only in a fragmentary way.

The truth is, we are here on perfectly new ground, and a ripening of experience is the first requisite. For very important reasons I should like to avoid over-hasty conclusions. We are dealing with a region of psychic life outside consciousness, and our way of observing it is indirect. As yet we do not know what depths we are trying to plumb. As I indicated above, it seems to me to be a question of some kind of centring process, for many pictures which patients feel to be decisive point in this direction. It is a process which brings into being a new centre of equilibrium, and it is as if the ego turned in an orbit round it. What the aim of this process may be remains at first obscure. We can only remark its important effect upon the conscious personality. From the fact that the change heightens the feeling for life and maintains the flow of life, we must conclude that a peculiar purposefulness is inherent in it. We might perhaps call this a new illusion—but what is illusion ? By what criterion do we judge something to be an illusion ? Does there exist for the psyche anything which we may call " illusion " ? What we are pleased to call such may be for the psyche a most important factor of life—something as indispensable as oxygen for the organism— a psychic actuality of prime importance. Presumably the psyche does not trouble itself about our categories of reality, and it would therefore be the better part of wisdom for us to say : everything that *acts* is actual.

He who would fathom the psyche must not confuse it with consciousness, else he veils from his own sight the object he wishes to explore. On the contrary, to recognize the psyche, even, he must learn to see how it differs from consciousness. It is highly probable that what we call illusion is actual for the psyche : for which reason we cannot take psychic actuality to be commensurable with conscious actuality. To the psychologist there is nothing more stupid than the standpoint of the missionary who pronounces the gods of the " poor heathen " to be illusions. But unfortunately we keep blundering along in the same dogmatic way, as if what we call the real were not equally full of illusion. In psychic life, as everywhere in our experience, all things that act are actual, regardless of the names man chooses to bestow on them. To understand that these happenings have actuality—that is what is important to us ; and not the attempt to give them one name instead of another. To the psyche the spirit is no less the spirit even though it be called sexuality.

I must repeat that the various technical terms and the changes rung upon them never touch the essence of the process described above. It cannot be compassed by the rational concepts of consciousness any more than life itself. It is because they feel the whole force of this truth that my patients turn to symbolical expression. In the representation and interpretation of symbols they find something more effective and adequate to their needs than rational explanations.

IV

A PSYCHOLOGICAL THEORY OF TYPES

CHARACTER is the fixed individual form of a human being. Since there is a form of body as well as of behaviour or mind, a general characterology must teach the significance of both physical and psychic features. The enigmatic oneness of the living being has as its necessary corollary the fact that bodily traits are not merely physical, nor mental traits merely psychic. The continuity of nature knows nothing of those antithetical distinctions which the human intellect is forced to set up as helps to understanding.

The distinction between mind and body is an artificial dichotomy, a discrimination which is unquestionably based far more on the peculiarity of intellectual understanding than on the nature of things. In fact, so intimate is the intermingling of bodily and psychic traits that not only can we draw far-reaching inferences as to the constitution of the psyche from the constitution of the body, but we can also infer from psychic peculiarities the corresponding bodily characteristics. It is true that the latter process is more difficult ; but this is surely not because there is a greater influence of the body over the mind than *vice versa*, but for quite another reason. In taking the mind as our starting-point we work our way from the relatively unknown to the known ; while in the opposite case we have the advantage of starting from something known, that is, from the visible

85

body.   Despite all the psychology we think we possess today, the psyche is still infinitely more obscure to us than the visible surface of the body.   The psyche is still a foreign, almost unexplored country of which we have only indirect knowledge ; it is mediated by conscious functions that are subject to almost endless possibilities of deception.

This being so, it appears safer for us to proceed from the outer world inward, from the known to the unknown, from the body to the mind.   Therefore all attempts at characterology have started from the outside world ; astrology, in ancient times, turned even to stellar space in order to determine those lines of fate whose beginnings are contained in man himself.   To the same class of interpretations from outward signs belong palmistry, Gall's phrenology, Lavater's study of physiognomy, and more recently, graphology, Kretschmer's physiological study of types and Rorschach's klexographic method.   As we can see, there are any number of paths leading from without inward, from the physical to the psychic, and it is necessary that research should follow this direction until certain elementary psychic facts are established with sufficient certainty.   But once having established these facts, we can reverse the procedure.   We can then put the question :   What are the bodily correlatives of a given psychic condition ?   Unfortunately we are not yet far enough advanced to answer this question even roughly.   The first requirement is to establish the primary facts of psychic life, and this has by no means as yet been accomplished.   Indeed, we have only just begun the work of compiling an inventory of the psyche, and our results have not always been successful.

Merely to establish the fact that certain people have this or that appearance is of no significance if it does not allow us to infer a psychic correlative. We have learned something only when we have determined what mental attributes go with a given bodily constitution. The body means as little to us without the psyche as the latter without the body. When we try to derive a psychic correlative from a physical characteristic, we are proceeding—as already stated—from the known to the unknown.

I must, unfortunately, stress this point, since psychology is the youngest of all the sciences, and therefore the one that suffers most from preconceived opinions. The fact that we have only recently discovered psychology shows plainly enough that it has taken us all this time to make a clear distinction between ourselves and the contents of our minds. Until this could be done, it was impossible to study the psyche objectively. Psychology, as a natural science, is actually our most recent acquisition; up to now it has been just as fantastic and arbitrary as was natural science in the Middle Ages. Heretofore it has been thought that psychology could dispense with empirical data and be created as it were by decree—a prejudice under which we are still labouring. Yet the events of psychic life are what is most immediate to us, and apparently what we know most about. Indeed, they are more than familiar to us, we yawn over them. We are amazed at the banality of these everlasting commonplaces; in short, we actually suffer under the immediacy of our psychic life and do everything in our power to avoid thinking about it. The psyche, then, being immediacy itself, and we ourselves being the psyche, we are almost forced to assume that we know it through and through in a way that cannot be questioned. This is why each of us has his own private opinion about psychology and is even convinced that he knows more about it than anyone else.   Psychiatrists, because they must struggle with their patients' families and guardians whose "understanding" is proverbial, are perhaps the first as a professional group to become aware of that blind prejudice which encourages every man to take himself as his own best authority in psychological matters.   But this of course does not prevent the psychiatrist also from becoming a "know-all".   One of them went so far as to confess : "There are only two normal people in this city—Professor B. is the other."

Since this is how matters stand in psychology today, we must admit that what is closest to us is the very thing we know least about, although it seems to be what we know best of all.   Furthermore, we must admit that everyone else probably understands us better than we do ourselves.   At any rate, as a starting-point, this would be a most useful heuristic principle.   As I have said, it is just because the psyche is so close to us that psychology has been discovered so late.   Being still in its initial stages as a science, we lack the concepts and definitions with which to grasp the facts. If concepts are lacking to us, facts are not ; on the contrary we are surrounded—almost buried—by these facts.   This is a striking contrast to the state of affairs in other sciences where the facts have first to be unearthed.   Here the classification of primary data results in the formation of descriptive concepts covering certain natural orders, as, for example, the grouping of the elements in chemistry and of genera in botany.   But it is quite different in the case of the psyche.   Here an empirical and descriptive standpoint leaves us at the mercy of the unchecked stream of our own subjective experiences, so that whenever any sort of inclusive generalization emerges from this welter of impressions, it is usually nothing more than a symptom. Because we ourselves are psyches, it is almost impossible for us to give free rein to psychic happenings without being practically dissolved in them and thus robbed of our ability to recognize distinctions and to make comparisons.

This is one difficulty. The other lies in the circumstance that the more we turn from special phenomena and come to deal with the spaceless psyche, the more impossible it becomes to determine anything by exact measurement. It becomes difficult even to establish facts. If, for example, I want to emphasize the unreality of something, I say that I merely thought it. I say: " I would never even have had this thought unless so-and-so had happened ; and besides, I never think things like that." Remarks of this kind are quite usual, and show how nebulous psychic facts are, or rather how vague they are on the subjective side—in reality they are just as objective and as definite as historical events. The truth is that I actually did think thus and thus, regardless of the conditions and stipulations I may attach to this fact. Many people have to wrestle with themselves in order to make this perfectly obvious admission, and it often costs them a great moral effort. These, then, are the difficulties we encounter when we draw inferences about the state of affairs in the psyche from the things we observe outside.

Now my more limited field of work is not the clinical determination of external characteristics, but the investigation and classification of the psychic data which can be inferred from them. The first result of this work is a descriptive study of the psyche, which enables us to formulate certain theories about its structure. From the empirical application of these theories there is finally developed a conception of psychological types.

Clinical studies are based upon the description of symptoms, and the step from this to the descriptive study of the psyche is comparable to the step from a purely symptomatic pathology to the pathology of the cell and of metabolism. That is to say that the descriptive study of the psyche brings into view those psychic processes in the hinterland of the mind which produce the clinical symptoms. As we know, this insight is gained by the application of analytical methods. We have today a substantial knowledge of those psychic processes which produce the neurotic symptoms, for our descriptive study of the psyche has advanced far enough to enable us to determine the complexes. Whatever else may be taking place within the obscure recesses of the psyche—and there are notoriously many opinions as to this matter—one thing is certain : it is first and foremost the so-called complexes (emotionally toned contents having a certain amount of autonomy) which play an important part there. The expression " autonomous complex " has often met with opposition, although, as it seems to me, unjustifiably. The active contents of the unconscious do behave in a way I cannot describe better than by the word " autonomous ". The term is used to indicate the fact that the complexes offer resistance to the conscious intentions, and come and go as they please. According to our best knowledge about them, complexes are psychic contents which are outside the control of the conscious mind. They have been split off from consciousness and lead a separate existence in the unconscious, being at all times ready to hinder or to reinforce the conscious intentions.

A further study of the complexes leads inevitably to the problem of their origin, and as to this a number of different theories are current. Apart from theories, experience shows us that complexes always contain something like a conflict—they are either the cause or the effect of a conflict. At any rate, the characteristics of conflict—that is, shock, upheaval, mental agony, inner strife—are peculiar to the complexes. They have been called in French *bêtes noires*, while we refer to them as " skeletons in the cupboard ". They are " vulnerable points " which we do not like to remember and still less to be reminded of by others, but which frequently come back to mind unbidden and in the most unwelcome fashion. They always contain memories, wishes, fears, duties, needs, or views, with which we have never really come to terms, and for this reason they constantly interfere with our conscious life in a disturbing and usually a harmful way.

Complexes obviously represent a kind of inferiority in the broadest sense—a statement I must at once qualify by saying that to have complexes does not necessarily indicate inferiority. It only means that something incompatible, unassimilated, and conflicting exists—perhaps as an obstacle, but also as a stimulus to greater effort, and so, perhaps, as an opening to new possibilities of achievement. Complexes are therefore, in this sense, focal or nodal points of psychic life which we would not wish to do without. Indeed they must not be lacking, for otherwise psychic activity would come to a fatal standstill. But they indicate the unresolved problems of the individual, the points at which he has suffered a defeat, at least for the time being, and where there is something he cannot evade or overcome—his weak spots in every sense of the word.

Now these characteristics of the complex throw a significant light on its genesis. It obviously arises from the clash between a requirement of adaptation and the individual's constitutional inability to meet the challenge. Seen in this light, the complex is a symptom which helps us to diagnose an individual disposition.

Experience shows us that complexes are infinitely varied, yet careful comparison reveals a relatively small number of typical primary patterns, all of which have their origins in the first experiences of childhood. This must necessarily be so, because the individual disposition is already a factor in childhood ; it is innate, and not acquired in the course of life. The parental complex is therefore nothing but the first manifestation of a clash between reality and the individual's constitutional inability to meet the requirements it demands of him. The first form of the complex cannot be other than a parental complex, because the parents are the first reality with which the child comes into conflict.

The existence of a parental complex therefore tells us little or nothing about the peculiar constitution of the individual. Practical experience soon teaches us that the crux of the matter does not lie in the presence of a parental complex, but rather in the special way in which the complex works itself out in the life of the individual. As to this we observe the most striking variations, and only a very small number can be attributed to the special traits of parental influence. There are often several children who are exposed to the same influence, and yet each reacts to it in a totally different way.

I have turned my attention to these very differences, because I believe that it is through them that specifically individual dispositions can be recognized. Why, in a neurotic family, does one child react with hysteria, another

with a compulsion neurosis, the third with a psychosis, and
the fourth apparently not at all ?   This problem of the
" choice of the neurosis ", with which Freud also was
confronted, robs the parental complex as such of all
ætiological meaning, and shifts the enquiry to the reacting
individual and his special disposition.

Although Freud's attempts to solve this problem leave
me entirely unsatisfied, I am myself unable to answer the
question.   Indeed, I think the time is not yet ripe for raising
this question of the choice of the neurosis.   Before we take
up this extremely difficult problem, we must know a great
deal more about the way in which the individual reacts.
The question is :   How does a person react to an obstacle ?
For instance, we come to a brook where there is no bridge.
The stream is too broad to step across, and we must jump.
To make this possible, we have at our disposal a complicated
functional system, namely, the psycho-motor system.   It
is completely developed and needs only to be released.
But before this happens, something of a purely psychic
nature takes place, that is, the decision is made about what
is to be done.   This is followed by activities which settle
the issue in some way and are different for each individual.
But, significantly enough, we rarely, if ever, recognize these
events as characteristic, for we cannot as a rule see ourselves
at all, or only at the very end.   This is to say that, just as
the psycho-motor apparatus is automatically at our disposal,
so there is an exclusively psychic apparatus ready for our
use in the making of decisions which works also by habit
and therefore unconsciously.

Opinions differ very widely as to what this apparatus is
like.   It is certain only that every individual has his
accustomed way of meeting decisions and of dealing with

difficulties. One person will say he jumped the brook for the fun of the thing ; another that it was because there was no alternative ; a third that every obstacle he meets challenges him to overcome it. A fourth person did not jump the brook because he hates useless effort, and a fifth refrained because he saw no urgent necessity for crossing to the other side.

I have purposely chosen this commonplace example in order to show how irrelevant these incentives seem. They appear so futile, indeed, that we push them all to one side and are inclined to substitute our own explanation. And yet it is just these variants that furnish us with valuable insight into the individual systems of psychic adaptation. If we examine, in other situations of life, the person who crossed the brook because it gave him pleasure to jump, we shall probably find that for the most part what he does and omits to do can be explained in terms of the pleasure it gives him. We shall observe that the one who sees no other means of getting across, goes through life carefully, but unwillingly, always making reluctant decisions. In all these cases special psychic systems are in readiness to carry out decisions offhand. We can easily imagine that the number of these attitudes is legion. The particular variations are certainly as innumerable as the variations of crystals which nevertheless may be recognized as belonging to one or another system. But just as crystals show basic uniformities which are relatively simple, so do these personal attitudes show certain fundamental traits which allow us to assign them to definite groups.

Since the earliest times, attempts have repeatedly been made to classify individuals according to types and thus to bring order into what was confusion. The oldest attempt of this sort known to us was made by oriental astrologers who devised the so-called trigons of the four elements, air, water, earth and fire. The trigon of the air as it appears in a horoscope consists of the three " aerial " signs of the zodiac, *Aquarius*, *Gemini* and *Libra* ; the trigon of fire is made up of *Aries*, *Leo* and *Sagittarius*. According to this age-old view, whoever is born in these trigons shares in their aerial or fiery nature and reveals a corresponding disposition and destiny. This ancient cosmological scheme is the parent of the physiological type-theory of antiquity according to which the four dispositions correspond to the four humours of the body. What was first represented by the signs of the zodiac was later expressed in the physiological terms of Greek medicine, giving us the classification into phlegmatic, sanguine, choleric, and melancholic. These are merely terms for the supposed humours of the body. As is well known, this classification lasted nearly seventeen centuries. As for the astrological type-theory, to the astonishment of the enlightened, it remains intact today, and is even enjoying a new vogue.

This historical retrospect may set our minds at rest as to the fact that our modern efforts to formulate a theory of types are by no means new and unprecedented, even if our scientific conscience no longer permits us to revert to these old, intuitive ways of handling the question. We must find our own answer to this problem—an answer which satisfies the demands of science.

And here we meet the chief difficulty of the problem of types—that is, the question of standards or criteria. The astrological criterion was simple ; it was given by the constellations. As to the way in which the elements of human character could be ascribed to the zodiacal signs and the planets, this is a question which reaches back into the grey mists of prehistory and remains unanswerable. The Greek classification according to the four physiological dispositions took as its criteria the appearance and behaviour of the individual, exactly as is done today in the case of modern physiological types. But where shall we seek our criterion for a psychological theory of types? Let us return to the previously mentioned instance of the various individuals who had to cross a brook. How, and from what standpoint, should we classify their habitual incentives? One person does it from pleasure, another acts because not to act is more troublesome, a third does not act because he has second thoughts, and so forth. The list of possibilities seems both endless and useless for purposes of classification.

I do not know how other people would set about the task. I can therefore only tell you how I myself have approached the matter, and I must submit to the reproach that my way of solving the problem is the outcome of my individual prejudice. Indeed, this objection is so entirely true, that I should not know how to meet it. I might, perhaps, content myself by referring to Columbus, who, by using subjective assumptions, a false hypothesis, and a route abandoned by modern navigation, nevertheless discovered America. Whatever we look at, and however we look at it, we see only through our own eyes. For this reason a science is never made by one man, but by many. The individual merely offers his contribution, and in this sense only do I dare to speak of my way of seeing things.

My profession has always forced me to take account of the peculiarities of individuals. This has made it necessary for me to establish certain average truths, as also has the circumstance that in the course of many years I have had to treat innumerable married couples and have been faced with the task of making the standpoints of husband and wife mutually plausible. How many times, for example, have I not had to say : " Look here, your wife has a very active nature, and it cannot be expected that her whole existence should centre round housekeeping." This is the beginning of a type-theory, a sort of statistical truth : there are active natures and passive ones. But this time-worn truth did not satisfy me. Therefore I next tried to say that there were some persons given to reflection, and others who were unreflective, because I had observed that apparently passive natures are in reality not so much passive as given to forethought. They first consider a situation and then act ; and because they do this habitually they miss opportunities where immediate action without forethought is called for, thus coming to be stigmatized as passive. The persons who did not reflect always seemed to me to jump into a situation without any forethought, only perhaps to observe afterwards that they had landed in a swamp. Thus they could be considered " unreflective ", and this seemed a more appropriate designation than "active ". Forethought is in certain cases a very important form of activity, just as it is a reasonable course of action in contrast to the effervescence of the person who must act at once at all costs. But I very soon discovered that the hesitation of the one was by no means always forethought, and that the quick action of the other was not necessarily want of reflection. The hesitation of the former often arises from habitual timidity, or at least from something like a customary shrinking backward as if faced with too heavy a task ; while the immediate activity of the second is frequently made possible by a predominating self-confidence with respect to the object. This observation caused me to formulate these typical distinctions in the following way : there is a whole class of men who at the moment of reaction to a given situation at first draw back a little as if with an unvoiced " No ", and only after that are able to react ; and there is another class who, in the same situation, come forward with an immediate reaction, apparently confident that their behaviour is obviously right. The former class would therefore be characterized by a certain negative relation to the object, and the latter by a positive one.

As we know, the former class corresponds to the introverted and the second to the extraverted attitude. But with these two terms in themselves as little is gained as when Molière's *bourgeois gentilhomme* discovered that he ordinarily spoke in prose. These distinctions attain meaning and value only when we realize all the other characteristics that go with the type.

One cannot be introverted or extraverted without being so in every respect. By the term " introverted " we mean that all psychic happenings take place in the way we posit as true of introverted people. Thus also, to establish the fact that a certain individual is extraverted would be as irrelevant as proving that his height is six feet, or that he has brown hair, or is brachycephalic. These statements bring little more to light than the bare fact they express. But the expression " extraverted " claims to have more meaning. It states that, when a person is extraverted, his consciousness as well as his unconscious have definite qualities ; that his general behaviour, his relation to people, and even the course of his life, show certain typical characteristics.

Introversion or extraversion, as a typical attitude, means an essential bias which conditions the whole psychic process, establishes the habitual reactions, and thus determines not only the style of behaviour, but also the nature of subjective experience. And not only so, but it also denotes the kind of compensatory activity of the unconscious which we may expect to find.

When the habitual reactions are determined, we can feel fairly certain of having hit the mark, because they govern external behaviour on the one hand, and on the other mould specific experience. A certain kind of behaviour brings corresponding results, and the subjective understanding of these results gives rise to the experiences which in turn influence behaviour, and thus close the circle of an individual's destiny.

Although there need be no doubt that with the habitual reactions we touch upon a decisive matter, there remains the delicate question as to whether we have satisfactorily characterized them. There can be an honest difference of opinion about this even among persons with an equally intimate knowledge of the special field. In my book on types [1] I have gathered together all that I could find in support of my conception, but I have made it very clear that I do not hold mine to be the only true or possible type-theory. This theory is simple enough, consisting as it does in the contrast between introversion and extraversion ; but simple formulations are unfortunately most open to doubt. They all too easily cover up the actual complexities, and so deceive us. I speak here from my own experience, for scarcely had I published the first formulation of my criteria, when I discovered to my dismay that somehow

[1] *Psychological Types*, Kegan Paul, Trench, Trubner & Co., London.

or other I had been taken in by it. Something was out of gear. I had tried to explain too much in too simple a way, as often happens in the first joy of discovery.

What struck me now was the undeniable fact that while people may be classed as introverts or extraverts, these distinctions do not cover all the dissimilarities between the individuals in either class. So great, indeed, are these differences that I was forced to doubt whether I had observed correctly in the first place. It took nearly ten years of observation and comparison to clear up this doubt.

The question as to the great variation observable among the members of each class entangled me in unforeseen difficulties which for a long time I could not master. To observe and recognize the differences gave me comparatively little trouble, the root of my difficulties being now, as before, the problem of criteria. How was I to find the right terms for the characteristic differences ? Here I realized for the first time and to the full extent how young psychology really is. It is still little more than a chaos of arbitrary opinions, the better part of which seems to have been produced in the study and consulting-room by spontaneous generation from the isolated and therefore Jovian brains of learned scholars. Without wishing to be irreverent, I cannot refrain from confronting the Professor of Psychology with the mentality of women, of the Chinese, and of Australian Negroes. Our psychology must embrace all life, otherwise we simply remain enclosed in the Middle Ages.

I have realized that no sound criteria are to be found in the chaos of contemporary psychology. They have first to be made—not out of whole cloth, of course, but on the basis of the invaluable preparatory work done by many men whose names no history of psychology will pass over in silence.

Within the limits of an essay, I cannot possibly mention all the separate observations that led me to pick out certain psychic functions as criteria for the designation of the differences under discussion. , I wish only to show how they appear to me as far as I have been able to grasp them. We must realize that an introvert does not simply draw back and hesitate before the object, but that he does so in a very definite way. Moreover he does not behave in all respects like every other introvert, but in a particular manner. Just as the lion strikes down his enemy or his prey with his fore-paw, in which his strength resides, and not with his tail like the crocodile, so our habitual reactions are normally characterized by the application of our most trustworthy and efficient function ; it is an expression of our strength. However, this does not prevent our reacting occasionally in a way that reveals our specific weakness. The predominance of a function leads us to construct or to seek out certain situations while we avoid others, and therefore to have experiences that are peculiar to us and different from those of other people. An intelligent man will make his adaptation to the world through his intelligence, and not in the manner of a sixth-rate pugilist, even though now and then, in a fit of rage, he may make use of his fists. In the struggle for existence and adaptation everyone instinctively uses his most developed function, which thus becomes the criterion of his habitual reactions.

The question now becomes : How is it possible to subsume all these functions under general concepts, so that they can be distinguished in the welter of merely contingent events ? In social life a rough grouping of this sort has long ago come about, and as a result we have types like the peasant, the worker, the artist, the scholar, the warrior, and so forth down the list of the various professions. But this sort of typification has very little to do with psychology, because—as a well-known scholar has maliciously remarked—there are savants who are merely " intellectual porters ".

A type-theory must be more subtle. It is not enough, for example, to speak of intelligence, for this is too general and too vague a concept. Almost any behaviour can be called intelligent if it works smoothly, quickly, effectively and to a purpose. Intelligence, like stupidity, is not a function but a modality ; the term tells us nothing more than how a function works. The same holds true of moral and æsthetic criteria. We must be able to designate what it is that functions outstandingly in the individual's habitual way of reacting. We are thus forced to resort to something which at first glance alarmingly resembles the old faculty psychology of the eighteenth century ; in reality, however, we are only returning to current ideas in daily speech, perfectly accessible and comprehensible to everyone. When, for instance, I speak of " thinking ", it is only the philosopher who does not know what I mean ; no layman will find it incomprehensible. He uses this word every day, and always in the same general sense, though it is true enough that he is not a little embarrassed if he is called upon suddenly to give an unequivocal definition of thinking. The same is true of " memory " or " feeling ". However difficult it is to define such notions scientifically and thus make of them psychological concepts, they are easily intelligible in current speech. Speech is a storehouse of images founded on experience, and therefore concepts which are too abstract do not easily take root in it, or quickly die out again for lack of contact with reality. But thinking and feeling are so obtrusively real that every language above the primitive level has absolutely unmistakable expressions for them. We can therefore be sure that these expressions coincide with perfectly definite psychic facts, no matter what the scientific definitions of these complex facts may be. Everyone knows, for example, what consciousness is, and nobody doubts that the concept covers a definite psychic condition, however far science may be from defining it satisfactorily.

So it came about that I simply formed my concepts of the psychic functions from the notions expressed in current speech, and used them as my criteria in judging the differences between persons of the same attitude-type. For example, I took thinking as it is generally understood, because I was struck by the fact that many persons habitually do more thinking than others, and accordingly give more weight to thought when making important decisions. They also use their thinking in trying to understand and adapt themselves to the world, and whatever happens to them is subjected to consideration and reflection, or at least reconciled with some principle sanctioned by thought. Other people conspicuously neglect thinking in favour of emotional factors, that is, feeling. They inveterately follow a "policy" dictated by feeling, and it takes an extraordinary situation to make them reflect. These persons exhibit a striking and unmistakable contrast to the former. This difference is most patent when, for example, a person of one kind is the partner in business or marriage of a person of the other kind. Now a man may give preference to thinking whether he be extraverted or introverted, but he always *uses* it in the way that is characteristic of his attitude-type.

However, the predominance of one or the other of these functions does not explain all the differences to be found. What I call the thinking or feeling types embrace two groups of persons who again have something in common which I cannot designate except by the word rationality. No one will dispute the statement that thinking is essentially rational, but when we come to feeling, certain objections may be raised which I do not want simply to overrule; on the contrary I freely admit that this problem of feeling has been one over which I have racked my brains. Yet, not to burden this essay with the various existing definitions of this concept, I shall confine myself briefly to my own view. The chief difficulty lies in the fact that the word " feeling " can be applied in all sorts of different ways. This is especially true in the German language, but is noticeable to some extent in English and French as well. First of all, then, we must make a careful distinction between the concepts of feeling and sensation, the latter being taken to cover the sensory processes. And in the second place we must recognize that a feeling of regret is something quite different from a " feeling " that the weather will change or that the price of our aluminium shares will go up. I have therefore proposed using the term " feeling " in the first instance, and dropping it—so far as psychological terminology is concerned—in the other two instances. Here we should speak of " sensation " when the sense organs are involved, and of intuition if we are dealing with a kind of perception which cannot be traced directly to conscious sensory experience. I have therefore defined sensation as perception through conscious sensory processes, and intuition as perception by way of unconscious contents and connections.

Obviously we could argue until Doomsday about the fitness of these definitions, but the discussion eventually turns upon a mere question of terms. It is as if we debated whether to call a certain animal a puma or a mountain-lion, when all that is needed is to know what we wish to designate in a given way.   Psychology is an unexplored field of study, and its particular idiom must first be fixed.   It is well known that temperature can be measured according to Réaumur, Celsius or Fahrenheit, but we must indicate which system we are using.

It is evident, then, that I take feeling as a function in itself and distinguish it from sensation and intuition. Whoever confuses these last two functions with feeling in this narrower sense, can obviously not acknowledge the rationality of feeling.   But if they are separated from feeling, it becomes quite clear that feeling values and feeling judgements—that is to say, our feelings—are not only reasonable, but are also as discriminating, logical and consistent as thinking.   Such a statement seems strange to a man of the thinking type, but we can understand this when we realize that in a person with a differentiated thinking function, the feeling function is always less developed, more primitive, and therefore contaminated with other functions —these being precisely the functions which are not rational, not logical, and not evaluating, namely, sensation and intuition.   These two last are by their very nature opposed to the rational functions.   When we think, it is in order to judge or to reach a conclusion, and when we feel it is in order to attach a proper value to something ; sensation and intuition, on the other hand, are perceptive—they make us aware of what is happening, but do not interpret or evaluate it.   They do not act selectively according to principles, but are simply receptive of what happens.   But "what happens" is merely nature, and therefore essentially non-rational. There are no modes of inference by which it can be proved that there must be so many planets, or so many species of warm-blooded animals of this or that sort.   Lack of rationality is a vice where thinking and feeling are called for—rationality is a vice where sensation and intuition should be trusted.

Now there are many persons whose habitual reactions are non-rational, because they are based chiefly upon sensation or intuition.   They cannot be based upon both at once, because sensation is just as antagonistic to intuition as thinking is to feeling.   When I try to assure myself with my eyes and ears of what actually occurs, I cannot at the same time give way to dreams and fantasies as to what lies round the corner.   As this is just what the intuitive type must do in order to give free play to the unconscious or to the object, it is easy to see that the sensation type is at the opposite pole to the intuitive.   Unfortunately, I cannot here take up the interesting variations which the extraverted or introverted attitude produces in non-rational types.

Instead, I prefer to add a word about the effects regularly produced upon the other functions when preference is given to one.   We know that a man can never be everything at once, never complete ; he always develops certain qualities at the expense of others, and wholeness is never attained. But what happens to those functions which are not developed by exercise and are not consciously brought into daily use ? They remain in a more or less primitive and infantile state, often only half-conscious, or even quite unconscious.   These relatively undeveloped functions constitute a specific inferiority which is characteristic of each type and is an integral part of the total character.   The one-sided emphasis on thinking is always accompanied by an inferiority in feeling, and differentiated sensation and intuition are mutually injurious. Whether a function is differentiated or not may easily be recognized from its strength, stability, constancy, trustworthiness and service in adaptedness. But inferiority in a function is often not so easily described or recognized. An essential criterion is its lack of self-sufficiency, and our resulting dependence on people and circumstances ; furthermore, its disposing us to moods and undue sensitivity, its untrustworthiness and vagueness, and its tendency to make us suggestible. We are always at a disadvantage in using the inferior function because we cannot direct it, being in fact even its victims.

Since I must restrict myself here to a mere sketch of the basic ideas of a psychological theory of types, I must unfortunately forego a detailed description of individual traits and actions in the light of this theory. The total result of my work in this field up to the present is the presentation of two general types covering the attitudes which I call extraversion and introversion. Besides these, I have worked out a fourfold classification corresponding to the functions of thinking, feeling, sensation and intuition. Each of these functions varies according to the general attitude, and thus eight variants are produced. I have been asked almost reproachfully why I speak of four functions and not of more or fewer. That there are exactly four is a matter of empirical fact. But as the following consideration will show, a certain completeness is attained by these four. Sensation establishes what is actually given, thinking enables us to recognize its meaning, feeling tells us its value, and finally intuition points to the possibilities of the whence and whither that lie within the immediate facts. In this way, we can orientate ourselves with respect to the immediate world as completely as when we locate a place geographically by latitude and longitude. The four functions are somewhat like the four points of the compass; they are just as arbitrary and just as indispensable. Nothing prevents our shifting the cardinal points as many degrees as we like in one direction or the other, nor are we precluded from giving them different names. It is merely a question of convention and comprehensibility.

But one thing I must confess : I would not for anything dispense with this compass on my psychological journeys of discovery. This is not merely for the obvious, all-too-human reason that everyone is in love with his own ideas. I value the type-theory for the objective reason that it offers a system of comparison and orientation which makes possible something that has long been lacking, a critical psychology.

V

THE STAGES OF LIFE

To discuss the problems connected with the stages of human development is an exacting task, for it means nothing less than unfolding a picture of psychic life in its entirety from the cradle to the grave. Within the narrow frame of this essay the task can be carried out only on the broadest lines, and it must be well understood that no attempt will be made to describe the normal psychic occurrences within the various stages. We shall rather restrict ourselves and deal only with certain " problems " ; that is, with things that are difficult, questionable or ambiguous ; in a word, with questions which allow of more than one answer—and, moreover, answers that are always open to doubt. For this reason there will be much to which we must add a question-mark in our thoughts. And—worse still—there will be some things which we must accept on faith, while now and then we must even indulge in speculations.

If psychic life consisted only of overt happenings—which on a primitive level is still the case—we could content ourselves with a sturdy empiricism. The psychic life of civilized man, however, is full of problems ; we cannot even think of it except in terms of problems. Our psychic processes are made up to a large extent of reflections, doubts and experiments, all of which are almost completely foreign to the unconscious, instinctive mind of primitive man.

It is the growth of consciousness which we must thank for the existence of problems; they are the dubious gift of civilization. It is just man's turning away from instinct— his opposing himself to instinct—that creates consciousness. Instinct is nature and seeks to perpetuate nature; while consciousness can only seek culture or its denial. Even when we turn back to nature, inspired by a Rousseauesque longing, we " cultivate " nature. As long as we are still submerged in nature we are unconscious, and we live in the security of instinct that knows no problems. Everything in us that still belongs to nature shrinks away from a problem; for its name is doubt, and wherever doubt holds sway, there is uncertainty and the possibility of divergent ways. And where several ways seem possible, there we have turned away from the certain guidance of instinct and are handed over to fear. For consciousness is now called upon to do that which nature has always done for her children—namely, to give a certain, unquestionable and unequivocal decision. And here we are beset by an all-too-human fear that consciousness—our Promethean conquest— may in the end not be able to serve us in the place of nature.

Problems thus draw us into an orphaned and isolated state where we are abandoned by nature and are driven to consciousness. There is no other way open to us; we are forced to resort to decisions and solutions where we formerly trusted ourselves to natural happenings. Every problem, therefore, brings the possibility of a widening of consciousness—but also the necessity of saying good-bye to childlike unconsciousness and trust in nature. This necessity is a psychic fact of such importance that it constitutes one of the essential symbolic teachings of the Christian religion. It is the sacrifice of the merely natural

man—of the unconscious, ingenuous being whose tragic
career began with the eating of the apple in Paradise. The
biblical fall of man presents the dawn of consciousness as
a curse. And as a matter of fact it is in this light that we
first look upon every problem that forces us to greater
consciousness and separates us even further from the paradise
of unconscious childhood. Every one of us gladly turns
away from his problems ; if possible, they must not be
mentioned, or, better still, their existence is denied. We
wish to make our lives simple, certain and smooth—and
for that reason problems are *tabu*. We choose to have
certainties and no doubts—results and no experiments—
without even seeing that certainties can arise only through
doubt, and results through experiment. The artful denial
of a problem will not produce conviction ; on the contrary,
a wider and higher consciousness is called for to give us
the certainty and clarity we need.

This introduction, long as it is, seemed to me necessary
in order to make clear the nature of our subject. When we
must deal with problems, we instinctively refuse to try
the way that leads through darkness and obscurity. We
wish to hear only of unequivocal results, and completely
forget that these results can only be brought about when
we have ventured into and emerged again from the darkness.
But to penetrate the darkness we must summon all the
powers of enlightenment that consciousness can offer ; as
I have already said, we must even indulge in speculations.
For in treating of the problems of psychic life we perpetually
stumble over questions of principle belonging to the private
domains of the most different branches of knowledge. We
disturb and anger the theologian no less than the philosopher,
the physician no less than the educator ; we even grope

about in the field of the biologist and of the historian. This
extravagant behaviour is not to be charged to our arrogance,
but to the circumstance that man's psyche is a unique
combination of factors which also make up the special
subjects of far-reaching lines of research. For it is out of
himself and out of his peculiar constitution that man
produced his sciences. They are symptoms of his psyche.

If, therefore, we ask ourselves the unavoidable question :
" Why does man, in obvious contrast to the animal world,
have problems ? "—we run into that inextricable tangle
of thoughts which many thousands of incisive minds have
brought about in the course of centuries. I shall not perform
the labours of a Sisyphus upon this masterpiece of confusion,
but will try to present quite simply my contribution toward
man's attempt to answer this basic question.

There are no problems without consciousness. We must
therefore put the question in another way : In what way
does consciousness arise ? Nobody can say with certainty ;
but we can observe small children in the process of becoming
conscious. Every parent can see it, if he pays attention.
And this is what we are able to observe : when the child
recognizes someone or something—when he " knows " a
person or a thing—then we feel that the child has consciousness. That, no doubt, is also why in Paradise it was the
tree of knowledge which bore such fateful fruit.

But what is recognition or knowledge in this sense ? We
speak of " knowing " something when we succeed in linking
a new perception to an already established context in such
a way that we hold in consciousness not only the new
perception but this context as well. " Knowing " is based,
therefore, upon a conscious connection between psychic
contents. We cannot have knowledge of disconnected

contents, and we cannot even be conscious of them. The first stage of consciousness, then, which we can observe consists in a mere connection between two or more psychic contents. At this level, consciousness is merely sporadic, being limited to the representation of a few connections, and the content is not remembered later on. It is a fact that in the early years of life there is no continuous memory ; at the most there are islands of consciousness which are like single lamps or lighted objects in the far-flung darkness. But these islands of memory are not the same as those initial connections between psychic contents ; they contain something more and something new. This something is that highly important series of related contents which constitutes the so-called ego. The ego—quite like the initial content-series—is an object in consciousness, and for this reason the child speaks of itself at first objectively, in the third person. Only later, when the ego-contents have been charged with energy of their own (very likely as a result of exercise), does the feeling of subjectivity or " I-ness " arise. This is no doubt the moment when the child begins to speak of itself in the first person. At this level the continuity of memory has its beginning. Essentially, therefore, it is a continuity in the ego-memories.

In the childish stage of consciousness there are as yet no problems ; nothing depends upon the subject, for the child itself is still wholly dependent upon its parents. It is as though it were not yet completely born, but were still enclosed in the psychic atmosphere of its parents. Psychic birth, and with it the conscious distinction of the ego from the parents, takes place in the normal course of things at the age of puberty with the eruption of sexual life. The physiological change is attended by a psychic revolution.

For the various bodily manifestations give such an emphasis to the ego that it often asserts itself without stint or measure. This is sometimes called " the unbearable age ".

Until this period is reached the psychic life of the individual is essentially governed by impulse, and few or no problems are met with. Even when external limitations oppose the subjective impulses, these restraints do not put the individual at variance with himself. He submits to them or circumvents them, remaining quite at one with himself. He does not yet know the state of inner tension which a problem brings about. This state only arises when what was an external limitation becomes an inner obstacle ; when one impulse opposes itself to another. Resorting to psychological terms we would say : the state induced by a problem—the state of being at variance with oneself—arises when, side by side with the series of ego-contents, a second series of equal intensity comes into being. This second series, because of its energy-value, has a functional significance equal to that of the ego-complex ; we might call it another, second ego which in a given case can wrest the leadership from the first. This brings about an estrangement from oneself— the state that betokens a problem.

With reference to what was said above we can epitomize as follows : the first stage of consciousness which consists of recognizing or " knowing " is an anarchic or chaotic state. The second—that of the developed ego-complex— is a monarchic or monistic phase. The third is another step forward in consciousness, and consists in the awareness of one's divided state ; it is a dualistic phase.

And here we take up our actual theme, namely the question of the stages of life. First of all we must deal with the period of youth. It extends roughly from the years just after puberty to middle life, which itself begins between the thirty-fifth and fortieth year.

I might well be asked why I choose to begin with the second period of human existence. Are there no difficult questions connected with childhood ? The complex psychic life of the child is of course a problem of the first magnitude to parents, educators and physicians ; but when normal, the child has no real problems of its own. It is only when a human being has grown up that he can have doubts about himself and be at variance with himself.

We are all thoroughly familiar with the sources of the problems which arise in the period of youth. For most people it is the demands of life which harshly put an end to the dream of childhood. If the individual is sufficiently well prepared, the transition to a professional career may take place smoothly. But if he clings to illusions that contradict reality, then problems will surely arise. No one takes the step into life without making certain presuppositions—and occasionally they are false. That is, they may not fit the conditions into which one is thrown. It is often a question of exaggerated expectations, of under-estimation of difficulties, of unjustified optimism or of a negative attitude. One could compile quite a list of the false presuppositions which give rise to the earliest, conscious problems.

But it is not always the contrast of subjective presuppositions with external facts that gives rise to problems; it may as often be inner, psychic disturbances. They may exist even when things run smoothly enough in the outer world. Very often it is the disturbance of the psychic equilibrium by the sexual impulse ; and perhaps just as often it is the feeling of inferiority which springs from an unbearable sensitivity.

These inner difficulties may exist even when adaptation to the outer world has been achieved without apparent effort. It even seems as if young people who have had to struggle hard for their existence are spared inner problems, while those for whom adaptation for some reason or other is made easy, run into problems of sex or conflicts growing from the sense of inferiority.

People whose own temperaments offer problems are often neurotic, but it would be a serious misunderstanding to confuse the existence of problems with neurosis. There is a marked distinction between the two in that the neurotic is ill because he is unconscious of his problems ; while the man with a difficult temperament suffers from his conscious problems without being ill.

If we try to extract the common and essential factors from the almost inexhaustible variety of individual problems found in the period of youth, we meet in nearly all cases with a particular feature : a more or less patent clinging to the childhood level of consciousness—a rebellion against the fateful forces in and around us which tend to involve us in the world. Something in us wishes to remain a child ; to be unconscious, or, at most, conscious only of the ego ; to reject everything foreign, or at least subject it to our will ; to do nothing, or in any case indulge our own craving for pleasure or power. In this leaning we observe something like the inertia of matter ; it is persistence in a hitherto existing state whose level of consciousness is smaller, narrower and more egoistic than that of the dualistic stage. For in the latter the individual finds himself compelled to recognize and to accept what is different and strange as a part of his own life—as a kind of " also-I ".

It is the extension of the horizon of life which is the

essential feature of the dualistic stage—and to which resistance is offered. To be sure, this enlargement—or this *diastole*, to use Goethe's expression—had started long before this. It begins at birth, when the child abandons the narrow confinement of the mother's womb ; and from then on it gains steadily until it reaches a critical point in that phase when, beset by problems, the individual begins to struggle against it.

What would happen to him if he simply changed himself into that other, foreign, " also-I ", and allowed the earlier ego to vanish into the past ? We might suppose this to be a quite practicable course. The very aim of religious education, from the exhortation to put off the old Adam, backward in time to the rebirth rituals of primitive races, is to transform a human being into a new—a future—man, and to allow the old forms of life to die away.

Psychology teaches us that, in a certain sense, there is nothing in the psyche that is old ; nothing that can really, definitively die away. Even Paul was left with a sting in his flesh. Whoever protects himself against what is new and strange and thereby regresses to the past, falls into the same neurotic condition as the man who identifies himself with the new and runs away from the past. The only difference is that the one has estranged himself from the past, and the other from the future. In principle both are doing the same thing ; they are salvaging a narrow state of consciousness. The alternative is to shatter it with the tension inherent in the play of opposites—in the dualistic stage—and thereby to build up a state of wider and higher consciousness.

This outcome would be ideal if it could be brought about in the second stage of life—but here is the rub. For one thing, nature cares nothing whatsoever about a higher level of consciousness ; quite the contrary. And then society does not value these feats of the psyche very highly ; its prizes are always given for achievement and not for personality—the latter being rewarded, for the most part, posthumously. This being so, a particular solution of the difficulty becomes compulsive : we are forced to limit ourselves to the attainable and to differentiate particular aptitudes, for in this way the capable individual discovers his social being.

Achievement, usefulness and so forth are the ideals which appear to guide us out of the confusion of crowding problems. They may be our lode-stars in the adventure of extending and solidifying our psychic existences—they may help us in striking our roots in the world ; but they cannot guide us in the development of that wider consciousness to which we give the name of culture. In the period of youth, at any rate, this course is the normal one and in all circumstances preferable to merely tossing about in the welter of problems.

The dilemma is often solved, therefore, in this way : whatever is given to us by the past is adapted to the possibilities and the demands of the future. We limit ourselves to the attainable, and this means the renunciation of all other potentialities. One man loses a valuable piece of his past, another a valuable piece of his future. Everyone can call to mind friends or schoolmates who were promising and idealistic youngsters, but who, when met with years later, seemed to have grown dry and cramped in a narrow mould. These are examples of the solution given above.

The serious problems of life, however, are never fully solved. If it should for once appear that they are, this is the sign that something has been lost. The meaning and design of a problem seem not to lie in its solution, but in our working at it incessantly. This alone preserves us from stultification and petrifaction. So also with that solution of the problems of the period of youth which consists in restricting ourselves to the attainable : it is only temporarily valid and not lasting in a deeper sense. Of course, to win for oneself a place in society and so to transform one's nature that it is more or less fitted to this existence, is in every instance an important achievement. It is a fight waged within oneself as well as outside, comparable to the struggle of the child to defend his ego. This struggle, we must grant, is for the most part unobserved because it happens in the dark ; but when we see how stubbornly childish illusions, presuppositions and egoistic habits are still clung to in later years we are able to realize the energy it took to form them. And so it is also with the ideals, convictions, guiding ideas and attitudes which in the period of youth lead us out into life—for which we struggle, suffer and win victories : they grow together with our own beings, we apparently change into them, and we therefore perpetuate them at pleasure and as a matter of course, just as the child asserts its ego in the face of the world and in spite of itself—occasionally even to spite itself.

The nearer we approach to the middle of life, and the better we have succeeded in entrenching ourselves in our personal standpoints and social positions, the more it appears as if we had discovered the right course and the right ideals and principles of behaviour. For this reason we suppose them to be eternally valid, and make a virtue of unchangeably clinging to them. We wholly overlook the essential fact that the achievements which society rewards are won at

the cost of a diminution of personality. Many—far too many
—aspects of life which should also have been experienced
lie in the lumber-room among dusty memories. Sometimes,
even, they are glowing coals under grey ashes.

Statistical tables show a rise in the frequency of cases of
mental depression in men about forty. In women the
neurotic difficulties generally begin somewhat earlier. We
see that in this phase of life—between thirty-five and forty—
a significant change in the human psyche is in preparation.
At first it is not a conscious and striking change ; it is rather
a matter of indirect signs of a change which seems to take
its rise from the unconscious. Often it is something like
a slow change in a person's character ; in another case
certain traits may come to light which had disappeared in
childhood ; or again, inclinations and interests begin to
weaken and others arise to take their places. It also
frequently happens that the convictions and principles which
have hitherto been accepted—especially the moral principles—commence to harden and to grow increasingly rigid
until, somewhere towards the age of fifty, a period of
intolerance and fanaticism is reached. It is then as if
the existence of these principles were endangered, and it
were therefore necessary to emphasize them all the
more.

The wine of youth does not always clear with advancing
years ; oftentimes it grows turbid. All the manifestations
mentioned above can be most clearly seen in rather one-sided
people, turning up sometimes sooner and sometimes later.
In my opinion, their appearance is often delayed by the
fact that a person's parents are still alive. It is then as
if the period of youth were unduly continued. I have seen
this especially in the cases of men whose fathers were long-

lived. The death of the father then has the effect of an overhurried—an almost catastrophic—ripening.

I know of a pious man who was a churchwarden and who, from the age of forty onward, showed a growing and finally unbearable intolerance in things of morality and religion. At the same time his disposition grew visibly worse. At last he was nothing more than a darkly lowering " pillar of the church ". In this way he got along until his fifty-fifth year when suddenly, one night, sitting up in bed, he said to his wife : " Now at last I've got it ! As a matter of fact I'm just a plain rascal." Nor did this self-realization remain without results. He spent his declining years in riotous living and in wasting a goodly part of his fortune. Obviously quite a likeable person, capable of both extremes !

The very frequent neurotic disturbances of adult years have this in common, that they betray the attempt to carry the psychic dispositions of youth beyond the threshold of the so-called years of discretion. Who does not know those touching old gentlemen who must always warm up the dish of their student days, who can fan the flames of life only by reminiscences of their heroic youth—and who for the rest, are stuck in a hopelessly wooden philistinism ? As a rule, to be sure, they have this one merit which it would be wrong to undervalue : they are not neurotic, but only boring or stereotyped. The neurotic is rather a person who can never have things as he would like them in the present, and who can therefore never enjoy the past.

As formerly the neurotic could not escape from childhood, so now he cannot part with his youth. He shrinks from the grey thoughts of approaching age ; and, feeling the prospect before him unbearable, is always straining to look behind him.   Just as a childish person shrinks back from the unknown in the world and in human existence, so the grown man shrinks back from the second half of life.   It is as if unknown and dangerous tasks were expected of him ;   or as if he were threatened with sacrifices and losses which he does not wish to accept ; or as if his life up to now seemed to him so fair and so precious that he could not do without it.

Is it perhaps at bottom the fear of death ?   That does not seem to me very probable, because as a rule death is still far in the distance, and is therefore regarded somewhat in the light of an abstraction.   Experience shows us rather that the basis and cause of all the difficulties of this transition are to be found in a deep-seated and peculiar change within the psyche.   In order to characterize it I must take for comparison the daily course of the sun—but a sun that is endowed with human feeling and man's limited consciousness.   In the morning it arises from the nocturnal sea of unconsciousness and looks upon the wide, bright world which lies before it in an expanse that steadily widens the higher it climbs in the firmament.   In this extension of its field of action caused by its own rising, the sun will discover its significance ;   it will see the attainment of the greatest possible height—the widest possible dissemination of its blessings—as its goal.   In this conviction the sun pursues its unforeseen course to the zenith ;   unforeseen, because its career is unique and individual, and its culminating point could not be calculated in advance.   At the stroke of noon the descent begins.   And the descent means the reversal of all the ideals and values that were cherished in the morning. The sun falls into contradiction with itself.   It is as though it should draw in its rays, instead of emitting them.   Light and warmth decline and are at last extinguished.

All comparisons are lame, but this simile is at least not lamer than others. A French aphorism sums it up with cynical resignation : *Si jeunesse savait, si vieillesse pouvait.*

Fortunately we men are not rising and setting suns, for then it would fare badly with our cultural values. But there is something sunlike within us ; and to speak of the morning and spring, of the evening and autumn of life is not mere sentimental jargon. We thus give expression to a psychological truth, even more, to physiological facts ; for the reversal at noon changes even bodily characteristics. Especially among southern races one can observe that older women develop rough and deep voices, incipient moustaches, hard facial expressions and other masculine traits. On the other hand, the masculine physique is toned down by feminine features, as for instance adiposity and softer facial expressions.

There is an interesting report in ethnological literature about an Indian warrior-chief to whom in middle age the Great Spirit appeared in a dream. The spirit announced to him that from then on he must sit among the women and children, wear women's clothes and eat the food of women. He obeyed the dream without suffering a loss of prestige. This vision is a true expression of the psychic revolution of life's noon—of the beginning of life's decline. Man's values and even his body tend to undergo a reversal into the opposite.

We might compare masculinity and femininity with their psychic components to a particular store of substances of which, in the first half of life, unequal use is made. A man consumes his large supply of masculine substance and has left over only the smaller amount of feminine substance, which he must now put to use. It is the other way round with a woman ; she allows her unused supply of masculinity to become active.

This transformation weighs more heavily still in the psychic realm than in the physical. How often it happens that a man of forty or fifty years winds up his business, and that his wife then dons the trousers and opens a little shop where he sometimes performs the duties of handyman. There are many women who only awake to social responsibility and to social consciousness after their fortieth year. In modern business life—especially in the United States— nervous breakdown in the forties or after is a very common occurrence. If one studies the victims a little closely one sees that the thing which has broken down is the masculine style of life which held the field up to now ; what is left over is an effeminate man. Contrariwise, one can observe women in these self-same business spheres who have developed in the second half of life an uncommon masculinity and an incisiveness which push the feelings and the heart aside. Very often the reversal is accompanied by all sorts of catastrophes in marriage ; for it is not hard to imagine what may happen when the husband discovers his tender feelings, and the wife her sharpness of mind.

The worst of it all is that intelligent and cultivated people have these leanings without even knowing of the possibility of such transformations. Wholly unprepared, they embark upon the second half of life. Or are there perhaps colleges for forty-year-olds which prepare them for their coming life and its demands as the ordinary colleges introduce our young people to a knowledge of the world and of life ? No, there are none. Thoroughly unprepared we take the step into the afternoon of life ; worse still, we take this step with the false presupposition that our truths and ideals will serve us as hitherto. But we cannot live the afternoon of life according to the programme of life's morning—for what was great in the morning will be little at evening, and what in the morning was true will at evening have become a lie. I have given psychological treatment to too many people of advancing years, and have looked too often into the secret chambers of their souls, not to be moved by this fundamental truth.

Ageing people should know that their lives are not mounting and unfolding, but that an inexorable inner process forces the contraction of life. For a young person it is almost a sin—and certainly a danger—to be too much occupied with himself; but for the ageing person it is a duty and a necessity to give serious attention to himself. After having lavished its light upon the world, the sun withdraws its rays in order to illumine itself. Instead of doing likewise, many old people prefer to be hypochondriacs, niggards, doctrinaires, applauders of the past or eternal adolescents—all lamentable substitutes for the illumination of the self, but inevitable consequences of the delusion that the second half of life must be governed by the principles of the first.

I said just now that we have no schools for forty-year-olds. That is not quite true. Our religions were always such schools in the past, but how many people regard them as such today? How many of us older persons have really been brought up in such a school and prepared for the second half of life, for old age, death and eternity?

A human being would certainly not grow to be seventy or eighty years old if this longevity had no meaning for the species to which he belongs. The afternoon of human life must also have a significance of its own and cannot be

merely a pitiful appendage to life's morning. The significance
of the morning undoubtedly lies in the development of the
individual, our entrenchment in the outer world, the pro-
pagation of our kind and the care of our children. This
is the obvious purpose of nature. But when this purpose
has been attained—and even more than attained—shall the
earning of money, the extension of conquests and the
expansion of life go steadily on beyond the bounds of all
reason and sense? Whoever carries over into the afternoon
the law of the morning—that is, the aims of nature—must
pay for so doing with damage to his soul just as surely as
a growing youth who tries to salvage his childish egoism
must pay for this mistake with social failure. Money-
making, social existence, family and posterity are nothing
but plain nature—not culture. Culture lies beyond the
purpose of nature. Could by any chance culture be the
meaning and purpose of the second half of life?

In primitive tribes we observe that the old people are
almost always the guardians of the mysteries and the laws,
and it is in these that the cultural heritage of the tribe is
expressed. How does the matter stand with us? Where
is the wisdom of our old people—where are their precious
secrets and their visions? For the most part our old people
try to compete with the young. In the United States it is
almost an ideal for the father to be the brother of his sons,
and for the mother if possible to be the younger sister of
her daughter.

I do not know how much of this confusion comes as a
reaction to an earlier exaggeration of the dignity of age,
and how much is to be charged to false ideals. These
undoubtedly exist, and the goal of those who hold them lies
behind, and not in front. Therefore they are always striving

to turn back. We have to grant to these persons that it is hard to see what other goal the second half of life can offer than the well-known goal of the first. Expansion of life, usefulness, efficiency, the cutting of a figure in social life, the shrewd steering of offspring into suitable marriages and good positions—are not these purposes enough? Unfortunately this is not enough meaning or purpose for many persons who see in the approach of old age a mere diminution of life, and who look upon their earlier ideals only as something faded and worn out. Of course, if these persons had filled up the beaker of life earlier and emptied it to the lees, they would feel quite differently about everything now; had they kept nothing back, all that wanted to catch fire would have been consumed, and the quiet of old age would be very welcome to them. But we must not forget that only a very few people are artists in life; that the art of life is the most distinguished and rarest of all the arts. Who ever succeeded in draining the whole cup with grace? So for many people all too much unlived life remains over— sometimes potentialities which they could never have lived with the best of wills; and so they approach the threshold of old age with unsatisfied claims which inevitably turn their glances backward.

It is particularly fatal for such people to look backward. For them a prospect and a goal in the future are indispensable. This is why all great religions hold the promise of a life beyond; it makes it possible for mortal man to live the second half of life with as much perseverance and aim as the first. For the man of today the enlargement of life and its culmination are plausible goals; but the idea of life after death seems to him questionable or beyond belief. And yet life's cessation, that is, death, can only be accepted as a goal when existence is so wretched that we are glad for it to end, or when we are convinced that the sun strives to its setting—" to illumine distant races "—with the same perseverance it showed in rising to the zenith. But to believe has become today such a difficult art, that people, and particularly the educated part of humanity, can hardly find their way there. They have become too accustomed to the thought that, with regard to immortality and such questions, there are many contradictory opinions and no convincing proofs. Since " science " has become the catchword which carries the weight of conviction in the contemporary world, we ask for " scientific " proofs. But educated people who can think, know that proof of this kind is out of the question. We simply know nothing whatever about it.

May I remark that, for the same reasons, we cannot know whether anything happens to a person after he is dead ? The answer is neither yes nor no. We simply have no definite scientific proofs about it one way or another, and are therefore in the same position as when we ask whether the planet Mars is inhabited or not. And the inhabitants of Mars, if there are any, are certainly not concerned whether we affirm or deny their existence. They may exist or not. And that is how it stands with so-called immortality—with which we may shelve the problem.

But here my physician's conscience awakes and urges me to say a word which is essential to this question. I have observed that a directed life is in general better, richer and healthier than an aimless one, and that it is better to go forwards with the stream of time than backwards against it. To the psychotherapist an old man who cannot bid farewell to life appears as feeble and sickly as a young man who is unable to embrace it. And as a matter of fact, in many cases it is a question of the selfsame childish covetousness, of the same fear, the same obstinacy and wilfulness, in the one as in the other. As a physician I am convinced that it is hygienic—if I may use the word—to discover in death a goal towards which one can strive ; and that shrinking away from it is something unhealthy and abnormal which robs the second half of life of its purpose. I therefore consider the religious teaching of a life hereafter consonant with the standpoint of psychic hygiene. When I live in a house which I know will fall about my head within the next two weeks, all my vital functions will be impaired by this thought ; but if on the contrary I feel myself to be safe, I can dwell there in a normal and comfortable way. From the standpoint of psychotherapy it would therefore be desirable to think of death as only a transition—one part of a life-process whose extent and duration escape our knowledge.

In spite of the fact that by far the larger part of mankind does not know why the body needs salt, everyone demands it none the less because of an instinctive need. It is the same in the things of the psyche. A large majority of people have from time immemorial felt the need of believing in a continuance of life. The demands of therapy, therefore, do not lead us into any bypaths, but down the middle of the roadway trodden by humankind. And therefore we are thinking correctly with respect to the meaning of life, even though we do not understand what we think.

Do we ever understand what we think ? We only understand that thinking which is a mere equation, and from which nothing comes out but what we have put in. That is the working of the intellect. But beyond that there is a **thinking** in primordial images—in symbols which are older than historical man ; which have been ingrained in him from earliest times, and, eternally living, outlasting all generations, still make up the groundwork of the human psyche. It is only possible to live the fullest life when we are in harmony with these symbols ; wisdom is a return to them. It is neither a question of belief nor of knowledge, but of the agreement of our thinking with the primordial images of the unconscious. They are the source of all our conscious thoughts, and one of these primordial thoughts is the idea of life after death. Science and these symbols are incommensurables. They are indispensable conditions of the imagination ; they are primary data—the materials whose expediency and warrant to exist science cannot deny offhand. It can only treat of them as given facts, much as it can explore a function like that of the thyroid gland, for example. Before the nineteenth century the thyroid was regarded as a meaningless organ, merely because it was not understood. It would be equally short-sighted of us today to call the primordial images senseless. For me these images are something like psychic organs, and I treat them with the very greatest care. It happens sometimes that I must say to an older patient : " Your picture of God or your idea of immortality is atrophied ; consequently your psychic metabolism is out of gear." The ancient *athanasias pharmakon*, the medicament of immortality, is more profound and meaningful than we supposed.

In this place I would like to return again for a moment to the comparison with the sun. The one hundred and eighty degrees of the arc of life are divisible into four parts. The first quarter, lying to the east, is childhood—that state in which we are a problem for others, but are not yet conscious of any problems of our own. Conscious problems fill out the second and third quarters ; while in the last— in extreme old age—we descend again into that condition where, unworried by our state of consciousness, we again become something of a problem for others. Childhood and extreme old age, to be sure, are utterly different, and yet they have one thing in common : submersion in unconscious psychic happenings. Since the mind of a child grows out of the unconscious, its psychic processes—though not easily accessible—are not as difficult to discern as those of a very old person who has plunged again into the unconscious, and who progressively vanishes within it. Childhood and old age are the stages of life without any conscious problems, for which reason I have not taken them into consideration here.

VI

FREUD AND JUNG—CONTRASTS

THE difference between Freud's views and my own ought really to be dealt with by someone who stands outside the circles of influence of those ideas which go under our respective names. Can I be credited with sufficient impartiality to rise above my own ideas ? Can any man do this ? I doubt it. If I were told that someone had rivalled Baron Münchausen by accomplishing such a feat, I should feel sure that his ideas were borrowed ones.

It is true that widely accepted ideas are never the personal property of their so-called author ; on the contrary, he is the bond-servant of his ideas. Impressive ideas which are hailed as truths have something peculiar to themselves. Although they come into being at a definite time, they are and have always been timeless ; they arise from that realm of procreative, psychic life out of which the ephemeral mind of the single human being grows like a plant that blossoms, bears fruit and seed, and then withers and dies. Ideas spring from a source that is not contained within one man's personal life. We do not create them ; they create us. To be sure, when we deal in ideas we inevitably make a confession, for they bring to the light of day not only the best that in us lies, but our worst insufficiencies and personal shortcomings as well. This is especially the case with ideas about psychology. Whence should they come except from

132

the most subjective side of life ? Can experience with the objective world save us from subjective prejudgements ? Is not every experience, even in the best of circumstances, to a large extent subjective interpretation ? On the other hand, the subject also is an objective fact, a piece of the world. What issues from it comes, after all, from the universal soil, just as the rarest and strangest organism is none the less supported and nourished by the earth which we all share in common. It is precisely the most subjective ideas which, being closest to nature and to the living being, deserve to be called the truest. But what is truth ?

For the purposes of psychology, I think it best to abandon the notion that we are today in anything like a position to make statements about the nature of the psyche that are " true " or " correct ". The best that we can achieve is true expression. By true expression I mean an open avowal and a detailed presentation of everything that is subjectively noted. One person will stress the forms into which this material can be worked, and will therefore believe that he has created what he finds within himself. Another will lay most weight upon the fact that he plays the part of an observer ; he will be conscious of his receptive attitude, and insist that his subjective material presents itself to him. The truth lies between the two. True expression consists in giving form to what is observed.

The modern psychologist, however unbounded his hopes, can hardly claim to have achieved more than the right sort of receptivity and a reasonable adequacy of expression. The psychology we at present possess is the testimony of a few individuals here and there regarding what they have found within themselves. The form in which they have cast it is sometimes adequate and sometimes not. Since each individual conforms more or less to a type, his testimony can be accepted as a fairly valid description of a large number of people. And since those who conform to other types belong none the less to the human species, we may conclude that the description applies, though less fully, to them too. What Freud has to say about sexuality, infantile pleasure, and their conflict with the " principle of reality ", as well as what he says about incest and the like, can be taken as the truest expression of his own psychic make-up. He has given adequate form to what he has noted in himself. I am no opponent of Freud's ; I am merely presented in that light by his own short-sightedness and that of his pupils. No experienced psychotherapist can deny having met with dozens of cases at least which answer in all essentials to Freud's descriptions. By his avowal of what he has found in himself, Freud has assisted at the birth of a great truth about man. He has devoted his life and his strength to the construction of a psychology which is a formulation of his own being.

Our way of looking at things is conditioned by what we are. And since other people are differently constituted, they see things differently and express themselves differently. Adler, one of Freud's earliest pupils, is a case in point. Working with the same empirical material as Freud, he approached it from a totally different standpoint. His way of looking at things is at least as convincing as Freud's, because he also represents a well-known type. I know that the followers of both schools flatly assert that I am in the wrong, but I may hope that history and all fair-minded persons will bear me out. Both schools, to my way of thinking, deserve reproach for over-emphasizing the pathological aspect of life and for interpreting man too exclusively in the light of his defects. A convincing example of this in Freud's case is his inability to understand religious experience, as is clearly shown in his book : *The Future of an Illusion.* For my part, I prefer to look at man in the light of what in him is healthy and sound, and to free the sick man from that point of view which colours every page Freud has written. Freud's teaching is definitely one-sided in that it generalizes from facts that are relevant only to neurotic states of mind ; its validity is really confined to those states. Within these limits Freud's teaching is true and valid even when it is in error, for error also belongs to the picture, and carries the truth of a true avowal. In any case, Freud's is not a psychology of the healthy mind.

The morbid symptom in Freud's psychology is this : it is based upon a view of the world that is uncriticized, or even unconscious, and this is apt to narrow the field of human experience and understanding to a considerable extent. It was a great mistake on Freud's part to turn his back on philosophy. Not once does he criticize his premises or even the assumptions that underlie his personal outlook. Yet to do so was necessary, as may be inferred from what I have said above ; for had he critically examined his assumptions, he would never have put his peculiar mental disposition naïvely on view, as he has done in *The Interpretation of Dreams.* At all events, he would have had a taste of the difficulties which I have met with. I have never refused the bitter-sweet drink of philosophical criticism, but have taken it with caution, a little at a time. All too little, my opponents will say ; almost too much, my own feeling tells me. All too easily does self-criticism poison one's naïveté, that priceless possession, or rather gift, which no creative man can be without. At any rate, philosophical criticism has helped me to see that every psychology—my own included —has the character of a subjective confession. And yet I must prevent my critical powers from destroying my creativeness. I know well enough that every word I utter carries with it something of myself—of my special and unique self with its particular history and its own particular world. Even when I deal with empirical data, I am necessarily speaking about myself. But it is only by accepting this as inevitable that I can serve the cause of man's knowledge of man—the cause which Freud also wished to serve, and which, in spite of everything, he has served. Knowledge rests not upon truth alone, but upon error also.

It is perhaps here, where the question arises of accepting the fact that every psychological teaching which is the work of one man is subjectively coloured, that the line between Freud and myself is most sharply drawn.

A further difference seems to me to consist in this, that I try to free myself from all unconscious and therefore uncriticized assumptions as to the world in general. I say " I try ", for who can be sure that he has freed himself from all his unconscious assumptions ? I try to save myself at least from the crassest prejudices, and am therefore inclined to recognize all manner of gods provided only that they are active in the human psyche. I do not doubt that the natural instincts or drives are forces of propulsion in human life, whether we call them sexuality or the will to power ; but I also do not doubt that these instincts come into collision with the spirit, for they are continually colliding with something, and why should not this something be called spirit ? I am far from knowing what spirit is in itself, and equally far from knowing what instincts are. The one is as mysterious to me as the other, yet I am unable to dismiss the one by explaining it in terms of the other. That would be to treat it as a mere misunderstanding. The fact that the earth has only one moon is not a misunderstanding. There are no misunderstandings in nature ; they are only to be found in the realms that man calls " understanding ". Certainly instinct and spirit are beyond my understanding. They are terms that we allow to stand for powerful forces whose nature we do not know.

As may be seen, I attribute a positive value to all religions. In their symbolism I recognize those figures which I have met with in the dreams and fantasies of my patients. In their moral teachings I see efforts that are the same as or similar to those made by my patients, when, guided by their own insight or inspiration, they seek the right way of dealing with the forces of the inner life. Ceremonial, ritual, initiation rites and ascetic practices, in all their forms and variations, interest me profoundly as so many techniques for bringing about a proper relation to these forces. I likewise attribute a positive value to biology, and to the empiricism of natural science in general, in which I see a herculean attempt to understand the human psyche by approaching it from the outer world. I regard the gnostic religions as an equally prodigious undertaking in the opposite direction : as an attempt to draw knowledge of the cosmos from within. In my picture of the world there is a vast outer realm and an equally vast inner realm ; between these two stands man, facing now one and now the other, and, according to his mood or disposition, taking the one for the absolute truth by denying or sacrificing the other.

This picture is hypothetical, of course, but it offers a hypothesis which is so valuable that I will not give it up. I consider it heuristically and empirically verified ; and,

what is more, it is supported by the *consensus gentium.*
This hypothesis certainly came to me from an inner source,
though I might imagine that empirical findings had led to
its discovery. Out of it has come my theory of types, and
also my reconciliation with views as different from my own
as those of Freud.

I see in all happening the play of opposites, and derive
from this conception my idea of psychic energy. I hold
that psychic energy involves the play of opposites in much
the same way as physical energy involves a difference of
potential, which is to say, the existence of such opposites
as warm and cold, high and low. Freud began by taking
sexuality as the only psychic driving power, and only after
my break with him did he grant an equal status to other
psychic activities as well. For my part, I have subsumed
the various psychic drives or forces under the concept of
energy in order to avoid the arbitrariness of a psychology
that deals with drives or impulses alone. I therefore speak,
not of separate drives or forces, but of " value intensities ".[1]
By what has just been said I do not mean to deny the
importance of sexuality in psychic life, though Freud
stubbornly maintains that I do deny it. What I seek is to
set bounds to the rampant terminology of sex which threatens
to vitiate all discussion of the human psyche ; I wish to
put sexuality itself in its proper place. Common-sense will
always return to the fact that sexuality is only one of the
life-instincts—only one of the psycho-physiological functions
—though one that is without doubt very far-reaching and
important.

Beyond all question, there is a marked disturbance today

[1] Compare the essay "On Psychical Energy" in *Contributions to
Analytical Psychology*, Kegan Paul, Trench, Trubner & Co., London, 1928.

in the realms of sexual life. It is well known that when we have a bad toothache, we can think of nothing else. The sexuality which Freud describes is unmistakably that sexual obsession which shows itself whenever a patient has reached the point where he needs to be forced or tempted out of a wrong attitude or situation. It is an over-emphasized sexuality piled up behind a dam ; and it shrinks at once to normal proportions as soon as the way to development is opened. It is being caught in the old resentments against parents and relations and in the boring emotional tangles of the family situation which most often brings about the damming-up of the energies of life. And it is this stoppage which shows itself unfailingly in that kind of sexuality which is called " infantile ". It is really not sexuality proper, but an unnatural discharge of tensions that belong to quite another province of life. This being so, what is the use of paddling about in this flooded country ? Surely, straight thinking will grant that it is more important to open up drainage canals. We should try to find, in a change of attitude or in new ways of life, that difference of potential which the pent-up energy requires. If this is not achieved a vicious circle is set up, and this is in fact the menace which Freudian psychology appears to offer. It points no way that leads beyond the inexorable cycle of biological events. This hopelessness would drive one to exclaim with Paul : " Wretched man that I am, who will deliver me from the body of this death ? " And our man of intellect comes forward, shaking his head, and says in Faust's words : " Thou art conscious only of the single urge ", namely of the fleshly bond leading back to father and mother or forward to the children that have sprung from our flesh— " incest " with the past and " incest " with the future, the original sin of the perpetuation of the family situation. There is nothing that can free us from this bond except that opposite urge of life, the spirit. It is not the children of the flesh, but the " children of God " who know freedom. In Ernst Barlach's tragic novel of family life, *Der Tote Tag*, the mother-dæmon says at the end : " The strange thing is that man will not learn that God is his father." That is what Freud would never learn, and what all those who share his outlook forbid themselves to learn. At least, they never find the key to this knowledge. Theology does not help those who are looking for the key, because theology demands faith, and faith cannot be made : it is in the truest sense a gift of grace. We moderns are faced with the necessity of rediscovering the life of the spirit ; we must experience it anew for ourselves. It is the only way in which we can break the spell that binds us to the cycle of biological events.

My position on this question is the third point of difference between Freud's views and my own. Because of it I am accused of mysticism. I do not, however, hold myself responsible for the fact that man has, everywhere and always, spontaneously developed religious forms of expression, and that the human psyche from time immemorial has been shot through with religious feelings and ideas. Whoever cannot see this aspect of the human psyche is blind, and whoever chooses to explain it away, or to " enlighten " it away, has no sense of reality. Or should we see in the father-complex which shows itself in all the members of the Freudian school, and in its founder as well, convincing evidence of any release worth mentioning from the inexorable family situation ? This father-complex, fanatically defended with such stubbornness and over-sensitivity, is a cloak for religiosity misunderstood ; it is a mysticism expressed in terms of biology and the family relation. As for Freud's idea of the " super-ego ", it is a furtive attempt to smuggle in his time-honoured image of Jehovah in the dress of psychological theory. When one does things like that, it is better to say so openly. For my part, I prefer to call things by the names under which they have always been known. The wheel of history must not be turned back, and man's advance toward a spiritual life, which began with the primitive rites of initiation, must not be denied. It is permissible for science to divide its field of enquiry and to set up limited hypotheses, for science must work in that way ; but the human psyche may not be parcelled out. It is a whole which embraces consciousness, and is the mother of consciousness. Scientific thought, being only one of its functions, can never exhaust all the possibilities of life. The psychotherapist must not allow his vision to be coloured by the glasses of pathology ; he must never allow himself to forget that the ailing mind is a human mind, and that, for all its ailments, it shares in the whole of the psychic life of man. The psychotherapist must even be able to admit that the ego is ill for the very reason that it is cut off from the whole, and has lost its connection with mankind as well as with the spirit. The ego is indeed the " place of fears ", as Freud says in *The Ego and the Id*, but only so long as it has not returned to the " father " and " mother ".[1] Freud ship-wrecks on the question of Nicodemus : " Can a man enter his mother's womb a second time and be born again ? " To compare small things with great, we might say that history repeats itself here, for the question once more comes to the front today in a domestic quarrel of modern psychology.

---

[1] *I.e.*, spirit and nature. (*Trans.*)

For thousands of years, rites of initiation have been teaching spiritual rebirth; yet, strangely enough, man forgets again and again the meaning of divine procreation. This is surely no evidence of a strong life of the spirit; and yet the penalty of misunderstanding is heavy, for it is nothing less than neurotic decay, embitterment, atrophy and sterility. It is easy enough to drive the spirit out of the door, but when we have done so the salt of life grows flat— it loses its savour. Fortunately, we have proof that the spirit always renews its strength in the fact that the central teaching of the ancient initiations is handed on from generation to generation. Ever and again human beings arise who understand what is meant by the fact that God is our father. The equal balance of the flesh and the spirit is not lost to the world.

The contrast between Freud and myself goes back to essential differences in our basic assumptions. Assumptions are unavoidable, and this being so, it is wrong to pretend that we have made no assumptions. That is why I have dealt with fundamental questions; with these as a starting-point, the manifold and detailed differences between Freud's views and my own can best be understood.

VII

ARCHAIC MAN

THE word " archaic " means primal—original. While it is
one of the most difficult and thankless of tasks to say anything of importance about civilized man of today, we are
apparently in a more favourable position with regard to
archaic man. In the first case we try to reach a commanding
point of view, but actually are caught in the same presuppositions and blinded by the same prejudices as are
those about whom we wish to speak. In the case of the
archaic man, however, we are far removed from his world
in time, and our mental capacities are more differentiated
than his. It is therefore apparently possible for us to occupy
a point of vantage from which we can overlook his world
and the meaning it held for him.

This sentence -delimits the subject to be covered in the
present essay. Save by restricting myself to the psychic
life of archaic man, I could hardly paint his picture in so
small a space. I shall confine myself to the task of making
this picture sufficiently inclusive, and shall not consider
the findings of anthropology with regard to primitive races.
When we speak of man in general, we do not have his anatomy
—the shape of his skull or the colour of his skin—in mind,
but mean rather his psychic world, his state of consciousness
and his mode of life. Since all this belongs to the subject-
matter of psychology, we shall be dealing here chiefly with

archaic or primitive mentality. Despite this limitation it turns out that we have actually widened our theme, because it is not only primitive man whose psychic processes are archaic. The civilized man of today shows these archaic processes as well, and not merely in the form of sporadic " throw-backs " from the level of modern social life. On the contrary, every civilized human being, whatever his conscious development, is still an archaic man at the deeper levels of his psyche. Just as the human body connects us with the mammals and displays numerous relics of earlier evolutionary stages going back even to the reptilian age, so the human psyche is likewise a product of evolution which, when followed up to its origins, shows countless archaic traits.

When first we come into contact with primitive peoples or read about primitive mentality in scientific works, we cannot fail to be deeply impressed with the strangeness of archaic man. Lévy-Brühl himself, an authority in the field of the psychology of primitive societies, never wearies of insisting upon the striking difference between the " pre-logical " state of mind and our conscious outlook. It seems to him, as a civilized man, inexplicable that the primitive should disregard the obvious lessons of experience, should flatly deny the most evident causal connections, and instead of accounting for things as accidents or on reasonable grounds, should simply take their " collective representa-tions " to be valid offhand. By "collective representations" Lévy-Brühl means widely current ideas whose truth is held to be self-evident, such as the primitive ideas regarding spirits, witchcraft, the power of medicines, and so forth. While it is perfectly understandable to us that people die of advanced age or as the result of diseases that are recognized to be fatal, this is not the case with primitive man. When old persons die, he does not believe it to be as a result of age. He argues that there are persons who have grown much older. Likewise, no one dies as the result of disease, for there have been other people who recovered from the same disease, or never contracted it. To him, the real explanation is always magic. Either a spirit has killed the man, or sorcery has done so. Many primitive tribes recognize death in battle as the only natural death. Still other tribes regard even death in battle as unnatural, holding that the adversary who brought it about must either have been a sorcerer or have used a charmed weapon. This grotesque idea can on occasions take an even more impressive form. For instance, two anklets were found in the stomach of a crocodile shot by a European. The natives recognized the anklets as the property of two women who, some time before, had been devoured by a crocodile. At once the charge of witchcraft was raised, for this quite natural occurrence, which would never have aroused the suspicions of a European, was given an unexpected interpretation in the light of one of those presuppositions which Lévy-Brühl calls " collective representations ". The natives said that an unknown sorcerer had summoned the crocodile and had bidden it to bring him the two women. The crocodile had carried out the command. But what about the anklets in the beast's stomach ? The natives maintained that crocodiles never ate people unless bidden to do so. The crocodile had received the anklets from the sorcerer as a reward.

This story is a perfect example of that capricious way of accounting for things which is a feature of the " pre-logical " state of mind. We call it pre-logical, because to us such an explanation seems absolutely illogical. But it only strikes us in this way because we start from assumptions wholly different from those of primitive man. If we were as con- vinced as he is of the existence of sorcerers and of mysterious powers, instead of believing in so-called natural causes, his inferences would seem to us perfectly reasonable. As a matter of fact, primitive man is no more logical or illogical than we are. His presuppositions are not the same as ours, and that is what distinguishes him from us. His thinking and his conduct are based on assumptions other than our own. To all that is in any way out of the ordinary and that therefore disturbs, frightens or astonishes him, he ascribes what we should call a supernatural origin. For him, of course, these things are not supernatural; on the contrary, they belong to his world of experience. We feel we are stating a natural sequence of events when we say : this house was burned down because the lightning struck it. Primitive man senses an equally natural sequence when he says : a sorcerer has used the lightning to set fire to this particular house. There is nothing whatever within the experience of primitive man—provided that it is at all unusual or impressive—that will not be accounted for on similar grounds. In explaining things in this way he is just like ourselves : he does not examine his assumptions. To him it is an unquestionable truth that disease and other ills are caused by spirits or witchcraft, just as for us it is a foregone conclusion that an illness has a natural cause. We would no more lay it down to sorcery than he to natural causes. His mental activity does not differ in any funda- mental way from ours. It is, as I have said, his assumptions alone that set him apart from ourselves.

It is often supposed that primitive man has other feelings

than we, and another moral outlook—that the " pre-
logical " state of mind differs from ours in these respects
also. Undoubtedly he has a different code of morals. When
questioned as to the distinction between good and bad
a negro chieftain declared : " When I steal my enemy's
wives, it is good, but when he steals mine, it is bad." In
many regions it is a terrible insult to tread upon a person's
shadow, and in others it is an unpardonable sin to scrape
a sealskin with an iron knife instead of a flint one. But
let us be honest. Do we not think it sinful to eat fish with
a steel knife, for a man to keep his hat on in a room, or to
greet a lady with a cigar in his mouth ? With us, as well as
with primitive man, such things have nothing to do with
ethics. There are true and loyal head-hunters, and there
are men who piously and conscientiously practise cruel
rites, or commit murder from righteous conviction. Primitive
man is no less prompt than we are to value an ethical
attitude. His good is just as good as ours, and his evil is
just as bad as ours. Only the forms under which good and
evil appear are different ; the process of ethical judgement
is the same.

It is likewise thought that primitive man has keener
sense-organs than we, or that they somehow differ from ours.
But his highly refined sense of direction or of hearing and
vision is entirely a question of his occupations. If he is
confronted with situations that are foreign to his experience,
he is amazingly slow and clumsy. I once showed some
native hunters, who were as keen-sighted as hawks,
magazine pictures in which any of our children would have
instantly recognized human figures. But my hunters
turned the pictures round and round until one of them,
tracing the outlines with his finger, finally exclaimed :

" These are white men." It was hailed by all as a great discovery.

The incredibly accurate sense of locality shown by many natives is a matter of practice. It is absolutely necessary that they should be able to find their way in forests and jungles. Even the European, after a short while in Africa, begins to notice things he would never have dreamed of noticing before; he does it out of the fear of going hopelessly astray in spite of his compass.

Nothing goes to show that primitive man thinks, feels, or perceives in a way that differs fundamentally from ours. His psychic functioning is essentially the same—only his primary assumptions are different. Compared to this it is a relatively unimportant fact that he has, or seems to have, a smaller area of consciousness than we, and that he is not very capable, or is quite incapable, of concentrated mental activity. This last, it is true, strikes the European as strange. For instance, I could never hold a palaver for longer than two hours, since by that time the natives always declared themselves tired. They said it was too difficult, and yet I had only asked quite simple questions in a desultory way. These same natives showed an astonishing concentration and endurance when out hunting or on a journey. My letter-carrier, for instance, could run seventy-five miles at a stretch. I saw a woman in her sixth month of pregnancy, carrying a baby on her back and smoking a long pipe of tobacco, dance almost the whole night through round a blazing fire when the temperature was $95°$, without collapsing. It cannot be denied that primitive people are capable of concentrating upon things that interest them. If we try to give our attention to uninteresting matters, we soon notice how feeble our powers of concentration are.

We ourselves, like them, are dependent upon emotional under-currents.

It is true that primitive man is simpler and more childlike than we, in good and evil alike. This in itself does not impress us as strange. And yet, when we approach the world of archaic man, we have the feeling of something prodigiously strange. As far as I have been able to analyse it, this feeling comes mainly from the fact that the primary assumptions of archaic man differ essentially from ours—that he lives, if I may use the expression, in a different world. Until we come to know his presuppositions, he is a riddle hard to read, but when we know them, all is relatively simple. We might equally well say that primitive man ceases to be a riddle when we have come to know our own presuppositions.

It is a rational presupposition of ours that everything has a natural and perceptible cause. We are convinced of this. Causality, so understood, is one of our most sacred dogmas. There is no legitimate place in our world for invisible, arbitrary and so-called supernatural forces—unless, indeed, we follow the modern physicist in his scrutiny of the minute and secret world of the atom wherein, as it appears, curious things come to pass. But that lies far from the beaten track. We distinctly resent the idea of invisible and arbitrary forces, for it is not so long ago that we made our escape from that frightening world of dreams and superstitions, and constructed for ourselves a picture of the cosmos worthy of rational consciousness—that latest and greatest achievement of man. We are now surrounded by a world that is obedient to rational laws. It is true that we do not know the causes of everything, but they will in time be discovered, and these discoveries will accord with our reasoned expectations. That is our hope, and we take it as much for granted as primitive man does his own assumptions. There are also chance occurrences, to be sure, but these are merely accidental, and we have granted them a causality of their own. Chance occurrences are repellent to the mind that loves order. They have a laughable and therefore irritating way of throwing out of gear the predictable course of events. We resent the idea of chance occurrences as much as that of invisible forces, for they remind us too much of Satanic imps or of the caprice of a *deus ex machina*. They are the worst enemies of our careful calculations and a continual threat to all our undertakings. Being admittedly contrary to reason, they deserve contempt, and yet we should not fail to give them their due. The Arab shows them greater respect than we. He writes on every letter *Insha-allah*, " If if please God ", for only then will the letter arrive. In spite of our reluctance to admit chance, and in spite of the fact that events run true to general laws, it is undeniable that we are always and everywhere exposed to incalculable accidents. And what is more invisible and arbitrary than chance ? What is more unavoidable and more annoying ?

If we consider the matter, we might as well say that the causal connection of events according to general laws is a theory which is borne out about half the time, while for the rest the demon of chance has his way. A chance occurrence also has its natural causes, and we must often discover to our sorrow that they are commonplace enough. It is not the fact that the cause of the accidents is unknown to us that annoys us ; the irritating thing about them is that they befall us here and now in an apparently arbitrary way. That is how it strikes us, at least. An accident is always irritating, and even the most dyed-in-the-wool rationalist may be moved to curse it. However we interpret an accidental event, we cannot alter the fact that it has the power to affect us. The more the conditions of existence become subject to regulation, the more is chance excluded and the less do we need to protect ourselves against it. None the less, everyone takes account of the possibility of accidental occurrences, or counts upon them, even though the official " credo " does not countenance this belief.

It is our assumption, amounting to a positive conviction, that everything has causes which we call natural and which we at least suppose to be perceptible. Primitive man, on the other hand, assumes that everything is brought about by invisible, arbitrary powers—in other words, that everything is chance. Only he does not call it chance, but intention. Natural causation is to him a mere semblance and not worthy of mention. If three women go to the river to draw water, and a crocodile seizes the one in the centre and pulls her under, our view of things leads us to the verdict that it was pure chance that that particular woman was seized. The fact that the crocodile seized her seems to us natural enough, for these beasts occasionally do eat human beings. For primitive man such an explanation completely obliterates the facts, and accounts for no aspect of the whole exciting story. Archaic man is right in holding our view of the matter to be superficial or even absurd, for the accident might not have happened and still the same interpretation would fit the case. The prejudice of the European does not allow him to see how little he really explains things in such a way.

Primitive man expects more of an explanation. What we call chance is to him arbitrary power. It was therefore the intention of the crocodile—as everyone could observe—

to seize the woman who stood between the other two. If it had not had this intention it would have taken one of the others. But why did the crocodile have this intention? These animals do not ordinarily eat human beings. This assertion is correct—quite as correct as the statement that there is no rainfall in the Sahara. Crocodiles are really timid animals, and are easily frightened. Considering their numbers, they kill astonishingly few people, and it is an unexpected and unnatural event when they devour a man. Such an event calls for explanation. Of his own accord the crocodile would not take a human life. By whom, then, was he ordered to do so?

It is on the facts of the world around him that primitive man bases his verdicts. When the unexpected occurs he is justifiably astonished and wishes to know the specific causes. To this extent he behaves exactly as we do. But he goes further than we. He has one or more theories about the arbitrary power of chance. We say: Nothing but chance. He says: Calculating intention. He lays the chief stress upon the confusing and confused breaks in the chain of causation—upon those occurrences that fail to show the causal connections which science expects, and that constitute the other half of happenings in general. He has long ago adapted himself to nature in so far as it conforms to general laws; what he fears is unpredictable chance whose power makes him see in it an arbitrary and incalculable agent. Here again he is right. It is quite understandable that everything out of the ordinary should frighten him. Ant-eaters are fairly numerous in the regions south of Mount Elgon where I stayed for some time. The anteater is a shy, nocturnal animal that is rarely seen. If one happens to be seen by day, it is an extraordinary and unnatural event which astonishes the natives as much as the discovery of a brook that occasionally flows uphill would astonish us. If we knew of actual cases in which water suddenly overcame the force of gravity, such knowledge would cause us no little anxiety. We know that tremendous masses of water surround us, and can easily imagine what would happen if water no longer conformed to gravitational law. This is the situation in which primitive man finds himself with respect to the happenings in his world. He is thoroughly familiar with the habits of anteaters, but when one of them transgresses the laws of nature it acquires an incalculable sphere of action. Primitive man is so strongly impressed by things as they are, that a transgression of the laws of his world exposes him to unforeseen possibilities. Such an exception is a portent, an omen, comparable to a comet or an eclipse. Since in his view such an unnatural event as the appearance of an anteater by day can have no natural causes, some invisible power must be behind it. And the alarming manifestation of a power which can annul cosmic laws calls of course for extraordinary measures of placation or self-defence. The neighbouring villages must be aroused, and the anteater must be dug up with the utmost pains, and killed. The oldest maternal uncle of the man who saw the anteater must then sacrifice a bull. The man descends into the sacrificial pit and receives the first piece of the animal's flesh, whereupon the uncle and the other participants in the ceremony also eat. In this way the dangerous caprice of nature is expiated.

As for us, we should certainly be alarmed enough if water began to run uphill for unknown reasons, but are not when an anteater is seen by day, or an albino is born, or an eclipse takes place. We know the meaning and the sphere of action of such happenings, while primitive man does not. Ordinary events constitute for him a coherent whole in which he and all other creatures are embraced. He is therefore extremely conservative, and does what others have always done. If something happens, no matter where, to break the coherence of this whole, he feels there is a rift in his well-ordered world. Then anything may happen—heaven knows what. All occurrences that are in any way striking are at once brought into connection with the unusual event. For instance, a missionary set up a flagstaff in front of his house so that he could raise the Union Jack on Sundays. But this innocent pleasure cost him dear. It was a singular and disturbing action, and when shortly afterwards a devastating storm broke out, the flagstaff was of course made responsible. This sufficed to start a general uprising against the missionary. It is the regularity of common occurrences that assures primitive man of a sense of security in his world. Every exceptional event seems to him the threatening act of an arbitrary power that must be expiated. It is not only a momentary interruption of the ordinary course of things, but also the portent of other untoward events.

This strikes us as nothing less than absurd inasmuch as we forget how our grandparents and our great-grandparents still felt about the world. A calf is born with two heads and five legs. In the next village a cock has laid an egg. An old woman has had a dream, a comet appears in the sky, there is a great fire in the nearest town, and the following year a war breaks out. In this way history was always written from remote antiquity on down to the eighteenth century. This juxtaposition of facts, so meaningless to us, is significant and convincing to primitive man. And, contrary to all expectation, he is right to find it so. His powers of observation can be trusted. From age-old experience he knows that such connections actually exist. What seems to us a wholly senseless heaping-up of single, haphazard occurrences—because we pay attention only to single events and their particular causes—is for primitive man a completely logical sequence of omens and of happenings indicated by them. It is a fatal outbreak of demonic power showing itself in a thoroughly consistent way.

The calf with two heads and the war are one and the same, for the calf was only an anticipation of the war. Primitive man finds this connection so unquestionable and convincing because the caprice of chance seems to him a far more important factor in the happenings of the world than regularity and conformity to laws. Thanks to his close attention to the unusual he has preceded us in discovering that chance events arrange themselves in groups or series. The law of the duplication of cases is known to all doctors engaged in clinical work. An old professor of psychiatry at Würzburg always used to say of a particularly rare clinical case : " Gentlemen, this is an absolutely unique case—tomorrow we shall have another just like it." I have myself often observed the same thing during my eight years' practice in an insane asylum. On one occasion a person was committed for a rare twilight-state of consciousness—the first case of this kind I had ever seen. Within two days we had a similar case, and that was the last. " Duplication of cases " is with us a joke of the clinics, but it has also been, from time immemorial, a fact of primitive science. A recent investigator has ventured the statement : " Magic is the science of the jungle." Astrology and other methods of divination may undoubtedly be called the science of antiquity.

What happens regularly is easily observed because we are prepared for it. Knowledge and skill are only needed in situations where the course of events is arbitrarily disrupted in a way hard to fathom. Generally it is one of the cleverest and shrewdest men of the tribe who is entrusted with the observation of events. His knowledge must suffice to explain all unusual occurrences, and his art to combat them. He is the scholar, the specialist, the expert on the subject of chance occurrences, and at the same time the keeper of the archives of the tribe's traditional lore. Surrounded by respect and fear, he enjoys great authority, yet not so great but that his tribe is secretly convinced that their neighbours have a sorcerer who is stronger than theirs. The best medicine is never to be found close at hand, but as far away as possible. I stayed for a time with a tribe who held their old medicine-man in the greatest awe. Nevertheless he was consulted only for the minor ailments of cattle and men. In all serious cases a foreign authority was called in—a *M'ganga* (sorcerer) who was brought at a high price from Uganda—just as with us.

Chance events occur most often in larger or smaller series or groups. An old and well-tried rule for foretelling the weather is this, that when it has rained for several days it will also rain tomorrow. A proverb says: " Misfortunes never come singly." Another has it that " It never rains but it pours." Such proverbial wisdom is primitive science. The people believe it and hold it in awe, while the educated man smiles at it—until something unusual happens to him. I will tell you a disagreeable story. A woman I know was awakened one morning by a peculiar tinkling on her night-table. After looking about her for a while she discovered the cause : the rim of her tumbler had snapped off in a ring about a quarter of an inch wide. This struck her as peculiar, and she rang for another glass. About five minutes later she heard the same tinkling, and again the rim of the glass had broken off. This time she was greatly disquieted, and had a third glass brought. Within twenty minutes the rim broke off again with the same noise. Three such accidents in immediate succession were too much for her. She gave up her belief in natural causes on the spot, and brought out in its place a " collective representation "—the conviction that an arbitrary power was at work. Something like this happens to many modern people—provided they are not too hard-headed—when they are confronted with events which natural causation fails to explain. We naturally prefer to deny such occurrences. They are unpleasant because they disrupt the orderly course of our world and make anything seem possible. Their effect upon us shows that the primitive mind is not yet dead.

Primitive man's belief in arbitrary power does not arise out of thin air, as was always supposed, but is grounded in experience. What we have always called his superstition is justified by the grouping of chance occurrences. There is a real measure of probability that unusual events will coincide in time and place. We must not forget that our experience is not fully to be trusted in this regard. Our observation is inadequate because our point of view leads us to overlook these matters. For instance, in a serious mood it would never occur to us to take the following events as a sequence : in the morning a bird flies into your room, an hour later you witness an accident in the street, in the afternoon a relative dies, in the evening your cook drops the soup tureen, and, on coming home late at night, you find that you have lost your key. Primitive man would not have overlooked a single item in this chain of events, for every new link would have answered to his expectations. And he is right—he is much more nearly right than we are willing to admit. His anxious expectations are justified and serve a purpose. Such a day, he holds, is ill-omened, and on it nothing should be undertaken. In our world this would be reprehensible superstition, but in the world of primitive man it is highly appropriate shrewdness. In that world man is far more exposed to accidents than we in our protected and well-regulated existence. When you are in the wilderness you dare not take too many chances. The European soon comes to appreciate this.

When a Pueblo Indian does not feel in the right mood, he stays away from the men's council. When an ancient Roman stumbled on the threshold as he left his house, he gave up his plans for the day. This seems to us senseless, but under primitive conditions of life such an omen inclines one at least to be cautious. When I am not in full control of myself, my bodily movements may be under a certain constraint ; my attention is easily distracted ; I am somewhat absent-minded. As a result I knock against something, stumble, let something fall or forget something. Under civilized conditions these are mere trifles, but in the primeval forest they mean mortal danger. It is fatal to make a false step upon the rain-soaked trunk of a tree that serves as a bridge high over a river teeming with crocodiles. Suppose I lose my compass in the deep grass, or forget to load my rifle and blunder into a rhinoceros trail in the jungle. If I am preoccupied with my thoughts, I may tread upon a puff-adder. At nightfall I forget to put on my mosquito-boots in time, and eleven days later I die from an onset of tropical malaria. To forget to shut one's mouth while bathing suffices to bring on a fatal attack of dysentery. For us a distracted state of mind is the natural cause of such accidents. For primitive man they are objectively conditioned omens, or sorcery.

But it may be more than a question of inattention. In the Kitoshi region south of Mount Elgon I went for an excursion into the Kabras forest. There, in the thick grass, I nearly stepped on a puff-adder, and only managed to jump away just in time. In the afternoon my companion returned from a hunt, deathly pale and trembling in every limb. He had almost been bitten by a seven-foot mamba which darted at his back from a termite hill. Without a doubt he would have been killed had he not been able at the last moment to wound the animal with a shot. At nine o'clock that night our camp was attacked by a pack of ravenous hyenas which had surprised and mauled a man in his sleep the day before. In spite of the fire they swarmed into the hut of our cook who fled screaming over the stockade. Thenceforth there were no accidents throughout the whole of our journey. Such a day gave our negroes food for thought. For us it was a simple multiplication of accidents, but for them the inevitable fulfilment of an omen that had occurred upon the first day of our journey into the wilds. It so happened that we had fallen, car, bridge and all, into a stream we were trying to cross. Our boys had exchanged glances on that occasion as if to say : " Well, that's a fine start." To cap the climax a tropical thunderstorm blew up and soaked us so thoroughly that I was prostrated with fever for several days. On the evening of the day when my friend had had such a narrow escape out hunting, I could not help saying to him as we white men sat looking at one another : " It seems to me as if the trouble had begun still further back. Do you remember the dream you told me in Zürich just before we left ? " At that time he had had a very impressive nightmare. He dreamed that he was hunting in Africa, and was suddenly attacked by a huge mamba, so that he woke up with a cry of terror. The dream had greatly disturbed him, and he now confessed to the thought that it had portended the death of one of us. He had of course assumed that I was to die, because we always hope it is the " other fellow ". But it was he who later fell ill of a severe malarial fever that brought him to the edge of the grave.

To read of such a conversation in a corner of the world where there are no snakes and no malaria-bearing mosquitoes means very little. One must imagine the velvety blue of a tropical night, the overhanging black masses of gigantic trees standing in a virgin forest, the mysterious voices of the nocturnal spaces, a lonely fire with loaded rifles stacked beside it, mosquito-nets, boiled swamp-water to drink, and above all the conviction expressed by an old Afrikander who knew what he was saying : " This isn't man's country— it's God's country." There man is not king ; it is rather nature—the animals, plants and microbes. Given the mood that goes with the place, one understands how it is that we found a dawning significance in things that anywhere else would provoke a smile. That is the world of unrestrained, capricious powers with which primitive man has to deal day by day. The extraordinary event is no joke to him. He draws his own conclusions. " It is not a good place "— " The day is unfavourable "—and who knows what dangers he avoids by following such warnings ?

" Magic is the science of the jungle." A portent effects the immediate modification of a course of action, the abandonment of a planned undertaking, a change of psychic attitude. These are all highly expedient reactions in view of the fact that chance occurrences tend to fall in sequences and that primitive man is wholly unconscious of psychic causality. Thanks to our one-sided emphasis upon so-called natural causation, we have learned to distinguish what is subjective and psychic from what is objective and " natural ". For primitive man, on the contrary, the psychic and the objective coalesce in the external world. In the face of something extraordinary it is not he who is astonished, but rather the thing which is astonishing. It is *mana*—endowed with magic power. What we would call the powers of imagination and suggestion seem to him invisible forces which act upon him from without. His country is neither a geographical nor a political entity. It is that territory which contains his mythology, his religion, all his thinking and feeling in so far as he is unconscious of these functions. His fear is localized in certain places that are " not good ". The spirits of the departed inhabit such or such a wood. That cave harbours devils which strangle any man who enters. In yonder mountain lives the great serpent ; that hill is the grave of the legendary king ; near this spring or rock or tree every woman becomes pregnant ; that ford is guarded by snake-demons ; this towering tree has a voice that can call certain people. Primitive man is unpsychological. Psychic happenings take place outside him in an objective way. Even the things he dreams about seem to him real ; that is his only reason for paying attention to dreams. Our Elgonyi porters seriously maintained that they never had dreams—only the sorcerer had them. When I questioned the sorcerer, he declared that he had stopped having dreams when the British entered the land. His father had still had " big " dreams, he told me, and had known where the herds strayed, where the cows took their calves, and when there was going to be a war or a pestilence. It was now the District Commissioner who knew everything, and they knew nothing. He was as resigned as certain Papuans are who believe that the crocodiles have in good part gone over to the British Government. It happened that a native convict had escaped from the authorities and been badly mangled by a crocodile while trying to cross a river. They therefore concluded that it must have been a police crocodile. God now speaks in dreams to the British, and not to the medicine-man of the Elgonyi, he told me, because it is the British who have the power. Dream activity had emigrated. Occasionally the souls of the natives emigrate, and the medicine-man catches them in cages as if they were birds; or strange souls immigrate and cause diseases.

This projection of psychic happenings naturally gives rise to relations between men and men, or between men and animals or things, that to us are inconceivable. A white man shoots a crocodile. At once a crowd of people come running from the nearest village and excitedly demand compensation. They explain that the crocodile was a certain old woman in their village who had died at the moment when the shot was fired. The crocodile was obviously her bush-soul. Another man shot a leopard that was lying in wait for his cattle. Just then a woman died in a neighbouring village. She and the leopard were one and the same.

Lévy-Brühl has coined the expression *participation mystique* for these curious relationships. It seems to me that the word "mystical" is not well chosen. Primitive man does not see anything mystical in these matters, but considers them perfectly natural. It is only we who find anything strange about them, and the reason is that we seem to know nothing about such psychic phenomena.[1] In reality, however, they occur in us too, but we give them more civilized forms of expression. In daily life it happens all the time that we presume that the psychic processes of other people are the same as ours. We suppose that what is pleasing or desirable to us is the same to others, and that what seems bad to us must also seem bad to them. It is only of late that our courts of law have adopted a psychological standpoint and admitted the relativity of guilt in pronouncing sentence. Unsophisticated people are still moved to rancour by the tenet *quod licet Jovi non licet bovi.* Equality before the law still represents a great human achievement ; it has not yet been superseded. And we still attribute to " the other fellow " all the evil and inferior qualities that we do not like to recognize in ourselves. That is why we have to criticize and attack him. What happens in such a case, however, is that an inferior " soul " emigrates from one person to another. The world is still full of *bêtes noires* and of scapegoats, just as it formerly teemed with witches and werewolves.

Psychic projection is one of the commonest facts of psychology. It is the same as that *participation mystique* which Lévy-Brühl remarked as a peculiar trait of primitive man. We merely give it another name, and as a rule deny that we are guilty of it. Everything that is unconscious in ourselves we discover in our neighbour, and we treat him accordingly. We no longer subject him to the test of drinking poison ; we do not burn him or put the screws on him ; but we injure him by means of moral verdicts pronounced with

---

[1] *I.e.* dissociation and projection. (*Trans.*)

the deepest conviction. What we combat in him is usually our own inferior side.

The simple truth is that primitive man is somewhat more given to projection than we because of the undifferentiated state of his mind and his consequent inability to criticize himself. Everything to him is perfectly objective, and his language reflects this in a radical way. With a touch of humour we can picture to ourselves a leopard woman. We often represent a person as a goose, a cow, a hen, a snake, an ox, or an ass. As uncomplimentary epithets these images are familiar to us all. But when primitive man attributes a bush-soul to a person, the poison of the moral verdict is absent. Archaic man is too naturalistic for that ; he is too much impressed by things as they are to pass judgement readily, and is therefore much less prone to do so than we. The Pueblo Indians declared in a matter-of-fact way that I belonged to the Bear Totem—in other words, that I was a bear—because I did not come down a ladder frontwards like a man, but backwards, using my hands like a bear. If a European said that I had the nature of a bear this would come to much the same thing, with perhaps a slightly different shade of meaning. The theme of the bush-soul, which seems so strange when we meet with it in primitive societies, has become with us, like so much else, a mere figure of speech. If we take our metaphors in a concrete way we return to a primitive point of view. For instance we have the medical expression to " handle a patient ". In concrete terms this means to lay the hands upon—to work at with the hands. And this is precisely what the medicine-man does with his patients.

We find the bush-soul hard to understand because we are baffled by such a concrete way of looking at things. We cannot conceive of a " soul " as an entity that emigrates and takes up its abode in a wild animal. When we describe someone as an ass, we do not mean that he is in every respect the quadruped called an ass. We mean that he resembles an ass in some particular respect. As far as the person in question is concerned, we isolate a part of his personality or psyche and concretize this part of him in the image of an ass. So, for primitive man, the leopard-woman is a human being, and only her bush-soul is a leopard. Since all unconscious psychic life is concrete and objective for archaic man, he supposes that a person describable as a leopard has the soul of a leopard. If the concretizing goes further, he assumes that such a soul lives in the bush in the form of a real leopard.

These identifications, brought about by the projection of psychic happenings, create a world in which man is contained not only physically, but psychically as well. To a certain extent he coalesces with it. In no way is he master of this world, but rather its component. Primitive man, in Africa for instance, is still far from the glorification of human powers. He does not dream of regarding himself as the lord of creation. His zoological classification does not culminate in *homo sapiens*, but in the elephant. Next comes the lion, then the python or the crocodile, then man and the lesser beings. It never occurs to him that he might be able to rule nature ; it is civilized man who strives to dominate nature and therefore devotes his greatest efforts to the discovery of natural causes which will give him the key to nature's secret laboratory. That is why he strongly resents the idea of arbitrary powers and denies them. Their existence would amount to proof that his attempt to dominate nature is futile after all.

Summing up, we may say that the outstanding trait of archaic man is his attitude towards the capriciousness of chance which he considers a far more important factor in cosmic happening than natural causes. Chance occurrences have two aspects; on the one hand it is a fact that they tend to take place in series, and on the other that they are endowed with an apparent purposefulness through the projection of unconscious psychic contents—in other words by "*participation mystique*". Archaic man, to be sure, does not draw this distinction, for he projects psychic happenings so completely that they coalesce with physical events. An accident seems to him to be an arbitrary and intentional act—an interference by an animated being— because he does not realize that unusual events move him only in so far as he invests them with the force of his own astonishment or fear. Here, it is true, we move on treacherous ground. Is a thing beautiful because I attribute beauty to it? It is well known that great minds have wrestled with the question whether it is the glorious sun that illumines the worlds, or whether it is the human eye by virtue of its relation to the sun. Archaic man believes it to be the sun, and civilized man believes it is the eye—so far, at any rate, as he reflects at all and does not suffer from the disease of poets. He must strip nature of psychic attributes in order to dominate it; to see his world objectively he must take back all his archaic projections.

In the primitive world everything has psychic qualities. Everything is endowed with the elements of man's psyche —or let us say, of the human psyche, of the collective unconscious, for there is as yet no individual psychic life. Let us not forget, in this connection, that what the Christian sacrament of baptism purports to do is of the greatest importance for the psychic development of mankind. Baptism endows the human being with a unique soul. I do not mean, of course, the baptismal rite in itself as a magical act that is effective at one performance. I mean that the idea of baptism lifts a man out of his archaic identification with the world and changes him into a being who stands above it. The fact that mankind has risen to the level of this idea is baptism in the deepest sense, for it means the birth of spiritual man who transcends nature.

It is an axiom in the study of the unconscious that every relatively independent, psychic content is personified whenever the opportunity arises. We find the clearest instances of this in the hallucinations of the insane and in mediumistic communications. An invisible person arises wherever and whenever an autonomous psychic component is projected. This explains the spirits of an ordinary spiritualistic séance and the ghosts which appear to primitive man. If an important psychic content is projected upon a human being, he becomes *mana*—that is, endowed with the power of producing unusual effects. He or she becomes a sorcerer, a witch, a werewolf, or the like. The primitive belief that the medicine-man catches the souls that have wandered away by night and puts them into cages like birds, strikingly illustrates this. Psychic projections endow the medicine-man with *mana* ; they cause animals, trees and stones to speak ; because they are psychic activities, they compel the individual to obey them. For this reason an insane person is hopelessly at the mercy of his voices. That which is projected is his own psychic activity. Without knowing it, he is the one who speaks through his voices, just as he is the one who hears, sees and obeys.

From the psychological point of view, primitive man's

belief that the arbitrary power of chance answers to the intentions of spirits and of sorcerers is perfectly natural, because it is an unavoidable inference from the facts as he sees them. And let us not delude ourselves in this connection. If we explain our scientific views to an intelligent native he will credit us with a ludicrous superstitiousness and a disgraceful want of logic. He believes that the world is lighted by the sun, and not by the human eye. My friend Mountain Lake, a Pueblo chief, once called me sharply to account because I had given voice to the Augustinian tenet : *Non est hic sol Dominus noster, sed qui illum fecit.* Pointing to the sun, he declared indignantly : " He who goes there is our father. You can see him. From him comes all light, all life—there is nothing that he has not made." He became greatly excited, struggled for words, and finally exclaimed : " Even a man in the mountains who goes alone cannot make his fire without him." The archaic standpoint can hardly be more beautifully expressed than by these words. The power that rules us comes from the external world, and through it alone are we permitted to live. With us, religious thought still keeps alive the archaic state of mind, even though our time is bereft of gods. Untold millions of people still think in this way.

In speaking of primitive man's outlook upon the caprice of chance, I expressed the view that this attitude serves a purpose, and therefore has a meaning. Shall we, for the moment at least, venture the hypothesis that the primitive belief in arbitrary powers is justified by the facts and not merely from a psychological point of view ? This sounds alarming, but I have no intention of jumping from the frying-pan into the fire and trying to prove that witchcraft actually exists. I wish only to consider the conclusions to

which we shall be led if we follow primitive man in supposing
that all light comes from the sun, that things are beautiful
in themselves and that a human part-soul is a leopard. In
doing this we accept the primitive idea of *mana*. According
to this idea, the beautiful moves *us*, and it is not we who
create beauty. A certain person *is* a devil—we have not
projected our own evil upon him and in this way made a
devil out of him. There are people—*mana* personalities—
who are impressive in their own right, and in no way thanks
to our imagination. The *mana* conception has it that there
exists something like a widely distributed force in the
external world that produces all those effects which are out
of the common. Everything that exists, acts, for otherwise
it would not be actual. It is only actual thanks to its
inherent energy. Being is a field of force. The primitive
mana conception, as we can see, is of the nature of a crude
theory of energy.

So far we can easily follow this primitive idea. The
difficulty arises when we try to carry its implications further,
for they reverse the process of psychic projection of which I
have spoken. These implications are as follows : it is not
my imagination or my awe that makes a sorcerer of the
medicine-man ; on the contrary, he *is* a sorcerer and projects
his magical powers upon me. Ghosts are not hallucinations
of my mind, but appear to me of their own volition. Although such statements are logical derivatives of the *mana*
idea, we hesitate to accept them and begin to look around
us for our comfortable theory of psychic projection. The
question is nothing less than this : does the psychic in
general—that is, the spirit, or the unconscious—arise in us ;
or is the psyche, in the early stages of consciousness, actually
outside us in the form of arbitrary powers with intentions of

their own, and does it gradually come to take its place within us in the course of psychic development ? Were the dissociated psychic contents—to use our modern terms—ever parts of the psyches of individuals, or were they rather from the beginning psychic entities existing in themselves according to the primitive view as ghosts, ancestral spirits and the like ? Were they only by degrees embodied by man in the course of development, so that they gradually constituted in him that world which we now call the psyche ?

This whole idea strikes us as dangerously paradoxical, and yet we are able to conceive something of the kind. Not only the religious teacher, but the pedagogue as well, assumes that it is possible to implant in the human psyche something that was not previously there. The power of suggestion and influence is a fact ; even the most modern behaviourism expects far-reaching results from this quarter. The idea of a complicated building-up of the psyche is expressed in primitive form in many widespread beliefs—for instance, possession, the incarnation of ancestral spirits, the immigration of souls, and so forth. When someone sneezes, we still say : " God bless you ", and mean by it : " I hope your new soul will do you no harm." When in the course of our own development we grow out of many-sided contradictions and achieve a unified personality, we experience something like a complicated growing-together of the psyche. Since the human body is built up by inheritance out of a number of Mendelian units, it does not seem altogether out of the question that the human psyche is similarly put together.

The materialistic views of our day have a tendency which we can discern in archaic thought. Both lead to the conclusion that the individual is a mere resultant ; in the first case, he is the resultant of natural causes, and in the second, of chance occurrences. According to both accounts, human individuality is nothing in its own right, but rather the accidental product of forces contained in the objective environment. This is through and through the archaic conception of the world according to which the single human being is never considered unique, but always interchangeable with any other and easily dispensable. By way of a narrow view of causality, modern materialism has returned to the standpoint of archaic man. But the materialist is more radical, because he is more systematic, than primitive man. The latter has the advantage of being inconsistent; he makes an exception of the *mana* personality. In the course of history these *mana* personalities were exalted to the position of divine figures; they became heroes and kings who shared in the immortality of the gods by eating of their rejuvenating food. This idea of the immortality of the individual and of his imperishable worth is to be found in primitive societies, first of all in the belief in ghosts, and then in myths of the age when death had not yet gained an entrance into the world through human carelessness or folly.

Primitive man is not aware of this contradiction in his views. Our negro porters assured me that they had no idea what would happen to them after death. According to them a man is simply dead; he does not breathe any longer, and the corpse is carried into the bush where the hyenas eat it. That is what they think about it by day, but the night teems with the spirits of the dead who bring diseases to cattle and man, who attack and strangle the nocturnal traveller and indulge in other forms of violence. The primitive mind is full of such contradictions. They could worry a European out of his skin, and it would never occur to him that something quite similar is to be found in our civilized midst. We have universities where the idea of divine intervention is considered beneath dispute—but where theology is a part of the curriculum. A research worker in natural science may hold it obscene to attribute the smallest variation of an animal species to an act of God, but may have another drawer in his mind in which he keeps a full-blown Christian faith which he likes to parade on Sundays. Why should we excite ourselves about primitive inconsistency ?

It is not possible to derive any philosophical system from the elementary thoughts of primitive man. They furnish us only with antinomies. And yet it is just these which are the inexhaustible source of all mental effort and provide the problems of thought in all times and in all civilizations. Are the " collective representations " of archaic man really profound, or do they only seem so ? I cannot answer this most difficult of questions, but I can tell of an observation which I made among the mountain tribe of the Elgonyi. I searched and enquired far and wide for traces of religious ideas and ceremonies, and for weeks on end I discovered nothing. The natives let me see everything and were free with their information. I could talk with them without the hindrance of an interpreter, for many of the old men spoke Swahili. At first they were reluctant enough, but when the ice was broken, I was cordially received. They knew nothing of religious customs. But I never gave up, and finally, at the close of one of many fruitless palavers, an old man exclaimed : " In the morning, when the sun comes up, we leave our huts, spit in our hands, and hold them up to the sun." I got them to perform the ceremony for me and describe it exactly. They hold their hands before their mouths and spit or blow into them vigorously. Then they turn their hands round and hold the palms toward the sun. I asked them the meaning of what they did—why they blew or spat in their hands. My question was futile. " That is how it has always been done ", they said. It was impossible to get an explanation, and I was perfectly convinced that they knew only what they did, and not why they did it. They see no meaning in their action. They greet the new moon with the same gestures.

Let us suppose that I am a total stranger in Zürich and have come to this city to explore the customs of the place. First I settle down in the outskirts near some suburban homes, and come into neighbourly contact with their owners. I then say to Messrs. Müller and Meyer : " Please tell me something about your religious customs." Both gentlemen are taken aback. They never go to church, know nothing about it, and emphatically deny that they practise any such customs. One morning I surprise Mr. Müller at a curious occupation. He is busily running about the garden, hiding coloured eggs and setting up peculiar rabbit idols. I have caught him *in flagrante delicto*. " Why did you conceal this highly interesting ceremony from me ? " I ask him. " What ceremony ? " he retorts. " This is nothing. Everybody does this at Eastertime." " But what is the meaning of these idols and eggs—and why do you hide them ? " Mr. Müller is stunned. He does not know, and just as little does he know the meaning of the Christmas-tree. And yet he does these things. He is just like primitive man. Did the distant ancestors of the Elgonyi know what they did ? It is highly improbable. Archaic man does what he does—and only civilized man knows what he does.

What is the meaning of the Elgonyi ceremony just cited ?

Clearly it is an offering to the sun which for these natives is *mungu*—that is, *mana*, or divine—only at the moment of rising. If they have spittle on their hands, this is the substance which, according to primitive belief, contains the personal *mana*, the force that cures, conjures and sustains life. If they breathe upon their hands, breath is wind and spirit—it is *roho*, in Arabic *ruch*, in Hebrew *ruach*, and in Greek *pneuma*. The action means : I offer my living spirit to God. It is a wordless, acted prayer, which could equally well be spoken : " Lord, into thy hands I commend my spirit." Does this merely happen so, or was this thought already incubated and purposed before man existed ? I must leave this question unanswered.

VIII

PSYCHOLOGY AND LITERATURE

IT is obvious enough that psychology, being the study of psychic processes, can be brought to bear upon the study of literature, for the human psyche is the womb of all the sciences and arts. We may expect psychological research, on the one hand, to explain the formation of a work of art, and on the other to reveal the factors that make a person artistically creative. The psychologist is thus faced with two separate and distinct tasks, and must approach them in radically different ways.

In the case of the work of art we have to deal with a product of complicated psychic activities—but a product that is apparently intentional and consciously shaped. In the case of the artist we must deal with the psychic apparatus itself. In the first instance we must attempt the psychological analysis of a definitely circumscribed and concrete artistic achievement, while in the second we must analyse the living and creative human being as a unique personality. Although these two undertakings are closely related and even interdependent, neither of them can yield the explanations that are sought by the other. It is of course possible to draw inferences about the artist from the work of art, and *vice versa*, but these inferences are never conclusive. At best they are probable surmises or lucky guesses. A knowledge of Goethe's particular relation to his mother throws

some light upon Faust's exclamation : " The mothers—
mothers—how very strange it sounds ! " But it does not
enable us to see how the attachment to his mother could
produce the Faust drama itself, however unmistakably we
sense in the man Goethe a deep connection between the
two. Nor are we more successful in reasoning in the reverse
direction. There is nothing in *The Ring of the Nibelungs*
that would enable us to recognize or definitely infer the fact
that Wagner occasionally liked to wear womanish clothes,
though hidden connections exist between the heroic masculine
world of the Nibelungs and a certain pathological effeminacy
in the man Wagner.

The present state of development of psychology does not
allow us to establish those rigorous causal connections which
we expect of a science. It is only in the realm of the psycho-
physiological instincts and reflexes that we can confidently
operate with the idea of causality. From the point where
psychic life begins—that is, at a level of greater complexity
—the psychologist must content himself with more or less
widely ranging descriptions of happenings and with the
vivid portrayal of the warp and weft of the mind in all its
amazing intricacy. In doing this, he must refrain from
designating any one psychic process, taken by itself, as
" necessary ". Were this not the state of affairs, and could
the psychologist be relied upon to uncover the causal connections within a work of art and in the process of artistic
creation, he would leave the study of art no ground to stand
on and would reduce it to a special branch of his own science.
The psychologist, to be sure, may never abandon his claim
to investigate and establish causal relations in complicated
psychic events. To do so would be to deny psychology the
right to exist. Yet he can never make good this claim

in the fullest sense, because the creative aspect of life which finds its clearest expression in art baffles all attempts at rational formulation.   Any reaction to stimulus may be causally explained ; but the creative act, which is the absolute antithesis of mere reaction, will for ever elude the human understanding.   It can only be described in its manifestations ; it can be obscurely sensed, but never wholly grasped.   Psychology and the study of art will always have to turn to one another for help, and the one will not invalidate the other.   It is an important principle of psychology that psychic events are derivable.   It is a principle in the study of art that a psychic product is something in and for itself—whether the work of art or the artist himself is in question.   Both principles are valid in spite of their relativity.

I

The Work of Art

There is a fundamental difference of approach between the psychologist's examination of a literary work, and that of the literary critic.   What is of decisive importance and value for the latter may be quite irrelevant for the former. Literary products of highly dubious merit are often of the greatest interest to the psychologist.   For instance, the so-called " psychological novel " is by no means as rewarding for the psychologist as the literary-minded suppose.   Considered as a whole, such a novel explains itself.   It has done its own work of psychological interpretation, and the psychologist can at most criticize or enlarge upon this.   The important question as to how a particular author came to write a particular novel is of course left unanswered, but I wish to reserve this general problem for the second part of my essay.

The novels which are most fruitful for the psychologist are those in which the author has not already given a psycho-logical interpretation of his characters, and which therefore leave room for analysis and explanation, or even invite it by their mode of presentation. Good examples of this kind of writing are the novels of Benoît, and English fiction in the manner of Rider Haggard, including the vein exploited by Conan Doyle which yields that most cherished article of mass-production, the detective story. Melville's *Moby Dick*, which I consider the greatest American novel, also comes within this class of writings. An exciting narrative that is apparently quite devoid of psychological exposition is just what interests the psychologist most of all. Such a tale is built upon a groundwork of implicit psychological assump-tions, and, in the measure that the author is unconscious of them, they reveal themselves, pure and unalloyed, to the critical discernment. In the psychological novel, on the other hand, the author himself attempts to reshape his material so as to raise it from the level of crude contingency to that of psychological exposition and illumination—a procedure which all too often clouds the psychological sig-nificance of the work or hides it from view. It is precisely to novels of this sort that the layman goes for "psychology"; while it is novels of the other kind that challenge the psychologist, for he alone can give them deeper meaning.

I have been speaking in terms of the novel, but I am dealing with a psychological fact which is not restricted to this particular form of literary art. We meet with it in the works of the poets as well, and are confronted with it when we com-pare the first and second parts of the Faust drama. The love-tragedy of Gretchen explains itself; there is nothing that the psychologist can add to it that the poet has not already said in better words. The second part, on the other hand, calls for explanation. The prodigious richness of the imaginative material has so overtaxed the poet's formative powers that nothing is self-explanatory and every verse adds to the reader's need of an interpretation. The two parts of *Faust* illustrate by way of extremes this psychological distinction between works of literature.

In order to emphasize the distinction, I will call the one mode of artistic creation *psychological*, and the other *visionary*. The psychological mode deals with materials drawn from the realm of human consciousness—for instance, with the lessons of life, with emotional shocks, the experience of passion and the crises of human destiny in general—all of which go to make up the conscious life of man, and his feeling life in particular. This material is psychically assimilated by the poet, raised from the commonplace to the level of poetic experience, and given an expression which forces the reader to greater clarity and depth of human insight by bringing fully into his consciousness what he ordinarily evades and overlooks or senses only with a feeling of dull discomfort. The poet's work is an interpretation and illumination of the contents of consciousness, of the ineluctable experiences of human life with its eternally recurrent sorrow and joy. He leaves nothing over for the psychologist, unless, indeed, we expect the latter to expound the reasons for which Faust falls in love with Gretchen, or which drive Gretchen to murder her child! Such themes go to make up the lot of humankind; they repeat themselves millions of times and are responsible for the monotony of the police-court and of the penal code. No obscurity whatever surrounds them, for they fully explain themselves.

Countless literary works belong to this class : the many novels dealing with love, the environment, the family, crime and society, as well as didactic poetry, the larger number of lyrics, and the drama, both tragic and comic. Whatever its particular form may be, the psychological work of art always takes its materials from the vast realm of conscious human experience—from the vivid foreground of life, we might say. I have called this mode of artistic creation psychological because in its activity it nowhere transcends the bounds of psychological intelligibility. Everything that it embraces—the experience as well as its artistic expression—belongs to the realm of the understandable. Even the basic experiences themselves, though non-rational, have nothing strange about them ; on the contrary, they are that which has been known from the beginning of time— passion and its fated outcome, man's subjection to the turns of destiny, eternal nature with its beauty and its horror.

The profound difference between the first and second parts of *Faust* marks the difference between the psychological and the visionary modes of artistic creation. The latter reverses all the conditions of the former. The experience that furnishes the material for artistic expression is no longer familiar. It is a strange something that derives its existence from the hinterland of man's mind—that suggests the abyss of time separating us from pre-human ages, or evokes a super-human world of contrasting light and darkness. It is a primordial experience which surpasses man's understanding, and to which he is therefore in danger of succumbing. The value and the force of the experience are given by its enormity. It arises from timeless depths ; it is foreign and cold, many-sided, demonic and grotesque. A grimly ridiculous sample of the eternal chaos—a *crimen laesae majestatis humanae*, to use Nietzsche's words—it bursts asunder our human standards of value and of æsthetic form. The disturbing vision of monstrous and meaningless happenings that in every way exceed the grasp of human feeling and comprehension makes quite other demands upon the powers of the artist than do the experiences of the foreground of life. These never rend the curtain that veils the cosmos ; they never transcend the bounds of the humanly possible, and for this reason are readily shaped to the demands of art, no matter how great a shock to the individual they may be. But the primordial experiences rend from top to bottom the curtain upon which is painted the picture of an ordered world, and allow a glimpse into the unfathomed abyss of what has not yet become. Is it a vision of other worlds, or of the obscuration of the spirit, or of the beginning of things before the age of man, or of the unborn generations of the future ? We cannot say that it is any or none of these.

> Shaping—re-shaping—
> The eternal spirit's eternal pastime.[1]

We find such vision in *The Shepherd of Hermas*, in Dante, in the second part of *Faust*, in Nietzsche's Dionysian exuberance, in Wagner's *Nibelungenring*, in Spitteler's *Olympischer Frühling*, in the poetry of William Blake, in the *Ipnerotomachia* of the monk Francisco Colonna, and in Jacob Boehme's philosophic and poetic stammerings. In a more restricted and specific way, the primordial experience furnishes material for Rider Haggard in the fiction-cycle

---

[1] *Gestaltung, Umgestaltung,*
Des ew'gen Sinnes ew'ge Unterhaltung. (Goethe.)

that turns upon *She*, and it does the same for Benoît, chiefly in *L'Atlantide*, for Kubin in *Die Andere Seite*, for Meyrink in *Das Grüne Gesicht*—a book whose importance we should not undervalue—for Goetz in *Das Reich ohne Raum*, and for Barlach in *Der Tote Tag*. This list might be greatly extended.

In dealing with the psychological mode of artistic creation, we never need ask ourselves what the material consists of or what it means. But this question forces itself upon us as soon as we come to the visionary mode of creation. We are astonished, taken aback, confused, put on our guard or even disgusted—and we demand commentaries and explanations. We are reminded in nothing of everyday, human life, but rather of dreams, night-time fears and the dark recesses of the mind that we sometimes sense with misgiving. The reading public for the most part repudiates this kind of writing—unless, indeed, it is coarsely sensational—and even the literary critic feels embarrassed by it. It is true that Dante and Wagner have smoothed the approach to it. The visionary experience is cloaked, in Dante's case, by the introduction of historical facts, and, in that of Wagner, by mythological events—so that history and mythology are sometimes taken to be the materials with which these poets worked. But with neither of them does the moving force and the deeper significance lie there. For both it is contained in the visionary experience. Rider Haggard, pardonably enough, is generally held to be a mere inventor of fiction. Yet even with him the story is primarily a means of giving expression to significant material. However much the tale may seem to overgrow the content, the latter outweighs the former in importance.

The obscurity as to the sources of the material in visionary creation is very strange, and the exact opposite of what we find in the psychological mode of creation. We are even led to suspect that this obscurity is not unintentional. We are naturally inclined to suppose—and Freudian psychology encourages us to do so—that some highly personal experience underlies this grotesque darkness. We hope thus to explain ·these strange glimpses of chaos and to understand why it sometimes seems as though the poet had intentionally concealed his basic experience from us. It is only a step from this way of looking at the matter to the statement that we are here dealing with a pathological and neurotic art—a step which is justified in so far as the material of the visionary creator shows certain traits that we find in the fantasies of the insane. The converse also is true ; we often discover in the mental output of psychotic persons a wealth of meaning that we should expect rather from the works of a genius. The psychologist who follows Freud will of course be inclined to take the writings in question as a problem in pathology. On the assumption that an intimate, personal experience underlies what I call the " primordial vision "—an experience, that is to say, which cannot be accepted by the conscious outlook—he will try to account for the curious images of the vision by calling them cover-figures and by supposing that they represent an attempted concealment of the basic experience. This, according to his view, might be an experience in love which is morally or æsthetically incompatible with the personality as a whole or at least with certain fictions of the conscious mind. In order that the poet, through his ego, might repress this experience and make it unrecognizable (unconscious), the whole arsenal of a pathological fantasy was brought into action. Moreover, this attempt to replace reality by fiction, being unsatisfactory, must be repeated in a long series of creative embodiments.

This would explain the proliferation of imaginative forms, all monstrous, demonic, grotesque and perverse. On the one hand they are substitutes for the unacceptable experience, and on the other they help to conceal it.

Although a discussion of the poet's personality and psychic disposition belongs strictly to the second part of my essay, I cannot avoid taking up in the present connection this Freudian view of the visionary work of art. For one thing, it has aroused considerable attention. And then it is the only well-known attempt that has been made to give a " scientific " explanation of the sources of the visionary material or to formulate a theory of the psychic processes that underlie this curious mode of artistic creation. I assume that my own view of the question is not well known or generally understood. With this preliminary remark, I will now try to present it briefly.

If we insist on deriving the vision from a personal experience, we must treat the former as something secondary— as a mere substitute for reality. The result is that we strip the vision of its primordial quality and take it as nothing but a symptom. The pregnant chaos then shrinks to the proportions of a psychic disturbance. With this account of the matter we feel reassured and turn again to our picture of a well-ordered cosmos. Since we are practical and reasonable, we do not expect the cosmos to be perfect ; we accept these unavoidable imperfections which we call abnormalities and diseases, and we take it for granted that human nature is not exempt from them. The frightening revelation of abysses that defy the human understanding is dismissed as illusion, and the poet is regarded as a victim and perpetrator of deception. Even to the poet, his primordial experience was " human—all too human ", to such a degree that he could not face its meaning but had to conceal it from himself.

We shall do well, I think, to make fully explicit all the implications of that way of accounting for artistic creation which consists in reducing it to personal factors. We should see clearly where it leads. The truth is that it takes us away from the psychological study of the work of art, and confronts us with the psychic disposition of the poet himself. That the latter presents an important problem is not to be denied, but the work of art is something in its own right, and may not be conjured away. The question of the significance to the poet of his own creative work—of his regarding it as a trifle, as a screen, as a source of suffering or as an achievement—does not concern us at the moment, our task being to interpret the work of art psychologically. For this undertaking it is essential that we give serious consideration to the basic experience that underlies it—namely, to the vision. We must take it least as seriously as we do the experiences that underlie the psychological mode of artistic creation, and no one doubts that they are both real and serious. It looks, indeed, as if the visionary experience were something quite apart from the ordinary lot of man, and for this reason we have difficulty in believing that it is real. It has about it an unfortunate suggestion of obscure metaphysics and of occultism, so that we feel called upon to intervene in the name of a well-intentioned reasonableness. Our conclusion is that it would be better not to take such things too seriously, lest the world revert again to a benighted superstition. We may, of course, have a predilection for the occult; but ordinarily we dismiss the visionary experience as the outcome of a rich fantasy or of a poetic mood—that is to say, as a kind of poetic licence psychologically understood. Certain of the poets encourage this interpretation in order to put a wholesome distance between themselves and their work. Spitteler, for example, stoutly maintained that it was one and the same whether the poet sang of an Olympian Spring or to the theme: "May is here!" The truth is that poets are human beings, and that what a poet has to say about his work is often far from being the most illuminating word on the subject. What is required of us, then, is nothing less than to defend the importance of the visionary experience against the poet himself.

It cannot be denied that we catch the reverberations of an initial love-experience in *The Shepherd of Hermas*, in the *Divine Comedy* and in the *Faust* drama—an experience which is completed and fulfilled by the vision. There is no ground for the assumption that the second part of *Faust* repudiates or conceals the normal, human experience of the first part, nor are we justified in supposing that Goethe was normal at the time when he wrote *Part I*, but in a neurotic state of mind when he composed *Part II*. *Hermas*, Dante and Goethe can be taken as three steps in a sequence covering nearly two thousand years of human development, and in each of them we find the personal love-episode not only connected with the weightier visionary experience, but frankly subordinated to it. On the strength of this evidence which is furnished by the work of art itself and which throws out of court the question of the poet's particular psychic disposition, we must admit that the vision represents a deeper and more impressive experience than human passion. In works of art of this nature—and we must never confuse them with the artist as a person—we cannot doubt that the vision is a genuine, primordial experience, regardless of what reason-mongers may say. The vision is not something derived or secondary, and it is not a symptom of something else. It is true symbolic expression—that is, the expression of something existent in its own right, but imperfectly known. The love-episode is a real experience really suffered, and the same statement applies to the vision. We need not try to determine whether the content of the vision is of a physical, psychic or metaphysical nature. In itself it has psychic reality, and this is no less real than physical reality. Human passion falls within the sphere of conscious experience, while the subject of the vision lies beyond it. Through our feelings we experience the known, but our intuitions point to things that are unknown and hidden—that by their very nature are secret. If ever they become conscious, they are intentionally kept back and concealed, for which reason they have been regarded from earliest times as mysterious, uncanny and deceptive. They are hidden from the scrutiny of man, and he also hides himself from them out of *deisidae-monia*. He protects himself with the shield of science and the armour of reason. His enlightenment is born of fear; in the day-time he believes in an ordered cosmos, and he tries to maintain this faith against the fear of chaos that besets him by night. What if there were some living force whose sphere of action lies beyond our world of every day ? Are there human needs that are dangerous and unavoidable ? Is there something more purposeful than electrons ? Do we delude ourselves in thinking that we possess and command our own souls ? And is that which science calls the " psyche " not merely a question-mark arbitrarily confined within the skull, but rather a door that opens upon the human world from a world beyond, now and again allowing strange and unseizable potencies to act upon man and to remove him, as if upon the wings of the night, from the level of common

humanity to that of a more than personal vocation ? When
we consider the visionary mode of artistic creation, it even
seems as if the love-episode had served as a mere release—
as if the personal experience were nothing but the prelude
to the all-important " divine comedy ".

It is not alone the creator of this kind of art who is in
touch with the night-side of life, but the seers, prophets,
leaders and enlighteners also. However dark this nocturnal
world may be, it is not wholly unfamiliar. Man has known
of it from time immemorial—here, there, and everywhere ;
for primitive man today it is an unquestionable part of his
picture of the cosmos. It is only we who have repudiated it
because of our fear of superstition and metaphysics, and
because we strive to construct a conscious world that is
safe and manageable in that natural law holds in it the
place of statute law in a commonwealth. Yet, even in our
midst, the poet now and then catches sight of the figures
that people the night-world—the spirits, demons and gods.
He knows that a purposiveness out-reaching human ends is
the life-giving secret for man ; he has a presentiment of
incomprehensible happenings in the pleroma. In short, he
sees something of that psychic world that strikes terror into
the savage and the barbarian.

From the very first beginnings of human society onward
man's efforts to give his vague intimations a binding form
have left their traces. Even in the Rhodesian cliff-drawings
of the Old Stone Age there appears, side by side with the
most amazingly life-like representations of animals, an
abstract pattern—a double cross contained in a circle. This
design has turned up in every cultural region, more or less,
and we find it today not only in Christian churches, but in
Tibetan monasteries as well. It is the so-called sun-wheel,

and as it dates from a time when no one had thought of
wheels as a mechanical device, it cannot have had its source
in any experience of the external world.   It is rather a symbol
that stands for a psychic happening ; it covers an experience
of the inner world, and is no doubt as lifelike a representation
as the famous rhinoceros with the tick-birds on its back.
There has never been a primitive culture that did not possess
a system of secret teaching, and in many cultures this system
is highly developed.   The men's councils and the totem-clans
preserve this teaching about hidden things that lie apart from
man's daytime existence—things which, from primeval
times, have always constituted his most vital experiences.
Knowledge about them is handed on to younger men in the
rites of initiation.   The mysteries of the Græco-Roman
world performed the same office, and the rich mythology of
antiquity is a relic of such experiences in the earliest stages
of human development.

   It is therefore to be expected of the poet that he will
resort to mythology in order to give his experience its most
fitting expression.   It would be a serious mistake to suppose
that he works with materials received at second-hand.   The
primordial experience is the source of his creativeness ; it
cannot be fathomed, and therefore requires mythological
imagery to give it form.   In itself it offers no words or
images, for it is a vision seen " as in a glass, darkly ".   It
is merely a deep presentiment that strives to find expression.
It is like a whirlwind that seizes everything within reach
and, by carrying it aloft, assumes a visible shape.   Since
the particular expression can never exhaust the possibilities
of the vision, but falls far short of it in richness of content,
the poet must have at his disposal a huge store of materials
if he is to communicate even a few of his intimations.   What

is more, he must resort to an imagery that is difficult to handle and full of contradictions in order to express the weird paradoxicality of his vision. Dante's presentiments are clothed in images that run the gamut of Heaven and Hell ; Goethe must bring in the Blocksberg and the infernal regions of Greek antiquity ; Wagner needs the whole body of Nordic myth ; Nietzsche returns to the hieratic style and recreates the legendary seer of prehistoric times ; Blake invents for himself indescribable figures, and Spitteler borrows old names for new creatures of the imagination. And no intermediate step is missing in the whole range from the ineffably sublime to the perversely grotesque.

Psychology can do nothing towards the elucidation of this colourful imagery except bring together materials for comparison and offer a terminology for its discussion. According to this terminology, that which appears in the vision is the collective unconscious. We mean by collective unconscious, a certain psychic disposition shaped by the forces of heredity ; from it consciousness has developed. In the physical structure of the body we find traces of earlier stages of evolution, and we may expect the human psyche also to conform in its make-up to the law of phylogeny. It is a fact that in eclipses of consciousness—in dreams, narcotic states and cases of insanity—there come to the surface psychic products or contents that show all the traits of primitive levels of psychic development. The images themselves are sometimes of such a primitive character that we might suppose them derived from ancient, esoteric teaching. Mythological themes clothed in modern dress also frequently appear. What is of particular importance for the study of literature in these manifestations of the collective unconscious is that they are compensatory to the conscious attitude. This is to say that they can bring a one-sided, abnormal, or dangerous state of consciousness into equilibrium in an apparently purposive way. In dreams we can see this process very clearly in its positive aspect. In cases of insanity the compensatory process is often perfectly obvious, but takes a negative form. There are persons, for instance, who have anxiously shut themselves off from all the world only to discover one day that their most intimate secrets are known and talked about by everyone.[1]

If we consider Goethe's *Faust*, and leave aside the possibility that it is compensatory to his own conscious attitude, the question that we must answer is this: In what relation does it stand to the conscious outlook of his time? Great poetry draws its strength from the life of mankind, and we completely miss its meaning if we try to derive it from personal factors. Whenever the collective unconscious becomes a living experience and is brought to bear upon the conscious outlook of an age, this event is a creative act which is of importance to everyone living in that age. A work of art is produced that contains what may truthfully be called a message to generations of men. So *Faust* touches something in the soul of every German. So also Dante's fame is immortal, while *The Shepherd of Hermas* just failed of inclusion in the New Testament canon. Every period has its bias, its particular prejudice and its psychic ailment. An epoch is like an individual; it has its own limitations of conscious outlook, and therefore requires a compensatory adjustment. This is effected by the collective unconscious in that a poet, a seer or a leader allows himself

---

[1] See my article: "Mind and the Earth", in *Contributions to Analytical Psychology*. Kegan Paul, Trench, Trubner & Co., London, 1928.

G*

to be guided by the unexpressed desire of his times and shows the way, by word or deed, to the attainment of that which everyone blindly craves and expects—whether this attainment results in good or evil, the healing of an epoch or its destruction.

It is always dangerous to speak of one's own times, because what is at stake in the present is too vast for comprehension. A few hints must therefore suffice.   Francesco Colonna's book is cast in the form of a dream, and is the apotheosis of natural love taken as a human relation ; without countenancing a wild indulgence of the senses, he leaves completely aside the Christian sacrament of marriage.   The book was written in 1453.   Rider Haggard, whose life coincides with the flowering-time of the Victorian era, takes up this subject and deals with it in his own way ; he does not cast it in the form of a dream, but allows us to feel the tension of moral conflict.   Goethe weaves the theme of Gretchen-Helen-Mater-Gloriosa like a red thread into the colourful tapestry of Faust.   Nietzsche proclaims the death of God, and Spitteler transforms the waxing and waning of the gods into a myth of the seasons.   Whatever his importance, each of these poets speaks with the voice of thousands and ten thousands, foretelling changes in the conscious outlook of his time.

II

THE POET

Creativeness, like the freedom of the will, contains a secret. The psychologist can describe both these manifestations as processes, but he can find no solution of the philosophical problems they offer.   Creative man is a riddle that we may try to answer in various ways, but always in vain, a truth that has not prevented modern psychology from turning now and again to the question of the artist and his art. Freud thought that he had found a key in his procedure of deriving the work of art from the personal experiences of the artist.[1] It is true that certain possibilities lay in this direction, for it was conceivable that a work of art, no less than a neurosis, might be traced back to those knots in psychic life that we call the complexes. It was Freud's great discovery that neuroses have a causal origin in the psychic realm—that they take their rise from emotional states and from real or imagined childhood experiences. Certain of his followers, like Rank and Stekel, have taken up related lines of enquiry and have achieved important results. It is undeniable that the poet's psychic disposition permeates his work root and branch. Nor is there anything new in the statement that personal factors largely influence the poet's choice and use of his materials. Credit, however, must certainly be given to the Freudian school for showing how far-reaching this influence is and in what curious ways it comes to expression.

Freud takes the neurosis as a substitute for a direct means of gratification. He therefore regards it as something inappropriate—a mistake, a dodge, an excuse, a voluntary blindness. To him it is essentially a shortcoming that should never have been. Since a neurosis, to all appearances, is nothing but a disturbance that is all the more irritating because it is without sense or meaning, few people will venture to say a good word for it. And a work of art is brought into questionable proximity with the neurosis when it is taken as something which can be analysed in

[1] See Freud's essay on Jensen's *Gradiva* and on Leonardo da Vinci.

terms of the poet's repressions. In a sense it finds itself in good company, for religion and philosophy are regarded in the same light by Freudian psychology. No objection can be raised if it is admitted that this approach amounts to nothing more than the elucidation of those personal determinants without which a work of art is unthinkable. But should the claim be made that such an analysis accounts for the work of art itself, then a categorical denial is called for. The personal idiosyncrasies that creep into a work of art are not essential; in fact, the more we have to cope with these peculiarities, the less is it a question of art. What is essential in a work of art is that it should rise far above the realm of personal life and speak from the spirit and heart of the poet as man to the spirit and heart of mankind. The personal aspect is a limitation—and even a sin—in the realm of art. When a form of " art " is primarily personal it deserves to be treated as if it were a neurosis. There may be some validity in the idea held by the Freudian school that artists without exception are narcissistic—by which is meant that they are undeveloped persons with infantile and auto-erotic traits. The statement is only valid, however, for the artist as a person, and has nothing to do with the man as an artist. In his capacity of artist he is neither auto-erotic, nor hetero-erotic, nor erotic in any sense. He is objective and impersonal—even inhuman—for as an artist he is his work, and not a human being.

Every creative person is a duality or a synthesis of contradictory aptitudes. On the one side he is a human being with a personal life, while on the other side he is an impersonal, creative process. Since as a human being he may be sound or morbid, we must look at his psychic make-up to find the determinants of his personality. But we can only understand him in his capacity of artist by looking at his creative achievement. We should make a sad mistake if we tried to explain the mode of life of an English gentleman, a Prussian officer, or a cardinal in terms of personal factors. The gentleman, the officer and the cleric function as such in an impersonal rôle, and their psychic make-up is qualified by a peculiar objectivity. We must grant that the artist does not function in an official capacity—the very opposite is nearer the truth. He nevertheless resembles the types I have named in one respect, for the specifically artistic disposition involves an overweight of collective psychic life as against the personal. Art is a kind of innate drive that seizes a human being and makes him its instrument. The artist is not a person endowed with free will who seeks his own ends, but one who allows art to realize its purposes through him. As a human being he may have moods and a will and personal aims, but as an artist he is "man" in a higher sense—he is " collective man "—one who carries and shapes the unconscious, psychic life of mankind. To perform this difficult office it is sometimes necessary for him to sacrifice happiness and everything that makes life worth living for the ordinary human being.

All this being so, it is not strange that the artist is an especially interesting case for the psychologist who uses an analytical method. The artist's life cannot be otherwise than full of conflicts, for two forces are at war within him— on the one hand the common human longing for happiness, satisfaction and security in life, and on the other a ruthless passion for creation which may go so far as to override every personal desire. The lives of artists are as a rule so highly unsatisfactory—not to say tragic—because of their inferiority on the human and personal side, and not because of a sinister dispensation. There are hardly any exceptions to the rule that a person must pay dearly for the divine gift of the creative fire. It is as though each of us were endowed at birth with a certain capital of energy. The strongest force in our make-up will seize and all but monopolize this energy, leaving so little over that nothing of value can come of it. In this way the creative force can drain the human impulses to such a degree that the personal ego must develop all sorts of bad qualities—ruthlessness, selfishness and vanity (so-called " auto-erotism ")—and even every kind of vice, in order to maintain the spark of life and to keep itself from being wholly bereft. The auto-erotism of artists resembles that of illegitimate or neglected children who from their tenderest years must protect themselves from the destructive influence of people who have no love to give them—who develop bad qualities for that very purpose and later maintain an invincible egocentrism by remaining all their lives infantile and helpless or by actively offending against the moral code or the law. How can we doubt that it is his art that explains the artist, and not the insufficiencies and conflicts of his personal life ? These are nothing but the regrettable results of the fact that he is an artist—that is to say, a man who from his very birth has been called to a greater task than the ordinary mortal. A special ability means a heavy expenditure of energy in a particular direction, with a consequent drain from some other side of life.

It makes no difference whether the poet knows that his work is begotten, grows and matures with him, or whether he supposes that by taking thought he produces it out of the void. His opinion of the matter does not change the fact that his own work outgrows him as a child its mother. The creative process has feminine quality, and the creative work arises from unconscious depths—we might say, from the realm of the mothers. Whenever the creative force predominates, human life is ruled and moulded by the unconscious as against the active will, and the conscious ego is swept along on a subterranean current, being nothing more than a helpless observer of events. The work in process becomes the poet's fate and determines his psychic development. It is not Goethe who creates *Faust*, but *Faust* which creates Goethe. And what is *Faust* but a symbol ? By this I do not mean an allegory that points to something all too familiar, but an expression that stands for something not clearly known and yet profoundly alive. Here it is something that lives in the soul of every German, and that Goethe has helped to bring to birth. Could we conceive of anyone but a German writing *Faust* or *Also sprach Zarathustra* ? Both play upon something that reverberates in the German soul —a " primordial·image ", as Jacob Burckhardt once called it—the figure of a physician or teacher·of mankind. The archetypal image of the wise man, the saviour or redeemer, lies buried and dormant in man's unconscious since the dawn of culture ; it is awakened whenever the times are out of joint and a human society is committed to a serious error. When people go astray they feel the need of a guide or teacher or even of the physician. These primordial images are numerous, but do not appear in the dreams of individuals or in works of art until they are called into being by the waywardness of the general outlook. When conscious life is characterized by one-sidedness and by a false attitude, then they are activated—one might say, " instinctively "—and come to light in the dreams of individuals and the visions of artists and seers, thus restoring the psychic equilibrium of the epoch.

In this way the work of the poet comes to meet the spiritual need of the society in which he lives, and for this reason his work means more to him than his personal fate, whether he is aware of this or not. Being essentially the instrument for his work, he is subordinate to it, and we have no reason for expecting him to interpret it for us. He has done the best that in him lies in giving it form, and he must leave the interpretation to others and to the future. A great work of art is like a dream ; for all its apparent obviousness it does not explain itself and is never unequivocal. A dream never says : " You ought ", or : " This is the truth ". It presents an image in much the same way as nature allows a plant to grow, and we must draw our own conclusions. If a person has a nightmare, it means either that he is too much given to fear, or else that he is too exempt from it ; and if he dreams of the old wise man it may mean that he is too pedagogical, as also that he stands in need of a teacher. In a subtle way both meanings come to the same thing, as we perceive when we are able to let the work of art act upon us as it acted upon the artist. To grasp its meaning, we must allow it to shape us as it once shaped him. Then we understand the nature of his experience. We see that he has drawn upon the healing and redeeming forces of the collective psyche that underlies consciousness with its isolation and its painful errors ; that he has penetrated to that matrix of life in which all men are embedded, which imparts a common rhythm to all human existence, and allows the individual to communicate his feeling and his striving to mankind as a whole.

The secret of artistic creation and of the effectiveness of art is to be found in a return to the state of *participation mystique*—to that level of experience at which it is man who lives, and not the individual, and at which the weal or woe of the single human being does not count, but only human existence. This is why every great work of art is objective and impersonal, but none the less profoundly moves us each and all. And this is also why the personal life of the poet cannot be held essential to his art—but at most a help or a hindrance to his creative task. He may go the way of a Philistine, a good citizen, a neurotic, a fool or a criminal. His personal career may be inevitable and interesting, but it does not explain the poet.

IX

THE BASIC POSTULATES OF ANALYTICAL
PSYCHOLOGY

IT was universally believed in the Middle Ages as well as in
the Græco-Roman world that the soul is a substance.[1]
Indeed, mankind as a whole has held this belief from its
earliest beginnings, and it was left for the second half of the
nineteenth century to develop a " psychology without the
soul ".[2]   Under the influence of scientific materialism,
everything that could not be seen with the eyes or touched
with the hands was held in doubt ; such things were even
laughed at because of their supposed affinity with metaphysics.   Nothing was considered " scientific " or admitted
to be true unless it could be perceived by the senses or traced
back to physical causes.   This radical change of view did
not begin with philosophical materialism, for the way was
being prepared long before.   When the spiritual catastrophe
of the Reformation put an end to the Gothic Age with its
impetuous yearning for the heights, its geographical confinement, and its restricted view of the world, the vertical
outlook of the European mind was forthwith intersected by
the horizontal outlook of modern times.   Consciousness
ceased to grow upward, and grew instead in breadth of

[1] Substance : i.e. that which has independent existence. (Trans.)
[2] " Psychologie ohne Seele "—compare the works of F. A. Lange (1828–
1875). It is to be noted that the German word Seele means psyche as well
as soul. (Trans.)

view, as well as in knowledge of the terrestrial globe.   This was the period of the great voyages, and of the widening of man's ideas of the world by empirical discoveries.   Belief in the substantiality of the spirit yielded more and more to the obtrusive conviction that material things alone have substance, till at last, after nearly four hundred years, the leading European thinkers and investigators came to regard the mind as wholly dependent on matter and material causation.

We are certainly not justified in saying that philosophy or natural science has brought about this complete *volte-face*. There were always a fair number of intelligent philosophers and scientists who had enough insight and depth of thought to accept this irrational reversal of standpoint only under protest ; a few even resisted it, but they had no following and were powerless against the popular attitude of un-reasoned, not to say emotional, surrender to the all-import-ance of the physical world.   Let no one suppose that so radical a change in man's outlook could be brought about by reasoning and reflection, for no chain of reasoning can prove or disprove the existence of either mind or matter. Both these concepts, as every intelligent man today may ascertain for himself, are mere symbols that stand for something unknown and unexplored, and this something is postulated or denied according to man's mood and dis-position or as the spirit of the age dictates.   There is nothing to prevent the speculative intellect from treating the psyche, on the one hand, as a complicated biochemical phenomenon, and at bottom a mere play of electrons, or, on the other, from regarding the unpredictable behaviour of electrons as the sign of mental life even in them.

The fact that a metaphysics of the mind was supplanted

in the nineteenth century by a metaphysics of matter, is a mere trick if we consider it as a question for the intellect ; yet regarded from the standpoint of psychology, it is an unexampled revolution in man's outlook upon the world. Other-worldliness is converted into matter-of-factness ; empirical boundaries are set to man's discussion of every problem, to his choice of purposes, and even to what he calls " meaning ". Intangible, inner happenings seem to have to yield place to things in the external, tangible world, and no value exists if it is not founded on a so-called fact. At least, this is how it appears to the simple mind.

It is futile, indeed, to attempt to treat this unreasoned change of opinion as a question of philosophy. We had better not try to do so, for if we maintain that mental phenomena arise from the activity of glands, we are sure of the thanks and respect of our contemporaries, whereas if we explain the break-up of the atom in the sun as an emanation of the creative *Weltgeist*, we shall be looked down upon as intellectual freaks. And yet both views are equally logical, equally metaphysical, equally arbitrary and equally symbolic. From the standpoint of epistemology it is just as admissible to derive animals from the human species, as man from animal species. But we know how ill Professor Daqué fared in his academic career because of his sin against the spirit of the age, which will not let itself be trifled with. It is a religion, or—even more—a creed which has absolutely no connection with reason, but whose significance lies in the unpleasant fact that it is taken as the absolute measure of all truth and is supposed always to have common-sense upon its side.

The spirit of the age cannot be compassed by the processes of human reason. It is an inclination, an emotional tendency that works upon weaker minds, through the unconscious, with an overwhelming force of suggestion that carries them along with it. To think otherwise than our contemporaries think is somehow illegitimate and disturbing ; it is even indecent, morbid or blasphemous, and therefore socially dangerous for the individual. He is stupidly swimming against the social current. Just as formerly the assumption was unquestionable that everything that exists takes its rise from the creative will of a God who is spirit, so the nineteenth century discovered the equally unquestionable truth that everything arises from material causes. Today the psyche does not build itself a body, but on the contrary, matter, by chemical action, produces the psyche. This reversal of outlook would be ludicrous if it were not one of the outstanding features of the spirit of the age. It is the popular way of thinking, and therefore it is decent, reasonable, scientific and normal. Mind must be thought to be an epiphenomenon of matter. The same conclusion is reached even if we say not " mind " but " psyche ", and in place of matter speak of brain, hormones, instincts or drives. To grant the substantiality of the soul or psyche is repugnant to the spirit of the age, for to do so would be heresy.

We have now discovered that it was intellectually unjustified presumption on our forefathers' part to assume that man has a soul ; that that soul has substance, is of divine nature and therefore immortal ; that there is a power inherent in it which builds up the body, supports its life, heals its ills and enables the soul to live independently of the body ; that there are incorporeal spirits with which the soul associates ; and that beyond our empirical present there is a spiritual world from which the soul receives knowledge of spiritual things whose origins cannot be discovered in this visible world. But people who are not above the general level of consciousness have not yet discovered that it is just as presumptuous and fantastic for us to assume that matter produces spirit; that apes give rise to human beings; that from the harmonious interplay of the drives of hunger, love, and power Kant's *Critique of Pure Reason* should have arisen; that the brain-cells manufacture thoughts, and that all this could not possibly be other than it is.

What or who, indeed, is this all-powerful matter? It is once more man's picture of a creative god, stripped this time of his anthropomorphic traits and taking the form of a universal concept whose meaning everyone presumes to understand. Consciousness today has grown enormously in breadth and extent, but unfortunately only in spatial dimensions; its temporal reach has not increased, for were that the case we should have a much more living sense of history. If our consciousness were not of today only, but had historical continuity, we should be reminded of similar transformations of the divine principle in Greek philosophy, and this might dispose us to be more critical of our present philosophical assumptions. We are, however, effectively prevented from indulging in such reflections by the spirit of the age. It looks upon history as a mere arsenal of convenient arguments that enables us, on occasion, to say: " Why, even old Aristotle knew that." This being the state of affairs, we must ask ourselves how the spirit of the age attains such an uncanny power. It is without doubt a psychic phenomenon of the greatest importance—at all events a prejudice so deeply rooted that until we give it proper consideration we cannot even approach the problem of the psyche.

As I have said, the irresistible tendency to account for everything on physical grounds corresponds to the horizontal development of consciousness in the last four centuries, and this horizontal perspective is a reaction against the exclusively vertical perspective of the Gothic Age. It is a manifestation of the crowd-mind, and as such is not to be treated in terms of the consciousness of individuals. Resembling in this the primitives, we are at first wholly unconscious of our actions, and only discover long afterwards why it was that we acted in a certain way. In the meantime, we content ourselves with all sorts of rationalized accounts of our behaviour, all of them equally inadequate.

If we were conscious of the spirit of the age, we should know why we are so inclined to account for everything on physical grounds ; we should know that it is because, up till now, too much was accounted for in terms of the spirit. This realization would at once make us critical of our bias. We should say : most likely we are now making as serious an error on the other side. We delude ourselves with the thought that we know much more about matter than about a " metaphysical " mind, and so we overestimate physical causation and believe that it alone affords us a true explanation of life. But matter is just as inscrutable as mind. As to the ultimate we can know nothing, and only when we admit this do we return to a state of equilibrium. This is in no way to deny the close connection of psychic happenings with the physiological structure of the brain, with the glands, and the body in general. We are once for all deeply convinced of the fact that the contents of consciousness are to a large part determined by our sense-perceptions. We cannot fail to recognize that unalterable characteristics of a physical as well as a psychic nature are unconsciously ingrained in us by heredity, and we are deeply struck by the power of the instincts which inhibit or reinforce or otherwise modify our mental capacities. Indeed, we must admit that as to cause, purpose and meaning, the human psyche—however we approach it—is first and foremost a close reflection of everything we call corporeal, empirical and mundane. And finally, in the face of all these admissions, we must ask ourselves if the psyche is not after all a secondary manifestation—an epiphenomenon—and completely dependent upon the body. In the light of reason and of our commitments as practical men to an actual world, we say yes. It is only our doubts as to the omnipotence of matter which could lead us to examine in a critical way this verdict of science upon the human psyche.

The objection has already been raised that this approach reduces psychic happenings to a kind of activity of the glands ; thoughts are regarded as secretions of the brain, and so we achieve a psychology without the psyche. From this standpoint, it must be confessed, the psyche does not exist in its own right ; it is nothing in itself, but is the mere expression of physical processes. That these processes have the qualities of consciousness is just an irreducible fact—were it otherwise, so the argument runs, we could not speak of the psyche at all ; there would be no consciousness, and so we should have nothing to say about anything. Consciousness, therefore, is taken as the *sine qua non* of psychic life—that is to say, as the psyche itself. And so it comes about that all modern " psychologies without the psyche " are studies of consciousness which ignore the existence of unconscious psychic life.

Yet there is not *one* modern psychology—there are several. This is curious enough when we remember that there is only one science of mathematics, of geology, zoology, botany and so forth. But there are so many psychologies that an American University was able to publish a thick volume under the title : *Psychologies of* 1930. I believe there are as many psychologies as philosophies, for there is also no one single philosophy, but many. I mention this for the reason that philosophy and psychology are linked by indissoluble bonds which are kept in being by the inter-relation of their subject-matters. Psychology takes the psyche for its subject-matter, and philosophy—to put it briefly—takes the world. Until recently psychology was a special branch of philosophy, but now we are coming to something which Nietzsche foresaw—the ascendance of psychology in its own right. It is even threatening to swallow philosophy. The inner resemblance of the two disciplines consists in this, that both are systems of opinion about subject-matter which cannot be fully experienced and therefore cannot be comprehended by a purely empirical approach. Both fields of study thus encourage speculation, with the result that opinions are formed in such variety and profusion that heavy volumes are needed to contain them all, whether they belong to the one field or to the other. Neither discipline can do without the other, and the one always furnishes the implicit—and frequently even unconscious—primary assumptions of the other.

The modern preference for physical grounds of explanation leads, as already remarked, to a " psychology without the psyche "—I mean, to the view that the psyche is nothing but a product of biochemical processes. As for a modern, scientific psychology which starts from the mind as such, there simply is none. No one today would venture to found a scientific psychology upon the postulate of an independent psyche that is not determined by the body. The idea of spirit in and for itself, of a self-contained world-system of the spirit that is the only adequate postulate for the belief in autonomous, individual souls, is extremely unpopular with us, to say the least. But I must remark that, in 1914, I attended at Bedford College, London, a joint session of the Aristotelian Society, the Mind Association and the British Psychological Society, at which a symposium was held on the question : Are individual minds contained in God or are they not ? Should anyone in England dispute the scientific standing of these societies, he would not receive a very cordial hearing, for their membership includes the outstanding minds of the country. And perhaps I was the only person in the audience who listened with surprise to arguments that had the ring of the thirteenth century. This instance may serve to show that the idea of an autonomous spirit whose existence is taken for granted has not died out everywhere in Europe or become a mere fossil left over from the Middle Ages.

If we keep this in mind, we can perhaps summon up the courage to consider the possibility of a " psychology with the psyche "—that is, of a field of study based on the assumption of an autonomous psyche. We need not be alarmed at the unpopularity of such an undertaking, for to postulate mind is no more fantastic than to postulate matter. Since we have literally no idea of the way in which what is psychic can arise from physical elements, and yet cannot deny the reality of psychic events, we are free to frame our assumptions the other way about for once, and to hold that the psyche arises from a spiritual principle which is as inaccessible to our understanding as matter. To be sure, this will not be a modern psychology, for to be modern is to deny such a

possibility. For better or worse, therefore, we must turn
back to the teachings of our forefathers, for they it was who
made such assumptions. The ancient view held that spirit
was essentially the life of the body, the life-breath, or a
kind of life-force which assumed spatial and corporeal form
at birth or after conception, and left the dying body again
after the final breath. The spirit in itself was considered as
a being without extension, and because it existed before
taking corporeal form and afterwards as well, it was considered as timeless and hence immortal. From the standpoint of modern, scientific psychology, this conception is of
course pure illusion. But as it is not our intention to indulge
in " metaphysics ", even of a modern variety, we will
examine this time-honoured notion for once in an unprejudiced way and test its empirical justification.

The names people give to their experiences are often
quite enlightening. What is the origin of the word *Seele* ?
Like the English word soul, it comes from the Gothic *saiwala*
and the Old German *saiwalô*, and these can be connected with
the Greek *aiolos*, mobile, coloured, iridescent. The Greek
word *psyche* also means butterfly. *Saiwalô* is related on the
other side to the old Slavonic word *sila*, meaning strength.
From these connections light is thrown on the original
meaning of the word *Seele* : it is moving force, that is,
life-force.

The Latin words *animus*, spirit, and *anima*, soul, are the
same as the Greek *anemos*, wind. The other Greek word for
wind, *pneuma*, means also spirit. In Gothic we find the
same word in *us-anan*, to breathe out, and in Latin *an-helare*,
to pant. In Old High German, *spiritus sanctus* was rendered
by *atun*, breath. In Arabic, wind is *rīh*, and *rūh* is soul,
spirit. There is a quite similar connection with the Greek

psyche, which is related to *psycho*, to breathe, *psychos*, cool, *psychros*, cold, and *phusa*, bellows.   These affinities show clearly how in Latin, Greek and Arabic the names given to the soul are related to the notion of moving air, the " cold breath of the spirit ".   And this also is why the primitive point of view endows the soul with an invisible breath-body.

It is quite evident that, since breath is the sign of life, breath is taken for life, as are also movement and moving force.   According to another primitive view the soul is regarded as fire or flame, because warmth also is a sign of life.   A very curious, but by no means rare, primitive conception identifies the soul with the name.   The name of an individual is his soul, and hence arises the custom of using the ancestor's name to reincarnate the ancestral soul in the new-born child.   We can infer from this that the ego-consciousness was recognized as an expression of the soul. Not infrequently the soul is identified with the shadow, for which reason it is a deadly insult to tread upon a person's shadow.   For the same reason, noon-day, the ghost-hour of southern latitudes, is considered threatening ;   the shadow then grows small, and this means that life is endangered. This conception of the shadow contains an idea which was indicated by the Greeks in the word *synopados*, " he who follows behind ".   They expressed in this way the feeling of an intangible, living presence—the same feeling which led to the belief that the souls of the departed were shadows.

These indications may serve to show how primitive man experienced the psyche.   To him the psyche appears as the source of life, the prime mover, a ghost-like presence which has objective reality.   Therefore the primitive knows how to converse with his soul ; it becomes vocal within him because it is not he himself and his consciousness.   To primitive man the psyche is not, as it is to us, the epitome of all that is subjective and subject to the will ; on the contrary, it is something objective, contained in itself, and living its own life.

This way of looking at the matter is empirically justified, for not only on the primitive level, but with civilized man as well, psychic happenings have an objective side. In large measure they are withdrawn from our conscious control. We are unable, for example, to suppress many of our emotions ; we cannot change a bad mood into a good one, and we cannot command our dreams to come or go. The most intelligent man may at times be obsessed with thoughts which he cannot drive away with the greatest effort of will. The mad tricks that memory plays sometimes leave us in helpless amazement, and at any time unexpected fantasies may run through our minds. We only believe that we are masters in our own house because we like to flatter ourselves. Actually, however, we are dependent to a startling degree upon the proper functioning of the unconscious psyche, and must trust that it does not fail us. If we study the psychic processes of neurotic persons, it seems perfectly ludicrous that any psychologist could take the psyche as the equivalent of consciousness. And it is well known that the psychic processes of neurotics differ hardly at all from those of so-called normal persons—for what man today is quite sure that he is not neurotic ?

This being so, we shall do well to admit that there is justification for the old view of the soul as an objective reality—as something independent, and therefore capricious and dangerous. The further assumption that this being, so mysterious and terrifying, is at the same time the source of life, is also understandable in the light of psychology.

Experience shows us that the sense of the " I "—the ego-consciousness—grows out of unconscious life. The small child has psychic life without any demonstrable ego-consciousness, for which reason the earliest years leave hardly any traces in memory. Where do all our good and helpful flashes of intelligence come from ? What is the source of our enthusiasms, inspirations, and of our heightened feeling for life ? The primitive senses in the depths of his soul the springs of life ; he is deeply impressed with the life-dispensing activity of his soul, and he therefore believes in everything that affects it—in magical practices of every kind. That is why, for him, the soul is life itself. He does not imagine that he directs it, but feels himself dependent upon it in every respect.

However preposterous the idea of the immortality of the soul may seem to us, it is nothing extraordinary to the primitive. After all, the soul is something out of the common. While everything else that exists takes up a certain amount of room, the soul cannot be located in space. We suppose, of course, that our thoughts are in our heads, but when it comes to our feelings we begin to be uncertain ; they appear to dwell in the region of the heart. Our sensations are distributed over the whole body. Our theory is that the seat of consciousness is in the head, but the Pueblo Indians told me that Americans were mad because they believed their thoughts were in their heads, whereas any sensible man knows that he thinks with his heart. Certain negro tribes locate their psychic functioning neither in the head nor in the heart, but in the belly.

To this uncertainty about the localization of psychic functions another difficulty is added. Psychic contents in general are non-spatial except in the particular realm of sensation.   What bulk can we ascribe to thoughts ?   Are they small, large, long, thin, heavy, fluid, straight, circular, or what ?   If we wished to form a vivid picture of a non-spatial being of the fourth dimension, we should do well to take thought, as a being, for our model.

It would all be so much simpler if we could only deny the existence of the psyche.   But here we are with our immediate experiences of something that *is*—something that has taken root in the midst of our measurable, ponderable, three-dimensional reality, that differs bafflingly from this in every respect and in all its parts, and yet reflects it.   The psyche may be regarded as a mathematical point and at the same time as a universe of fixed stars.   It is small wonder, then, if, to the unsophisticated mind, such a paradoxical being borders on the divine.   If it occupies no space, it has no body.   Bodies die, but can something invisible and incorporeal disappear ?   What is more, life and psyche existed for me before I could say " I ", and when this " I " disappears, as in sleep òr unconsciousness, life and psyche still go on, as our observation of other people and our own dreams inform us.   Why should the simple mind deny, in the face of such experiences, that the " soul " lives in a realm beyond the body ?   I must admit that I can see as little nonsense in this so-called superstition as in the findings of research regarding heredity or the basic instincts.

We can easily understand why higher and even divine knowledge was formerly ascribed to the psyche if we remember that in ancient cultures, beginning with primitive times, man always resorted to dreams and visions as a source of information.   It is a fact that the unconscious contains subliminal perceptions whose scope is nothing less than astounding.   In recognition of this fact, primitive societies used dreams and visions as important sources of information. Great and enduring civilizations like those of the Hindus and Chinese built upon this foundation and developed from it a discipline of self-knowledge which they brought to a high pitch of refinement both in philosophy and in practice.

A high regard for the unconscious psyche as a source of knowledge is by no means such a delusion as our Western rationalism likes to suppose. We are inclined to assume that, in the last resort, all knowledge comes from without. Yet today we know for certain that the unconscious contains contents which would mean an immeasurable increase of knowledge if they could only be made conscious. Modern investigation of animal instinct, as for example in insects, has brought together a rich fund of empirical findings which show that if man acted as certain insects do he would possess a higher intelligence than at present. It cannot, of course, be proved that insects possess conscious knowledge, but common-sense cannot doubt that their unconscious action-patterns are psychic functions. Man's unconscious likewise contains all the patterns of life and behaviour inherited from his ancestors, so that every human child, prior to consciousness, is possessed of a potential system of adapted psychic functioning. In the conscious life of the adult, as well, this unconscious, instinctive functioning is always present and active. In this activity all the functions of the conscious psyche are prepared for. The unconscious perceives, has purposes and intuitions, feels and thinks as does the conscious mind. We find sufficient evidence for this in the field of psycho-pathology and the investigation of dream-processes. Only in one respect is there an essential difference between the conscious and the unconscious

functioning of the psyche. While consciousness is intensive
and concentrated, it is transient and is directed upon the
immediate present and the immediate field of attention ;
moreover, it has access only to material that represents one
individual's experience stretching over a few decades. A
wider range of " memory " is artificially acquired and consists
mostly of printed paper. But matters stand very differently
with the unconscious. It is not concentrated and intensive,
but shades off into obscurity ; it is highly extensive and can
juxtapose the most heterogeneous elements in the most
paradoxical way. More than this, it contains, besides an
indeterminable number of subliminal perceptions, an immense fund of accumulated inheritance-factors left by one
generation of men after another, whose mere existence
marks a step in the differentiation of the species. If it were
permissible to personify the unconscious, we might call it a
collective human being combining the characteristics of both
sexes, transcending youth and age, birth and death, and,
from having at his command a human experience of one or
two million years, almost immortal. If such a being existed,
he would be exalted above all temporal change ; the present
would mean neither more nor less to him than any year in
the one hundredth century before Christ ; he would be a
dreamer of age-old dreams and, owing to his immeasurable
experience, he would be an incomparable prognosticator.
He would have lived countless times over the life of the
individual, of the family, tribe and people, and he would
possess the living sense of the rhythm of growth, flowering
and decay.

Unfortunately—or rather let us say, fortunately—this
being dreams. At least it seems to us as if the collective
unconscious, which appears to us in dreams, had no con-

sciousness of its own contents—though of course we cannot be sure of this, any more than we are in the case of insects. The collective unconscious, moreover, seems not to be a person, but something like an unceasing stream or perhaps an ocean of images and figures which drift into consciousness in our dreams or in abnormal states of mind.

It would be positively grotesque for us to call this immense system of experience of the unconscious psyche an illusion, for our visible and tangible body itself is just such a system. It still carries within it the discernible traces of primeval evolution, and it is certainly a whole that functions purposively—for otherwise we could not live. It would never occur to anyone to look upon comparative anatomy or physiology as nonsense. And so we cannot dismiss the collective unconscious as illusion, or refuse to recognize and study it as a valuable source of knowledge.

Looked at from without, the psyche appears to us to be essentially a reflection of external happenings—to be not only occasioned by them, but to have its origin in them. And it also seems to us that the unconscious can be understood only from without and from the side of consciousness. It is well known that Freud has attempted an explanation from this side—an undertaking which could only succeed if the unconscious were actually something which came into being with the existence and consciousness of the individual. But the truth is that the unconscious is always there beforehand as a potential system of psychic functioning handed down by generations of man. Consciousness is a late-born descendant of the unconscious psyche. It would certainly show perversity if we tried to explain the lives of our ancestors in terms of their late descendants; and it is just as wrong, in my opinion, to regard the unconscious as a derivative of consciousness. We are nearer the truth if we put it the other way round.

But this was the standpoint of past ages, which always held the individual soul to be dependent upon a world-system of the spirit. They could not fail to do so, because they were aware of the untold treasure of experience lying hidden beneath the threshold of the transient consciousness of the individual. These ages not only formed an hypothesis about the world system of the spirit, but they assumed without question that this system was a being with a will and consciousness—was even a person—and they called this being God, the quintessence of reality. He was for them the most real of beings, the first cause, through whom alone the soul could be understood. There is psychological justification for this supposition, for it is only appropriate to call divine an almost immortal being whose experience, compared to that of man, is nearly eternal.

In the foregoing I have shown where the problems lie for a psychology that does not explain everything upon physical grounds, but appeals to a world of the spirit whose active principle is neither matter and its qualities nor any state of energy, but God. We might be tempted at this juncture by modern philosophy to call energy or the *élan vital* God, and thus to blend into one spirit and nature. As long as this undertaking is restricted to the misty heights of speculative philosophy, no great harm is done. But if we should operate with this idea in the lower realm of practical psychology, where our way of explaining things bears fruit in daily conduct, we should find ourselves involved in the most hopeless difficulties. We do not profess a psychology shaped to the academic taste, or seek explanations that have no bearing on life. What we want is a practical

H*

psychology which yields approvable results—one which helps us to explain things in a way that is justified by the outcome for the patient.   In practical psychotherapy we strive to fit people for life, and we are not free to set up theories which do not concern our patients or which may even injure them. Here we come to a question which is often attended by mortal danger—the question whether we base our explanations upon matter or upon spirit.   We must never forget that everything spiritual is illusion from the naturalistic standpoint, and that the spirit, to ensure its own existence, must often deny and overcome an obtrusive, physical fact. If I recognize only naturalistic values, and explain everything in physical terms, I shall depreciate, hinder or even destroy the spiritual development of my patients.   And if I hold exclusively to a spiritual interpretation, then I shall misunderstand and do violence to the natural man in his right to existence as a physical being.   More than a few suicides in the course of psycho-therapeutic treatment are to be laid at the door of such mistakes.   Whether energy is God, or God is energy, concerns me very little, for how, in any case, can I know such things ?   But to give appropriate psychological explanations—this I must be able to do.

The modern psychologist occupies neither the one position nor the other, but finds himself between the two, dangerously committed to " this as well as that "—a situation which invitingly opens the way to a shallow opportunism.   This is undoubtedly the danger of the *coincidentia oppositorum*— of intellectual liberation from the opposites.   How should anything but a formless and aimless uncertainty result from giving equal value to contradictory postulates ?   In contrast to this, we can readily appreciate the advantage of an explanatory principle that is unequivocal.   It allows of a standpoint which can serve as a point of reference. Undoubtedly we are confronted here with a very difficult problem. We must be able to appeal to an explanatory principle founded on reality, and yet it is no longer possible for the modern psychologist to believe exclusively in the physical aspect of reality when once he has given the spiritual aspect its due. Nor will he be able to put weight on the latter alone, for he cannot ignore the relative validity of a physical interpretation.

The following train of thought shows my way of attempting the solution of this problem. The conflict of nature and mind is itself a reflection of the paradox contained in the psychic being of man. This reveals a material and a spiritual aspect which appear a contradiction as long as we fail to understand the nature of psychic life. Whenever, with our human understanding, we must pronounce upon something that we have not grasped or cannot grasp, then—if we are honest— we must be willing to contradict ourselves, and we must pull this something into its antithetical parts in order to deal with it at all. The conflict of the material and spiritual aspects of life only shows that the psychic is in the last resort an incomprehensible something. Without a doubt psychic happenings constitute our only, immediate experience. All that I experience is psychic. Even physical pain is a psychic event that belongs to my experience. My sense-impressions—for all that they force upon me a world of impenetrable objects occupying space—are psychic images, and these alone are my immediate experience, for they alone are the immediate objects of my consciousness. My own psyche even transforms and falsifies reality, and it does this to such a degree that I must resort to artificial means to determine what things are like apart from myself. Then I discover that a tone is a vibration of the air of such and such a frequency, or that a colour is a wave-length of light of such and such a length. We are in all truth so enclosed by psychic images that we cannot penetrate to the essence of things external to ourselves. All our knowledge is conditioned by the psyche which, because it alone is immediate, is superlatively real. Here there is a reality to which the psychologist can appeal—namely, psychic reality.

If we go more deeply into the meaning of this concept, it seems to us that certain psychic contents or images are derived from a material environment to which our bodies also belong, while others, which are in no way less real, seem to come from a mental source which appears to be very different from the physical environment. Whether I picture to myself the car I wish to buy, or try to imagine the state in which the soul of my dead father now is—whether it is an external fact or a thought that occupies me—both happenings are psychic reality. The only difference is that one psychic happening refers to the physical world, and the other to the mental world. If I change my concept of reality in such a way as to admit that all psychic happenings are real—and no other use of the concept is valid—this puts an end to the conflict of matter and mind as contradictory explanatory principles. Each becomes a mere designation for the particular source of the psychic contents that crowd into my field of consciousness. If a fire burns me I do not question the reality of the fire, whereas if I am beset by the fear that a ghost will appear, I take refuge behind the thought that it is only an illusion. But just as the fire is the psychic image of a physical process whose nature is unknown so my fear of the ghost is a psychic image from a mental source; it is just as real as the fire, for my fear is as real as the pain caused by the fire. As for the mental process that finally underlies my fear of the ghost—it is as unknown to me as the ultimate nature of matter. And just as it never occurs to me to account for the nature of fire except by the concepts of chemistry and physics, so I would never think of trying to explain my fear of ghosts except in terms of mental processes.

The fact that all immediate experience is psychic and that immediate reality can only be psychic, explains why it is that primitive man puts the appearance of ghosts and the effects of magic on a plane with physical events. He has not yet torn his naïve experiences into their antithetical parts. In his world mind and matter still interpenetrate each other, and his gods still wander through forest and field. He is like a child, only half-born, still enclosed in a dream-state within his own psyche and the world as it actually is, a world not yet distorted by the difficulties in understanding that beset a dawning intelligence. When the primitive world disintegrated into spirit and nature, the West rescued nature for itself. It was prone to a belief in nature, and only became the more entangled in it with every painful effort to make itself spiritual. The East, on the contrary, took mind for its own, and by explaining away matter as mere illusion (*maya*), continued to dream in Asiatic filth and misery. But since there is only *one* earth and *one* mankind, East and West cannot rend humanity into two different halves. Psychic reality exists in its original oneness, and awaits man's advance to a level of consciousness where he no longer believes in the one part and denies the other, but recognizes both as constituent elements of one psyche.

We may well point to the idea of psychic reality as the most important achievement of modern psychology, though it is scarcely recognized as such. It seems to me only a question of time for this idea to be generally accepted. It must be accepted, for it alone enables us to do justice to psychic manifestations in all their variety and uniqueness. Without this idea it is unavoidable that we should explain our psychic experiences in a way that does violence to a good half of them, while with it we can give its due to that side of psychic experience which expresses itself in superstition and mythology, religion and philosophy. And this aspect of psychic life is not to be undervalued. Truth that appeals to the testimony of the senses may satisfy reason, but it offers nothing that stirs our feelings and expresses them by giving a meaning to human life. Yet it is most often feeling that is decisive in matters of good and evil, and if feeling does not come to the aid of reason, the latter is usually powerless. Did reason and good intentions save us from the World War, or have they ever saved us from any other catastrophic nonsense? Have any of the great spiritual and social revolutions sprung from reasoning—let us say the transformation of the Græco-Roman world into the age of feudalism, or the explosive spread of Islamic culture?

As a physician I am of course not directly concerned with these world-questions; my duties lie with people who are ill. Medicine has until recently gone on the supposition that illness should be treated and cured by itself; yet voices are now heard which declare this view to be wrong, and demand the treatment of the sick person, and not of the illness. The same demand is forced upon us in the treatment of psychic suffering. More and more we turn our attention from the visible disease and direct it upon the man as a whole. We have come to understand that psychic suffering is not a definitely localized, sharply delimited phenomenon, but rather the symptom of a wrong attitude assumed by the total personality. We can therefore not hope for a thorough cure to result from a treatment restricted to the trouble itself, but only from a treatment of the personality as a whole.

I am reminded of a case which is very instructive in this connection. It concerns a highly intelligent young man who had worked out a detailed analysis of his own neurosis after a serious study of medical literature. He brought me his findings in the form of a precise and well-written monograph fit for publication, and asked me to read the manuscript and to tell him why he was not cured. He should have been according to the verdict of science as he understood it. After reading his monograph I was forced to grant him that, if it were only a question of insight into the causal connections of a neurosis, he should in all truth be cured. Since he was not, I supposed this must be due to the fact that his attitude to life was somehow fundamentally wrong —though I had to admit that his symptoms did not betray it. In reading his account of his life I had noticed that he often spent his winters at St. Moritz or Nice. I therefore asked him who paid for these holidays, and it thereupon came out that a poor school-teacher who loved him had cruelly deprived herself to indulge the young man in these visits to pleasure-resorts. His want of conscience was the cause of his neurosis, and it is not hard to see why scientific understanding failed to help him. His fundamental error lay in his moral attitude. He found my way of looking at the question shockingly unscientific, for morals have nothing to do with science. He supposed that, by invoking scientific thought, he could spirit away the immorality which he himself could not stomach. He would not even admit that a conflict existed, because his mistress gave him the money of her free will.

We can take what scientific position we choose, there remains the fact that the large majority of civilized persons simply cannot tolerate such behaviour. The moral attitude is a real factor in life with which the psychologist must reckon if he is not to commit the gravest errors. The psychologist must also remember that certain religious convictions not founded on reason are a necessity of life for many persons. It is again a matter of psychic realities which can cause and cure diseases. How often have I heard a patient exclaim : " If only I knew that my life had some meaning and purpose, then there would be no silly story about my nerves ! " Whether the person in question is rich or poor, has family and social position or not, alters nothing, for outer circumstances are far from giving his life a meaning. It is much more a question of his unreasoned need of what we call a spiritual life, and this he cannot obtain from universities, libraries, or even churches. He cannot accept what these have to offer because it touches only his head, and does not stir his heart. In such cases, the physician's recognition of the spiritual factors in their true light is vitally important, and the patient's unconscious helps him in his need by producing dreams whose contents are undeniably religious. Not to recognize the spiritual source of such contents means faulty treatment and failure.

General conceptions of a spiritual nature are indispensable constituents of psychic life. We can point them out among all peoples whose level of consciousness makes them in some degree articulate. Their relative absence or their denial by a civilized people is therefore to be regarded as a sign of

degeneration. Whereas in its development up to the present
psychology has dealt chiefly with psychic processes in the
light of physical causation, the future task of psychology
will be the investigation of théir spiritual determinants. But
the natural history of the mind is no further advanced today
than was natural science in the thirteenth century. We
have only begun to take scientific note of our spiritual
experiences.

If modern psychology can boast of having removed any
of the coverings which concealed the picture of the human
psyche, it is only that one which hid from the investigator
its biological aspect. We may compare the present situation
with the state of medicine in the sixteenth century, when
people began to study anatomy but had not as yet even the
faintest idea of physiology. The spiritual aspect of the
psyche is at present known to us only in a fragmentary way.
We have learned that there are spiritually conditioned
processes of transformation in the psyche which underlie,
for example, the well-known initiation rites of primitive
peoples and the states induced by the practice of Hindu
yoga. But we have not yet succeeded in determining their
particular uniformities or laws. We only know that a large
part of the neuroses arise from a disturbance in these processes. Psychological research has not as yet drawn aside
all the many veils from the picture of the human psyche ;
it remains as unapproachable and obscure as all the deep
secrets of life. We can speak only of what we have tried
to do, and what we hope to do in the future, in the way of
attempting a solution of the great riddle.

X

THE SPIRITUAL PROBLEM OF MODERN MAN [1]

THE spiritual problem of modern man is one of those questions which belong so intimately to the present in which we are living that we cannot judge of them fully. The modern man is a newly formed human being ; a modern problem is a question which has just arisen and whose answer lies in the future. In speaking, therefore, of the spiritual problem of modern man we can at most state a question—and we should perhaps put this statement in different terms if we had but the faintest inkling of the answer. The question, moreover, seems rather vague ; but the truth is that it has to do with something so universal that it exceeds the grasp of any single human being. We have reason enough, therefore, to approach such a problem with true moderation and with the greatest caution. I am deeply convinced of this, and wish it stressed the more because it is just such problems which tempt us to use high-sounding words—and because I shall myself be forced to say certain things which may sound immoderate and incautious.

To begin at once with an example of such apparent lack of caution, I must say that the man we call modern, the man who is aware of the immediate present, is by no means the average man. He is rather the man who stands upon a

[1] The author has made some changes in this essay since its publication in German. (*Trans.*)

226

peak, or at the very edge of the world, the abyss of the future before him, above him the heavens, and below him the whole of mankind with a history that disappears in primeval mists. The modern man—or, let us say again, the man of the immediate present—is rarely met with. There are few who live up to the name, for they must be conscious to a superlative degree. Since to be wholly of the present means to be fully conscious of one's existence as a man, it requires the most intensive and extensive consciousness, with a minimum of unconsciousness. It must be clearly understood that the mere fact of living in the present does not make a man modern, for in that case everyone at present alive would be so. He alone is modern who is fully conscious of the present.

The man whom we can with justice call " modern " is solitary. He is so of necessity and at all times, for every step towards a fuller consciousness of the present removes him further from his original *" participation mystique "* with the mass of men—from submersion in a common unconsciousness. Every step forward means an act of tearing himself loose from that all-embracing, pristine unconsciousness which claims the bulk of mankind almost entirely. Even in our civilizations the people who form, psychologically speaking, the lowest stratum, live almost as unconsciously as primitive races. Those of the succeeding stratum manifest a level of consciousness which corresponds to the beginnings of human culture, while those of the highest stratum have a consciousness capable of keeping step with the life of the last few centuries. Only the man who is modern in our meaning of the term really lives in the present ; he alone has a present-day consciousness, and he alone finds that the ways of life which correspond to earlier levels pall upon him. The values and strivings of those past worlds no longer interest him save from the historical standpoint. Thus he has become " unhistorical " in the deepest sense and has estranged himself from the mass of men who live entirely within the bounds of tradition. Indeed, he is completely modern only when he has come to the very edge of the world, leaving behind him all that has been discarded and outgrown, and acknowledging that he stands before a void out of which all things may grow.

These words may be thought to be but empty sound, and their meaning reduced to mere banality. Nothing is easier than to affect a consciousness of the present. As a matter of fact, a great horde of worthless people give themselves the air of being modern by overleaping the various stages of development and the tasks of life they represent. They appear suddenly by the side of the truly modern man as uprooted human beings, bloodsucking ghosts, whose emptiness is taken for the unenviable loneliness of the modern man and casts discredit upon him. He and his kind, few in number as they are, are hidden from the un-discerning eyes of mass-men by those clouds of ghosts, the pseudo-moderns. It cannot be helped ; the " modern " man is questionable and suspect, and has always been so, even in the past.

An honest profession of modernity means voluntarily declaring bankruptcy, taking the vows of poverty and chastity in a new sense, and—what is still more painful—renouncing the halo which history bestows as a mark of its sanction. To be " unhistorical " is the Promethean sin, and in this sense modern man lives in sin. A higher level of consciousness is like a burden of guilt. But, as I have said, only the man who has outgrown the stages of consciousness belonging to the past and has amply fulfilled the duties appointed for him by his world, can achieve a full consciousness of the present. To do this he must be sound and proficient in the best sense—a man who has achieved as much as other people, and even a little more. It is these qualities which enable him to gain the next highest level of consciousness.

I know that the idea of proficiency is especially repugnant to the pseudo-moderns, for it reminds them unpleasantly of their deceits. This, however, cannot prevent us from taking it as our criterion of the modern man. We are even forced to do so, for unless he is proficient, the man who claims to be modern is nothing but an unscrupulous gambler. He must be proficient in the highest degree, for unless he can atone by creative ability for his break with tradition, he is merely disloyal to the past. It is sheer juggling to look upon a denial of the past as the same thing as consciousness of the present. "Today" stands between "yesterday" and "tomorrow", and forms a link between past and future; it has no other meaning. The present represents a process of transition, and that man may account himself modern who is conscious of it in this sense.

Many people call themselves modern—especially the pseudo-moderns. Therefore the really modern man is often to be found among those who call themselves old-fashioned. He takes this stand for sufficient reasons. On the one hand he emphasizes the past in order to hold the scales against his break with tradition and that effect of guilt of which I have spoken. On the other hand he wishes to avoid being taken for a pseudo-modern.

Every good quality has its bad side, and nothing that is good can come into the world without directly producing a corresponding evil. This is a painful fact. Now there is the danger that consciousness of the present may lead to an elation based upon illusion : the illusion, namely, that we are the culmination of the history of mankind, the fulfilment and the end-product of countless centuries. If we grant this, we should understand that it is no more than the proud acknowledgement of our destitution : we are also the disappointment of the hopes and expectations of the ages. Think of nearly two thousand years of Christian ideals followed, instead of by the return of the Messiah and the heavenly millennium, by the World War among Christian nations and its barbed-wire and poison-gas. What a catastrophe in heaven and on earth !

In the face of such a picture we may well grow humble again. It is true that modern man is a culmination, but tomorrow he will be surpassed ; he is indeed the end-product of an age-old development, but he is at the same time the worst conceivable disappointment of the hopes of humankind. The modern man is aware of this. He has seen how beneficent are science, technology and organization, but also how catastrophic they can be. He has likewise seen that well-meaning governments have so thoroughly paved the way for peace on the principle " in time of peace prepare for war ", that Europe has nearly gone to rack and ruin. And as for ideals, the Christian church, the brotherhood of man, international social democracy and the "solidarity" of economic interests have all failed to stand the baptism of fire—the test of reality. Today, fifteen years after the war, we observe once more the same optimism, the same organization, the same political aspirations, the same phrases and catch-words at work. How can we but fear that they will inevitably lead to further catastrophes ?

Agreements to outlaw war leave us sceptical, even while we wish them all possible success. At bottom, behind every such palliative measure, there is a gnawing doubt. On the whole, I believe I am not exaggerating when I say that modern man has suffered an almost fatal shock, psychologically speaking, and as a result has fallen into profound uncertainty.

These statements, I believe, make it clear enough that my being a physician has coloured my views. A doctor always spies out diseases, and I cannot cease to be a doctor. But it is essential to the physician's art that he should not discover diseases where none exists. I will therefore not make the assertion that the white races in general, and occidental nations in particular, are diseased, or that the Western world is on the verge of collapse. I am in no way competent to pass such a judgement.

It is of course only from my own experience with other persons and with myself that I draw my knowledge of the spiritual problem of modern man. I know something of the intimate psychic life of many hundreds of educated persons, both sick and healthy, coming from every quarter of the civilized, white world ; and upon this experience I base my statements. No doubt I can draw only a one-sided picture, for the things I have observed are events of psychic life ; they lie within us—on the *inner side*, if I may use the expression. I must point out that this is not always true of psychic life ; the psyche is not always and everywhere to be found on the inner side. It is to be found on the *outside* in whole races or periods of history which take no account of psychic life as such. As examples we may choose any of the ancient cultures, but especially that of Egypt with its imposing objectivity and its naïve confession of sins that have not been committed.[1] We can no more feel the Pyramids and the Apis tombs of Sakkara to be expressions of personal problems or personal emotions, than we can feel this of the music of Bach.

Whenever there is established an external form, be it ritual or spiritual, by which all the yearnings and hopes of the soul are adequately expressed—as for instance in some living religion—then we may say that the psyche is outside, and no spiritual problem, strictly speaking, exists. In consonance with this truth, the development of psychology falls entirely within the last decades, although long before that man was introspective and intelligent enough to recognize the facts that are the subject-matter of psychology. The same was the case with technical knowledge. The Romans were familiar with all the mechanical principles and physical facts on the basis of which they could have constructed the steam-engine, but all that came of it was the toy made by Hero of Alexandria. There was no urgent necessity to go further. It was the division of labour and specialization in the nineteenth century which gave rise to the need to apply all available knowledge. So also a spiritual need has produced in our time our "discovery" of psychology. There has never, of course, been a time when the psyche did not manifest itself, but formerly it attracted no attention—no one noticed it. People got along without heeding it. But today we can no longer get along unless we give our best attention to the ways of the psyche.

It was men of the medical profession who were the first to notice this ; for the priest is concerned only to establish

---

[1] According to Egyptian tradition, when the dead man meets his judges in the underworld, he makes a detailed confession of the crimes he has *not* committed, but leaves unmentioned his actual sins. (*Trans.*)

an undisturbed functioning of the psyche within a recognized system of belief. As long as this system gives true expression to life, psychology can be nothing but a technical adjuvant to healthy living, and the psyche cannot be regarded as a problem in itself. While man still lives as a herd-being he has no " things of the spirit " of his own ; nor does he need any, save the usual belief in the immortality of the soul. But as soon as he has outgrown whatever local form of religion he was born to—as soon as this religion can no longer embrace his life in all its fulness—then the psyche becomes something in its own right which cannot be dealt with by the measures of the Church alone. It is for this reason that we of today have a psychology founded on experience, and not upon articles of faith or the postulates of any philosophical system. The very fact that we have such a psychology is to me symptomatic of a profound convulsion of spiritual life. Disruption in the spiritual life of an age shows the same pattern as radical change in an individual. As long as all goes well and psychic energy finds its application in adequate and well-regulated ways, we are disturbed by nothing from within. No uncertainty or doubt besets us, and we *cannot* be divided against ourselves. But no sooner are one or two of the channels of psychic activity blocked, than we are reminded of a stream that is dammed up. The current flows backward to its source ; the inner man wants something which the visible man does not want, and we are at war with ourselves. Only then, in this distress, do we discover the psyche; or, more precisely, we come upon something which thwarts our will, which is strange and even hostile to us, or which is incompatible with our conscious standpoint. Freud's psychoanalytic labours show this process in the clearest way. The very first thing he discovered was the existence of sexually perverse and criminal fantasies which at their face value are wholly incompatible with the conscious outlook of a civilized man. A person who was activated by them would be nothing less than a mutineer, a criminal or a madman.

We cannot suppose that this aspect of the unconscious or of the hinterland of man's mind is something totally new. Probably it has always been there, in every culture. Each culture gave birth to its destructive opposite, but no culture or civilization before our own was ever forced to take these psychic undercurrents in deadly earnest. Psychic life always found expression in a metaphysical system of some sort. But the conscious, modern man, despite his strenuous and dogged efforts to do so, can no longer refrain from acknowledging the might of psychic forces. This distinguishes our time from all others. We can no longer deny that the dark stirrings of the unconscious are effective powers—that psychic forces exist which cannot, for the present at least, be fitted in with our rational world-order. We have even enlarged our study of these forces to a science—one more proof of the earnest attention we bring to them. Previous centuries could throw them aside unnoticed ; for us they are a shirt of Nessus which we cannot strip off.

The revolution in our conscious outlook, brought about by the catastrophic results of the World War, shows itself in our inner life by the shattering of our faith in ourselves and our own worth. We used to regard foreigners—the other side—as political and moral reprobates ; but the modern man is forced to recognize that he is politically and morally just like anyone else. Whereas I formerly believed it to be my bounden duty to call other persons to order, I now admit that I need calling to order myself. I admit this the more readily because I realize only too well that I am losing my faith in the possibility of a rational organization of the world, that old dream of the millennium, in which peace and harmony should rule, has grown pale. The modern man's scepticism regarding all such matters has chilled his enthusiasm for politics and world-reform ; more than that, it does not favour any smooth application of psychic energies to the outer world. Through his scepticism the modern man is thrown back upon himself ; his energies flow towards their source and wash to the surface those psychic contents which are at all times there, but lie hidden in the silt as long as the stream flows smoothly in its course. How totally different did the world appear to mediæval man ! For him the earth was eternally fixed and at rest in the centre of the universe, encircled by the course of a sun that solicitously bestowed its warmth. Men were all children of God under the loving care of the Most High, who prepared them for eternal blessedness ; and all knew exactly what they should do and how they should conduct themselves in order to rise from a corruptible world to an incorruptible and joyous existence. Such a life no longer seems real to us, even in our dreams. Natural science has long ago torn this lovely veil to shreds. That age lies as far behind as childhood, when one's own father was unquestionably the handsomest and strongest man on earth.

The modern man has lost all the metaphysical certainties of his mediæval brother, and set up in their place the ideals of material security, general welfare and humaneness. But it takes more than an ordinary dose of optimism to make it appear that these ideals are still unshaken. Material security, even, has gone by the board, for the modern man begins to see that every step in material "progress" adds just so much force to the threat of a more stupendous catastrophe. The very picture terrorizes the imagination. What are we to imagine when cities today perfect measures of defence against poison-gas attacks and practise them in " dress rehearsals " ? We cannot but suppose that such attacks have been planned and provided for—again on the principle " in time of peace prepare for war ". Let man but accumulate his materials of destruction and the devil within him will soon be unable to resist putting them to their fated use. It is well known that fire-arms go off of themselves if only enough of them are together

An intimation of the law that governs blind contingency, which Heraclitus called the rule of *enantiodromia* (conversion into the opposite), now steals upon the modern man through the by-ways of his mind, chilling him with fear and paralysing his faith in the lasting effectiveness of social and political measures in the face of these monstrous forces. If he turns away from the terrifying prospect of a blind world in which building and destroying successively tip the scale, and if he then turns his gaze inward upon the recesses of his own mind, he will discover a chaos and a darkness there which he would gladly ignore. Science has destroyed even the refuge of the inner life. What was once a sheltering haven has become a place of terror.

And yet it is almost a relief for us to come upon so much evil in the depths of our own minds. We are able to believe, at least, that we have discovered the root of the evil in mankind. Even though we are shocked and disillusioned at first, we yet feel, because these things are manifestations of our own minds, that we hold them more or less in our own hands and can therefore correct or at least effectively suppress them. We like to assume that, if we succeeded in this, we should have rooted out some fraction of the evil in the world. We like to think that, on the basis of a widespread knowledge of the unconscious and its ways, no one could be deceived by a statesman who was unaware of his own bad motives ; the very newspapers would pull him up : " Please have yourself analysed ; you are suffering from a repressed father-complex."

I have purposely chosen this grotesque example to show to what absurdities we are led by the illusion that because something is psychic it is under our control. It is, however, true that much of the evil in the world is due to the fact that man in general is hopelessly unconscious, as it is also true that with increasing insight we can combat this evil at its source in ourselves. As science enables us to deal with injuries inflicted from without, so it helps us to treat those arising from within.

The rapid and world-wide growth of a " psychological " interest over the last two decades shows unmistakably that modern .man has to some extent turned his attention from material things to his own subjective processes. Should we call this mere curiosity ? At any rate, art has a way of anticipating future changes in man's fundamental outlook, and expressionist art has taken this subjective turn well in advance of the more general change.

This " psychological " interest of the present time shows that man expects something from psychic life which he has not received from the outer world : something which our religions, doubtless, ought to contain, but no longer do contain—at least for the modern man. The various forms of religion no longer appear to the modern man to come from within—to be expressions of his own psychic life ; for him they are to be classed with the things of the outer world.

He is vouchsafed no revelation of a spirit that is not of this world ; but he tries on a number of religions and convictions as if they were Sunday attire, only to lay them aside again like worn-out clothes.

Yet he is somehow fascinated by the almost pathological manifestations of the unconscious mind. We must admit the fact, however difficult it is for us to understand that something which previous ages have discarded should suddenly command our attention. That there is a general interest in these matters is a truth which cannot be denied, their offence to good taste notwithstanding. I am not thinking merely of the interest taken in psychology as a science, or of the still narrower interest in the psychoanalysis of Freud, but of the widespread interest in all sorts of psychic phenomena as manifested in the growth of spiritualism, astrology, theosophy, and so forth. The world has seen nothing like it since the end of the seventeenth century. We can compare it only to the flowering of Gnostic thought in the first and second centuries after Christ. The spiritual currents of the present have, in fact, a deep affinity with Gnosticism. There is even a Gnostic church in France today, and I know of two schools in Germany which openly declare themselves Gnostic. The modern movement which is numerically most impressive is undoubtedly Theosophy, together with its continental sister, Anthroposophy ; these are pure Gnosticism in a Hindu dress. Compared with these movements the interest in scientific psychology is negligible. What is striking about Gnostic systems is that they are based exclusively upon the manifestations of the unconscious, and that their moral teachings do not baulk at the shadow-side of life. Even in the form of its European revival, the Hindu *Kundalini-Yoga* shows this clearly. And as every

person informed on the subject of occultism will testify, the
statement holds true in this field as well.

The passionate interest in these movements arises undoubtedly from psychic energy which can no longer be
invested in obsolete forms of religion. For this reason such
movements have a truly religious character, even when they
pretend to be scientific. It changes nothing when Rudolf
Steiner calls his Anthroposophy " spiritual science ", or
Mrs. Eddy discovers a " Christian Science ". These attempts
at concealment merely show that religion has grown suspect
—almost as suspect as politics and world-reform.

I do not believe that I am going too far when I say that
modern man, in contrast to his nineteenth-century brother,
turns his attention to the psyche with very great expectations ; and that he does so without reference to any traditional creed, but rather in the Gnostic sense of religious
experience. We should be wrong in seeing mere caricature
or masquerade when the movements already mentioned try
to give themselves scientific airs ; their doing so is rather an
indication that they are actually pursuing " science " or
knowledge instead of the *faith* which is the essence of Western
religions. The modern man abhors dogmatic postulates
taken on faith and the religions based upon them. He holds
them valid only in so far as their knowledge-content seems
to accord with his own experience of the deeps of psychic
life. He wants to know—to experience for himself. Dean
Inge of St. Paul's has called attention to a movement in the
Anglican Church with similar objectives.

The age of discovery has only just'come to a close in our
day when no part of the earth remains unexplored ; it
began when men would no longer *believe* that the Hyper-
boreans inhabited the land of eternal sunshine, but wanted

to find out and to see with their own eyes what existed beyond the boundaries of the known world. Our age is apparently bent on discovering what exists in the psyche outside of consciousness. The question asked in every spiritualistic circle is : What happens when the medium has lost consciousness ? Every Theosophist asks : What shall I experience at higher levels of consciousness ? The question which every astrologer puts is this : What are the effective forces and determinants of my fate beyond the reach of my conscious intention ? And every psychoanalyst wants to know : What are the unconscious drives behind the neurosis ?

Our age wishes to have actual experiences in psychic life. It wants to experience for itself, and not to make assumptions based on the experience of other ages. Yet this does not preclude its trying anything in a hypothetical way—for instance, the recognized religions and the genuine sciences. The European of yesterday will feel a slight shudder run down his spine when he gazes at all deeply into these delvings. Not only does he consider the subject of this research all too obscure and uncanny, but even the methods employed seem to him a shocking misuse of man's finest intellectual attainments. What can we expect an astronomer to say when he is told that at least a thousand horoscopes are drawn today to one three hundred years ago ? What will the educator and the advocate of philosophical enlightenment say to the fact that the world has not been freed of one single superstition since Greek antiquity ? Freud himself, the founder of psychoanalysis, has thrown a glaring light upon the dirt, darkness and evil of the psychic hinterland, and has presented these things as so much refuse and slag ; he has thus taken the utmost pains to discourage people from seeking anything behind them. He did not succeed, and his warning has even brought about the very thing he wished to prevent : it has awakened in many people an admiration for all this filth. We are tempted to call this sheer perversity ; and we could hardly explain it save on the ground that it is not a love of dirt, but the fascination of the psyche, which draws these people.

There can be no doubt that from the beginning of the nineteenth century—from the memorable years of the French Revolution onwards—man has given a more and more prominent place to the psyche, his increasing attentiveness to it being the measure of its growing attraction for him. The enthronement of the Goddess of Reason in Nôtre Dame seems to have been a symbolic gesture of great significance to the Western world—rather like the hewing down of Wotan's oak by the Christian missionaries. For then, as at the Revolution, no avenging bolt from heaven struck the blasphemer down.

It is certainly more than an amusing coincidence that just at that time a Frenchman, Anquetil du Perron, was living in India, and, in the early eighteen-hundreds, brought back with him a translation of the *Oupnek'hat*—a collection of fifty *Upanishads*—which gave the Western world its first deep insight into the baffling mind of the East. To the historian this is mere chance without any factors of cause and effect. But in view of my medical experience I cannot take it as accident. It seems to me rather to satisfy a psychological law whose validity in personal life, at least, is complete. For every piece of conscious life that loses its importance and value—so runs the law—there arises a compensation in the unconscious. We may see in this an analogy to the conservation of energy in the physical world, for our psychic processes have a quantitative aspect also. No psychic value can disappear without being replaced by another of equivalent intensity. This is a rule which finds its pragmatic sanction in the daily practice of the psychotherapist ; it is repeatedly verified and never fails. Now the doctor in me refuses point blank to consider the life of a people as something that does not conform to psychological law. A people, in the doctor's eyes, presents only a somewhat more complex picture of psychic life than the individual. Moreover, taking it the other way round, has not a poet spoken of the " nations " of his soul ? And quite correctly, as it seems to me, for in one of its aspects the psyche is not individual, but is derived from the nation, from collectivity, or from humanity even. In some way or other we are part of an all-embracing psychic life, of a single " greatest " man, to quote Swedenborg.

And so we can draw a parallel : just as in me, a single human being, the darkness calls forth the helpful light, so does it also in the psychic life of a people. In the crowds that poured into Nôtre Dame, bent on destruction, dark and nameless forces were at work that swept the individual off his feet ; these forces worked also upon Anquetil du Perron, and provoked an answer which has come down in history. For he brought the Eastern mind to the West, and its influence upon us we cannot as yet measure. Let us beware of underestimating it ! So far, indeed, there is little of it to be seen in Europe on the intellectual surface : some orientalists, one or two Buddhist enthusiasts, and a few sombre celebrities like Madame Blavatsky and Annie Besant. These manifestations make us think of tiny, scattered islands in the ocean of mankind ; in reality they are like the peaks of submarine mountain-ranges of considerable size. The Philistine believed until recently that astrology had been disposed of long since, and was something that could be safely laughed at. But today, rising out of the social deeps, it knocks at the doors of the universities from which it was banished some three hundred years ago. The same is true of the thought of the East; it takes root in the lower social levels and slowly grows to the surface. Where did the five or six million Swiss francs for the Anthroposophist temple at Dornach come from? Certainly not from one individual. Unfortunately there are no statistics to tell us the exact number of avowed Theosophists today, not to mention the unavowed. But we can be sure that there are several millions of them. To this number we must add a few million Spiritualists of Christian or Theosophic leanings.

Great innovations never come from above; they come invariably from below; just as trees never grow from the sky downward, but upward from the earth, however true it is that their seeds have fallen from above. The upheaval of our world and the upheaval in consciousness is one and the same. Everything becomes relative and therefore doubtful. And while man, hesitant and questioning, contemplates a world that is distracted with treaties of peace and pacts of friendship, democracy and dictatorship, capitalism and Bolshevism, his spirit yearns for an answer that will allay the turmoil of doubt and uncertainty. And it is just people of the lower social levels who follow the unconscious forces of the psyche; it is the much-derided, silent folk of the land—those who are less infected with academic prejudices than great celebrities are wont to be. All these people, looked at from above, present mostly a dreary or laughable comedy; and yet they are as impressively simple as those Galileans who were once called blessed. Is it not touching to see the refuse of man's psyche gathered together in compendia a foot thick ? We find recorded in *Anthropophyteia* with scrupulous care the merest babblings, the most absurd actions and the wildest fantasies, while men like Havelock Ellis and Freud have dealt with the like matters in serious treatises which have been accorded all scientific honours. Their reading public is scattered over the breadth of the civilized, white world. How are we to explain this zeal, this almost fanatical worship of repellent things ? In this way : the repellent things belong to the psyche, they are of the substance of the psyche and therefore as precious as fragments of manuscript salvaged from ancient ruins. Even the secret and noisome things of the inner life are valuable to modern man because they serve his purpose. But what purpose ?

Freud has prefixed to his *Interpretation of Dreams* the citation : *Flectere si nequeo superos Acheronta movebo*—" If I cannot bend the gods on high, I will at least set Acheron in uproar ". But to what purpose ?

The gods whom *we* are called to dethrone are the idolized values of our conscious world. It is well known that it was the love-scandals of the ancient deities which contributed most to their discredit ; and now history is repeating itself. People are laying bare the dubious foundations of our belauded virtues and incomparable ideals, and are calling out to us in triumph : " There are your man-made gods, mere snares and delusions tainted with human baseness— whited sepulchres full of dead men's bones and of all un- cleanness ". We recognize a familiar strain, and the Gospel words, which we never could make our own, now come to life again.

I am deeply convinced that these are not vague analogies.

There are too many persons to whom Freudian psychology is dearer than the Gospels, and to whom the Russian Terror means more than civic virtue. And yet all these people are our brothers, and in each of us there is at least *one* voice which seconds them—for in the end there is a psychic life which embraces us all.

The unexpected result of this spiritual change is that an uglier face is put upon the world. It becomes so ugly that no one can love it any longer—we cannot even love ourselves—and in the end there is nothing in the outer world to draw us away from the reality of the life within. Here, no doubt, we have the true significance of this spiritual change. After all, what does Theosophy, with its doctrines of *karma* and reincarnation, seek to teach except that this world of appearance is but a temporary health-resort for the morally unperfected ? It depreciates the present-day world no less radically than does the modern outlook, but with the help of a different technique ; it does not vilify our world, but grants it only a relative meaning in that it promises other and higher worlds. The result is in either case the same.

I grant that all these ideas are extremely " unacademic ", the truth being that they touch modern man on the side where he is least conscious.   Is it again a mere coincidence that modern thought has had to come to terms with Einstein's relativity theory and with ideas about the structure of the atom which lead us away from determinism and visual representation ?   Even physics volatilizes our material world. It is no wonder, then, in my opinion, if the modern man falls back upon the reality of psychic life and expects from it that certainty which the world denies him.

But spiritually the Western world is in a precarious

situation—and the danger is greater the more we blind ourselves to the merciless truth with illusions about our beauty of soul. The Occidental burns incense to himself, and his own countenance is veiled from him in the smoke. But how do we strike men of another colour ? What do China and India think of us ? What feelings do we arouse in the black man ? And what is the opinion of all those whom we deprive of their lands and exterminate with rum and venereal disease ?

I have a Red Indian friend who is the governor of a pueblo. When we were once speaking confidentially about the white man, he said to me : " We don't understand the whites ; they are always wanting something—always restless— always looking for something. What is it ? We don't know. We can't understand them. They have such sharp noses, such thin, cruel lips, such lines in their faces. We think they are all crazy."

My friend had recognized, without being able to name it, the Aryan bird of prey with his insatiable lust to lord it in every land—even those that concern him not at all. And he had also noted that megalomania of ours which leads us to suppose, among other things, that Christianity is the only truth, and the white Christ the only Redeemer. After setting the whole East in turmoil with our science and technology, and exacting tribute from it, we send our missionaries even to China. The stamping out of polygamy by the African missions has given rise to prostitution on such a scale that in Uganda alone twenty thousand pounds sterling is spent yearly on preventatives of venereal infection, not to speak of the moral consequences, which have been of the worst. And the good European pays his missionaries for these edifying achievements ! No need to mention also the story of suffering in Polynesia and the blessings of the opium trade.

That is how the European looks when he is extricated from the cloud of his own moral incense. No wonder that to unearth buried fragments of psychic life we have first to drain a miasmal swamp. Only a great idealist like Freud could devote a lifetime to the unclean work. This is the beginning of our psychology. For us acquaintance with the realities of psychic life could start only at this end, with all that repels us and that we do not wish to see.

But if the psyche consisted for us only of evil and worthless things, no power in the world could induce a normal man to pretend to find it attractive. This is why people who see in Theosophy nothing but regrettable intellectual superficiality, and in Freudian psychology nothing but sensationalism, prophesy an early and inglorious end for these movements. They overlook the fact that they derive their force from the fascination of psychic life. No doubt the passionate interest that is aroused by them may find other expressions; but it will certainly show itself in these forms until they are replaced by something better. Superstition and perversity are after all one and the same. They are transitional or embryonic stages from which new and riper forms will emerge.

Whether from the intellectual, the moral or the æsthetic viewpoint, the undercurrents of the psychic life of the West present an uninviting picture. We have built a monumental world round about us, and have slaved for it with unequalled energy. But it is so imposing only because we have spent upon the outside all that is imposing in our natures—and what we find when we look within must necessarily be as it is, shabby and insufficient.

I am aware that in saying this I somewhat anticipate the

actual growth of consciousness. There is as yet no general insight into these facts of psychic life. Westerners are only on the way to a recognition of these facts, and for quite understandable reasons they struggle violently against it. Of course Spengler's pessimism has exerted some influence, but this has been safely confined to academic circles. As for psychological insight, it always trespasses upon personal life, and therefore meets with personal resistances and denials. I am far from considering these resistances meaningless ; on the contrary I see in them a healthy reaction to something which threatens destruction. Whenever relativism is taken as a fundamental and final principle it has a destructive effect. When, therefore, I call attention to the dismal undercurrents of the psyche, it is not in order to sound a pessimistic note ; I wish rather to emphasize the fact that the unconscious has a strong attraction not only for the sick, but for healthy, constructive minds as well—and this in spite of its alarming aspect. The psychic depths are nature, and nature is creative life. It is true that nature tears down what she has herself built up—yet she builds it once again. Whatever values in the visible world are destroyed by modern relativism, the psyche will produce their equivalents. At first we cannot see beyond the path that leads downward to dark and hateful things—but no light or beauty will ever come from the man who cannot bear this sight. Light is always born of darkness, and the sun never yet stood still in heaven to satisfy man's longing or to still his fears. Does not the example of Anquetil du Perron show us how psychic life survives its own eclipse ? China hardly believes that European science and technology are preparing her ruin. Why should we believe that we must be destroyed by the secret, spiritual influence of the East ?

But I forget that we do not yet realize that while we are turning upside down the material world of the East with our technical proficiency, the East with its psychic proficiency is throwing our spiritual world into confusion. We have never yet hit upon the thought that while we are overpowering the Orient from without, it may be fastening its hold upon us from within. Such an idea strikes us as almost insane, because we have eyes only for gross material connections, and fail to see that we must lay the blame for the intellectual confusion of our middle class at the doors of Max Müller, Oldenberg, Neumann, Deussen, Wilhelm and others like them. What does the example of the Roman Empire teach us ? After the conquest of Asia Minor, Rome became Asiatic ; even Europe was infected by Asia, and remains so today. Out of Cilicia came the Mithraic cult— the religion of the Roman army—and it spread from Egypt to fog-bound Britain. Need I point to the Asiatic origin of Christianity ?

We have not yet clearly grasped the fact that Western Theosophy is an amateurish imitation of the East. We are just taking up astrology again, and that to the Oriental is his daily bread. Our studies of sexual life, originating in Vienna and in England, are matched or surpassed by Hindu teachings on this subject. Oriental texts ten centuries old introduce us to philosophical relativism, while the idea of indetermination, newly broached in the West, furnishes the very basis of Chinese science. Richard Wilhelm has even shown me that certain complicated processes discovered by analytical psychology are recognizably described in ancient Chinese texts. Psychoanalysis itself and the lines of thought to which it gives rise—surely a distinctly Western development—are only a beginner's attempt compared to what is an immemorial art in the East. It should be mentioned that the parallels between psychoanalysis and yoga have already been traced by Oskar A. H. Schmitz.

The Theosophists have an amusing idea that certain Mahatmas, seated somewhere in the Himalayas or Tibet, inspire or direct every mind in the world. So strong, in fact, can be the influence of the Eastern belief in magic upon Europeans of a sound mind, that some of them have assured me that I am unwittingly inspired by the Mahatmas with every good thing I say, my own inspirations being of no account whatever. This myth of the Mahatmas, widely circulated and firmly believed in the West, far from being nonsense, is—like every myth—an important psychological truth. It seems to be quite true that the East is at the bottom of the spiritual change we are passing through today. Only this East is not a Tibetan monastery full of Mahatmas, but in a sense lies within us. It is from the depths of our own psychic life that new spiritual forms will arise ; they will be expressions of psychic forces which may help to subdue the boundless lust for prey of Aryan man. We shall perhaps come to know something of that circumscription of life which has grown in the East into a dubious quietism ; also something of that stability which human existence acquires when the claims of the spirit become as imperative as the necessities of social life. Yet in this age of Americanization we are still far from anything of the sort, and it seems to me that we are only at the threshold of a new spiritual epoch. I do not wish to pass myself off as a prophet, but I cannot outline the spiritual problem of modern man without giving emphasis to the yearning for rest that arises in a period of unrest, or to the longing for security that is bred of insecurity. It is from need and distress that new forms of life take their rise, and not from mere wishes or from the requirements of our ideals.

To me, the crux of the spiritual problem of today is to be found in the fascination which psychic life exerts upon modern man. If we are pessimists, we shall call it a sign of decadence ; if we are optimistically inclined, we shall see in it the promise of a far-reaching spiritual change in the Western world. At all events, it is a significant manifestation. It is the more noteworthy because it shows itself in broad sections of every people ; and it is the more important because it is a matter of those imponderable psychic forces which transform human life in ways that are unforeseen and —as history shows—unforeseeable. These are the forces, still invisible to many persons today, which are at the bottom of the present " psychological " interest. When the attractive power of psychic life is so strong that man is neither repelled nor dismayed by what he is sure to find, then it has nothing of sickliness or perversion about it.

Along the great highroads of the world everything seems desolate and outworn. Instinctively the modern man leaves the trodden ways to explore the by-paths and lanes, just as the man of the Græco-Roman world cast off his defunct Olympian gods and turned to the mystery-cults of Asia. The force within us that impels us to the search, turning outward, annexes Eastern Theosophy and magic ; but it also turns inward and leads us to give our thoughtful attention to the unconscious psyche. It inspires in us the selfsame scepticism and relentlessness with which a Buddha swept aside his two million gods that he might come to the pristine experience which alone is convincing.

And now we must ask a final question. Is what I have said of the modern man really true, or is it perhaps the result of

ɪ

an optical illusion ? There can be no doubt whatever that
the facts I have cited are wholly irrelevant contingencies in
the eyes of many millions of Westerners, and seem only
regrettable errors to a large number of educated persons.
But I may ask : What did a cultivated Roman think of
Christianity when he saw it spreading among the people of
the lowest classes ? The biblical God is still a living person
in the Western world—as living as Allah ˙ beyond the
Mediterranean. One kind of believer holds the other an
ignoble heretic, to be pitied and tolerated if he cannot be
changed. What is more, a clever European is convinced
that religion and such things are good enough for the masses
and for women, but are of little weight compared to
economic and political affairs.

So I am refuted all along the line, like a man who predicts
a thunderstorm when there is not a cloud in the sky. Perhaps
it is a storm beneath the horizon that he senses—and it may
never reach us. But what is significant in psychic life is
always below the horizon of consciousness, and when we
speak of the spiritual problem of modern man we are dealing
with things that are barely visible—with the most intimate
and fragile things—with flowers that open only in the night.
In daylight everything is clear and tangible ; but the night
lasts as long as the day, and we live in the night-time also.
There are persons who have bad dreams which even spoil
their days for them. And the day's life is for many people
such a bad dream that they long for the night when the
spirit awakes. I even believe that there are nowadays a
great many such people, and this is why I maintain that the
spiritual problem of modern man is much as I have presented
it. I must plead guilty, indeed, to the charge of one-sidedness, for I have not mentioned the modern spirit of commit-

ment to a practical world about which everyone has much to say because it lies in such full view. We find it in the ideal of internationalism or supernationalism which is embodied in the League of Nations and the like ; and we find it also in sport and, very expressively, in the cinema and in jazz music.

These are certainly characteristic symptoms of our time ; they show unmistakably how the ideal of humanism is made to embrace the body also. Sport represents an exceptional valuation of the human body, as does also modern dancing. The cinema, on the other hand, like the detective story, makes it possible to experience without danger all the excitement, passion and desirousness which must be repressed in a humanitarian ordering of life. It is not difficult to see how these symptoms are connected with the psychic situation. The attractive power of the psyche brings about a new self-estimation—a re-estimation of the basic facts of human nature. We can hardly be surprised if this leads to the rediscovery of the body after its long depreciation in the name of the spirit. We are even tempted to speak of the body's revenge upon the spirit. When Keyserling sarcastically singles out the chauffeur as the culture-hero of our time, he has struck, as he often does, close to the mark. The body lays claim to equal recognition ; like the psyche, it also exerts a fascination. If we are still caught by the old idea of an antithesis between mind and matter, the present state of affairs means an unbearable contradiction ; it may even divide us against ourselves. But if we can reconcile ourselves with the mysterious truth that spirit is the living body seen from within, and the body the outer manifestation of the living spirit—the two being really one—then we can understand why it is that the attempt to transcend the

present level of consciousness must give its due to the body.
We shall also see that belief in the body cannot tolerate an
outlook that denies the body in the name of the spirit. These
claims of physical and psychic life are so pressing compared
to similar claims in the past, that we may be tempted to see
in this a sign of decadence. Yet it may also signify a
rejuvenation, for as Hölderlin says :

> Danger itself
> Fosters the rescuing power.[1]

What we actually see is that the Western world strikes up
a still more rapid tempo—the American tempo—the very
opposite of quietism and resigned aloofness. An enormous
tension arises between the opposite poles of outer and inner
life, between objective and subjective reality. Perhaps it is
a final race between ageing Europe and young America ;
perhaps it is a desperate or a wholesome effort of conscious
man to cheat the laws of nature of their hidden might and
to wrest a yet greater, more heroic victory from the sleep of
the nations. This is a question which history will answer.

In coming to a close after so many bold assertions, I
would like to return to the promise made at the outset to
be mindful of the need for moderation and caution. Indeed,
I do not forget that my voice is but one voice, my experience
a mere drop in the sea, my knowledge no greater than the
visual field in a microscope, my mind's eye a mirror that
reflects a small corner of the world, and my ideas—a
subjective confession.

---

[1] *Wo Gefahr ist,*
Wächst das Rettende auch. (Hölderlin.)

XI

PSYCHOTHERAPISTS OR THE CLERGY

It is the urgent psychic problems of patients, much more than the questions put by scientific workers, which have given effective impetus to the newer developments in medical psychology and psychotherapy. The science of medicine has avoided all contact with strictly psychic problems. It has held to this position in spite of the patient's urgent needs, but on the partly justified assumption that psychic problems belong to other fields of study. And yet it has been forced to widen its scope so as to include experimental psychology, just as it has been driven time and time again—in view of man's biological homogeneity—to borrow from such branches of science as chemistry, physics and biology.

It was natural that a new direction should be given to these adopted branches of science. We can characterize the change by saying that instead of being regarded as ends in themselves, they were valued because of their possible application to human beings. Psychiatry, for example, helped itself out of the treasure-chest of experimental psychology and funded its borrowings in that inclusive body of knowledge called psychopathology—a general name for the study of complex psychic manifestations. Psychopathology is built for one part upon the findings of psychiatry in the strict sense of the term, and for the other upon the findings of neurology—a field of study which originally embraced the so-called psychogenetic neuroses, and still does so in academic parlance. In practice, however, a gulf has opened in the last few decades between the trained neurologist and the psychotherapist, this rift being traceable to the first researches in hypnotism. There was no preventing this divergence, for neurology is the study of organic nervous diseases in particular, while the psychogenetic neuroses are not organic diseases in the usual sense of the term. Nor do these neuroses fall within the realm of psychiatry, whose particular field of study is the psychoses, or mental diseases —for the psychogenetic neuroses are not mental diseases as this term is commonly understood. Rather do they constitute a special field by themselves which has no hard and fast boundaries, and they show many transitional forms which point in two directions : towards mental disease on the one hand, and disease of the nerves on the other.

The unmistakable feature of the neuroses is the fact that their causes are psychic, and that their cure depends entirely upon psychic methods of treatment. The attempts to delimit and to explore this special field—both from the side of psychiatry and from that of neurology—have led to a discovery which is very unwelcome to the science of medicine : namely, the discovery that the psyche is an ætiological or causal factor in disease. In the course of the nineteenth century medicine shaped its methods and theory in such a way as to become one of the disciplines of natural science, and it also adopted that primary assumption of natural science : material causation. For medicine the psyche did not exist in its own right, and experimental psychology also did its best to constitute itself a psychology without the psyche.

Investigation, however, has established beyond a doubt that the crux of the psycho-neuroses is to be found in the psychic factor ; that this is the essential cause of the pathological state, and must therefore be recognized in its own right along with other admitted pathogenic factors such as inheritance, disposition, bacterial infection, and so forth. All attempts to explain the psychic factor in terms of more elementary physical factors were doomed to failure. There was more promise in the attempt to delimit the psychic factor by the concept of the drive or instinct [1]—a concept taken over from biology. It is well known that instincts are observable physiological urges which are traceable to the functioning of the glands, and that, as experience shows, they condition or influence psychic processes. What could seem more plausible, therefore, than to seek the specific cause of the psycho-neuroses, not in the mystical notion of the " soul ", but in a disturbance of the impulses which might possibly be curable in the last resort by medicinal treatment of the glands ? As a matter of fact, this is Freud's standpoint when establishing his well-known theory which explains the neuroses in terms of disturbances of the sexual impulse. Adler likewise resorts to the concept of the drive, and explains the neuroses in terms of disturbances of the urge to power. We must admit, indeed, that this concept is further removed from physiology, and is of a more psychic nature, than that of the sexual drive.

The concept of instinct is anything but well defined in the scientific sense. It applies to a biological manifestation of great complexity, and is not much more than a notion of quite indefinite content standing for an unknown quantity.

[1] The German word *Trieb* covers both. (Trans.)

I do not wish to enter here upon a critical discussion of the concept of instinct. Instead I will consider the possibility that the psychic factor is just a combination of instincts which for their part may again be reduced to the functioning of the glands. We may even discuss the possibility that everything that is usually called psychic is embraced in the sum-total of instincts, and that the psyche itself is therefore only an instinct or a conglomerate of instincts, being in the last analysis nothing but the functioning of the glands. A psycho-neurosis would thus be a glandular disease. This statement, however, has not been proved, and no glandular extract that will cure a neurosis has as yet been found. On the other hand, we have been taught by all too many mistakes that organic medicine fails completely in the treatment of neuroses, while psychic methods cure them. These psychic methods are just as effective as we might suppose the glandular extracts would be. So far, then, as our present experience goes, neuroses are to be influenced or cured by considering them, not from the side of their irreducible elements, the glandular secretions, but from that of psychic activity, which must be taken as a reality. For example, a suitable explanation or a comforting word to the patient may have something like a healing effect which may even influence the glandular secretions. The doctor's words, to be sure, are " only " vibrations in the air, yet they con- stitute a particular set of vibrations corresponding to a particular psychic state in the doctor. The words are effective only in so far as they convey a meaning or have significance. It is their meaning which is effective. But " meaning " is something mental or spiritual. Call it a fiction if you like. None the less it enables us to influence the course of the disease in a far more effective way than with chemical preparations. We can even influence the biochemical processes of the body by it. Whether the fiction arises in me spontaneously, or reaches me from without by way of human speech, it can make me ill or cure me. Nothing is surely more intangible and unreal than fictions, illusions and opinions; and yet nothing is more effective in the psychic and even the psychophysical realm.

It was by recognizing these facts that science discovered the psyche, and we are now in honour bound to admit its reality. It has been shown that the drive, or instinct, is a condition of psychic activity, while at the same time the psychic processes seem to condition the instincts.

It is no reproach to the Freudian and Adlerian theories that they are based upon the drives; the only trouble is that they are one-sided. The kind of psychology they represent leaves out the psyche, and is suited to people who believe that they have no spiritual needs or aspirations. In this matter both the doctor and the patient deceive themselves. Although the theories of Freud and Adler come much nearer to getting at the bottom of the neuroses than does any earlier approach to the question from the side of medicine, they still fail, because of their exclusive concern with the drives, to satisfy the deeper spiritual needs of the patient. They are still bound by the premises of nineteenth-century science, and they are too self-evident—they give too little value to fictional and imaginative processes. In a word, they do not give meaning enough to life. And it is only the meaningful that sets us free.

Everyday reasonableness, sound human judgement, and science as a compendium of common sense, certainly help us over a good part of the road; yet they do not go beyond that frontier of human life which surrounds the commonplace

1*

and matter-of-fact, the merely average and normal. They afford, after all, no answer to the question of spiritual suffering and its innermost meaning. A psycho-neurosis must be understood as the suffering of a human being who has not discovered what life means for him. But all creativeness in the realm of the spirit as well as every psychic advance of man arises from a state of mental suffering, and it is spiritual stagnation, psychic sterility, which causes this state.

The doctor who realizes this truth sees a territory opened before him which he approaches with the greatest hesitation. He is now confronted with the necessity of conveying to his patient the healing fiction, the meaning that quickens—for it is this that the patient longs for, over and above all that reason and science can give him. The patient is looking for something that will take possession of him and give meaning and form to the confusion of his neurotic mind.

Is the doctor equal to this task ? To begin with, he will probably hand over his patient to the clergyman or the philosopher, or abandon him to that perplexity which is the special note of our day. As a doctor he is not required to have a finished outlook on life, and his professional conscience does not demand it of him. But what will he do when he sees only too clearly why his patient is ill ; when he sees that it arises from his having no love, but only sexuality ; no faith, because he is afraid to grope in the dark ; no hope, because he is disillusioned by the world and by life ; and no understanding, because he has failed to read the meaning of his own existence ?

There are many well-educated patients who flatly refuse to consult the clergyman. With the philosopher they will have even less to do, for the history of philosophy leaves them cold, and intellectual problems seem to them more barren than the desert. And where are the great and wise men who do not merely talk about the meaning of life and of the world, but really possess it ? Human thought cannot conceive any system or final truth that could give the patient what he needs in order to live : that is, faith, hope, love and insight.

These four highest achievements of human effort are so many gifts of grace, which are neither to be taught nor learned, neither given nor taken, neither withheld nor earned, since they come through experience, which is something *given*, and therefore beyond the reach of human caprice. Experiences cannot be *made*. They happen—yet fortunately their independence of man's activity is not absolute but relative. We can draw closer to them—that much lies within our human reach. There are ways which bring us nearer to living experience, yet we should beware of calling these ways " methods ". The very word has a deadening effect. The way to experience, moreover, is anything but a clever trick ; it is rather a venture which requires us to commit ourselves with our whole being.

Thus, in trying to meet the demands made upon him, the doctor is confronted by a question which seems to contain an insuperable difficulty. How can he help the sufferer to attain the liberating experience which will bestow upon him the four great gifts of grace and heal his sickness ? We can of course advise the patient with the very best intentions that he should have true love, or true faith, or true hope ; and we can admonish him with the phrase : " Know thyself ". But how is the patient, before he has come to experience, to obtain that which only experience can give him ?

Saul owed his conversion neither to true love, nor to true

faith, nor to any other truth. It was solely his hatred of the Christians that set him upon the road to Damascus, and to that decisive experience which was to decide the whole course of his life. He was brought to this experience by following with conviction the course in which he was most completely mistaken. This opens up for us an approach to the problems of life which we can hardly take too seriously. And it confronts the psychotherapist with a question which brings him shoulder to shoulder with the clergyman : the question of good and evil.

It is in reality the priest or the clergyman, rather than the doctor, who should be most concerned with the problem of spiritual suffering. But in most cases the sufferer consults the doctor in the first place, because he supposes himself to be physically ill, and because certain neurotic symptoms can be at least alleviated by drugs. But if, on the other hand, the clergyman is consulted, he cannot persuade the sick man that the trouble is psychic. As a rule he lacks the special knowledge which would enable him to discern the psychic factors of the disease, and his judgement is without the weight of authority.

There are, however, persons who, while well aware of the psychic nature of their complaint, nevertheless refuse to turn to the clergyman. They do not believe that he can really help them. Such persons distrust the doctor for the same reason, and they are justified by the fact that both doctor and clergyman stand before them with empty hands, if not—what is even worse—with empty words. We can hardly expect the doctor to have anything to say about the ultimate questions of the soul. It is from the clergyman, not from the doctor, that the sufferer should expect such help. But the Protestant clergyman often finds himself face to face with an almost impossible task, for he has to cope with practical difficulties that the Catholic priest is spared. Above all, the priest has the authority of his Church behind him, and his economic position is secure and independent. This is far less true of the Protestant clergy-man who may be married and burdened with the respon-sibility of a family, and cannot expect, if all else fails, to be supported by his community or taken into a monastery. But the priest, if he is also a Jesuit, even has at his disposal the psychological teaching of the present day. I know, for instance, that my own writings were seriously studied in Rome long before any Protestant pastor thought them worthy of a glance.

We have come to a serious pass. The exodus from the German Protestant Church is only one of many symptoms which should make it plain to the clergy that mere admoni-tions to believe, or to perform acts of charity, do not give modern man what he is looking for. The fact that many clergymen seek support or practical help from Freud's theory of sexuality or Adler's theory of power is astonishing, inasmuch as both these theories are hostile to spiritual values, being, as I have said, psychology without the psyche. They are rational methods of treatment which actually hinder the realization of meaningful experience. By far the larger number of psychotherapists are disciples of Freud or of Adler. This means that the great majority of patients are necessarily alienated from a spiritual standpoint—a fact which cannot be a matter of indifference to one who has the realization of spiritual values much at heart. The wave of interest in psychology which at present is sweeping over the Protestant countries of Europe is far from receding. It is coincident with the general exodus from the Church.

Quoting a Protestant minister, I may say : " Nowadays people go to the psychotherapist rather than to the clergyman."

I am convinced that this statement is true only of relatively educated persons, not of mankind in the mass. However, we must not forget that it will be some twenty years before the ordinary run of people begin to think the thoughts of the educated person of today. For instance, Büchner's work, *Force and Matter*, became one of the most widely read books in German public libraries about twenty years after educated persons had begun to forget about it. I am persuaded that what is today a vital interest in psychology among educated persons will tomorrow be shared by everyone.

I should like to call attention to the following facts. During the past thirty years, people from all the civilized countries of the earth have consulted me. I have treated many hundreds of patients, the larger number being Protestants, a smaller number Jews, and not more than five or six believing Catholics. Among all my patients in the second half of life—that is to say, over thirty-five—there has not been one whose problem in the last resort was not that of finding a religious outlook on life. It is safe to say that every one of them fell ill because he had lost that which the living religions of every age have given to their followers, and none of them has been really healed who did not regain his religious outlook. This of course has nothing whatever to do with a particular creed or membership of a church.

Here, then, the clergyman stands before a vast horizon. But it would seem as if no one had noticed it. It also looks as though the Protestant clergyman of today was insufficiently equipped to cope with the urgent psychic needs of our age.   It is indeed high time for the clergyman and the psychotherapist to join forces to meet this great spiritual task.

Here is a concrete example which goes to show how closely this problem touches us all.   Somewhat more than two years ago the leaders of the Christian Students' Conference at Aarau (Switzerland) laid before me the question whether people in spiritual distress prefer nowadays to consult the doctor rather than the clergyman, and what are the causes of their choice.   This was a very direct and concrete question.   At that time I knew nothing more than the fact that my own patients obviously had consulted the doctor rather than the clergyman.   It seemed to me to be open to doubt whether this was generally the case or not.   At any rate, I was unable to give a definite reply.   I therefore set on foot an enquiry, through acquaintances of mine, among people whom I did not know ; I sent out a questionnaire which was answered by Swiss, German, and French Protestants, as well as by a few Catholics.   The results are very interesting, as the following general summary shows.   Those who decided for the doctor represented 57 per cent. of the Protestants and only 25 per cent. of the Catholics, while those who decided for the divine formed 8 per cent. of the Protestants and 58 per cent. of the Catholics.   These were the unequivocal decisions. There were some 35 per cent. of the Protestants who could not make up their minds, while only 17 per cent of the Catholics were undecided.

The reason given for not consulting the minister of the church was generally his lack of psychological knowledge and insight, and this covered 52 per cent. of the answers.

Some 28 per cent. were to the effect that he was prejudiced in his views and showed a dogmatic and traditional bias. Curiously enough, there was even one clergyman who decided for the doctor, while another made the irritated retort : " Theology has nothing to do with the treatment of human beings ". All the relatives of clergymen who answered my questionnaire pronounced themselves against the clergy.

In so far as this enquiry was restricted to educated persons, it is only a straw in the wind. I am convinced that the uneducated classes would have reacted differently. But I am inclined to accept the results as a more or less valid indication of the views of educated people, the more so as it is a well-known fact that their indifference in matters of the Church and religion is steadily growing. And we must not forget that truth of social psychology to which I have already referred : that it takes about twenty years for a general outlook upon life to percolate down from the educated class to the uneducated masses. Who, for instance, would have dared to prophesy twenty years ago, or even ten, that Spain, the most Catholic of European countries, would undergo the unexampled spiritual transformation we are witnessing today ? And yet it has broken out with the violence of a cataclysm.

It seems to me, that, side by side with the decline of religious life, the neuroses grow noticeably more frequent. There are as yet no statistics which enable us to prove this increase in actual numbers. But of one thing I am sure, that everywhere the mental state of European man shows an alarming lack of balance. We are living undeniably in a period of the greatest restlessness, nervous tension, confusion and disorientation of outlook. Among my patients

from many countries, all of them educated persons, there
is a considerable number who came to see me, not because
they were suffering from a neurosis, but because they could
find no meaning in life or were torturing themselves with
questions which neither present-day philosophy nor religion
could answer. Some of them perhaps thought that I knew
of a magic formula, but I was soon forced to tell them that
I, too, had no answer to give. And this brings us to practical
considerations.

Let us take for example that most ordinary and frequent
of questions : What is the meaning of my life, or of life in
general ? Men to-day believe that they know only too well
what the clergyman will say—or, rather, must say—to this.
They smile at the very thought of the philosopher's answer,
and in general do not expect much of the physician. But
from the psychotherapist who analyses the unconscious—
from him one might doubtless learn something. He has
perhaps dug up from the depths of his mind, among other
things, a meaning for life which could be bought for a fee !
It must be a relief to every serious-minded person to hear
that the psychotherapist also does not know what to say.
Such a confession is often the beginning of the patient's
confidence in him.

I have found that modern man has an ineradicable aversion
for traditional opinions and inherited truths. He is a
Bolshevist for whom all the spiritual standards and forms
of the past have lost their validity, and who therefore wants
to experiment in the world of the spirit as the Bolshevist
experiments with economics. When confronted with this
modern attitude, every ecclesiastical system is in a parlous
state, be it Catholic, Protestant, Buddhist or Confucian.
Among these moderns there are of course certain of those

denigrating, destructive and perverse natures—unbalanced eccentrics—who are never satisfied anywhere, and who therefore flock to every new banner, much to the hurt of these movements and undertakings, in the hope of finding something *for once* which will atone at a low cost for their own insufficiency. It goes without saying that, in my professional work, I have come to know a great many modern men and women, and such pathological pseudo-moderns among them. But I prefer to leave these aside. Those of whom I am thinking are by no means sickly eccentrics, but are most often exceptionally able, courageous and upright persons who have repudiated our traditional truths for honest and decent reasons, and not from wicked-ness of heart. Every one of them has the feeling that our religious truths have somehow or other grown empty. Either they cannot reconcile the scientific and the religious outlooks, or Christian tenets have lost their authority and their psychological justification. People no longer feel themselves to have been redeemed by the death of Christ ; they cannot believe—they cannot compel themselves to believe, however happy they may deem the man who has a belief. Sin has for them become something quite relative : what is evil for the one, is good for the other. After all, why should not Buddha be in the right, also ?

There is no one who is not familiar with these questions and doubts. Yet Freudian analysis would brush all these matters aside as irrelevant. It holds the position that the basic problem is that of repressed sexuality, and that philo-sophical or religious doubts only mask the true state of affairs. If we closely examine the individual case, we do actually discover peculiar disturbances in the sexual sphere as well as in the sphere of the unconscious impulses in general.

It is Freud's way to see in these disturbances an explanation of the psychic disturbance as a whole ; he is interested only in the causal interpretation of the sexual symptoms. He completely overlooks the fact that, in certain cases, the supposed causes of the neurosis were always present, but had no pathological effect until a disturbance of the conscious attitude set in and led to a neurotic upset. It is as though, when a ship was sinking because of a leak, the crew only interested itself in the chemical constitution of the water that was pouring in. Disturbances in the sphere of the unconscious drives are not primary, but secondary phenomena. When conscious life has lost its meaning and promise, it is as though a panic had broken loose and we heard the exclamation : " Let us eat and drink, for tomorrow we die ! " It is this mood, born of the meaninglessness of life, that causes the disturbance in the unconscious and provokes the painfully curbed impulses to break out anew. The causes of a neurosis lie in the present as well as in the past ; and only a still existing cause can keep a neurosis active. A man is not tubercular because he was infected twenty years ago with bacilli, but because foci of infection are still active today. The questions when and how the infection took place are even quite irrelevant to his present condition. Even the most accurate knowledge of the previous history of the case cannot cure tuberculosis. And the same holds true of the neuroses.

This is why I regard the religious problems which the patient brings before me as relevant to the neurosis and as possible causes of it. But if I take them seriously, I must admit to the patient that his feelings are justified. " Yes, I agree, Buddha may be right as well as Jesus. Sin is only relative, and it is difficult to see how we can feel ourselves in any way redeemed by the death of Christ." As a doctor

I can easily admit these doubts, while it is hard for the clergyman to do so. The patient feels my attitude to be one of understanding, while the pastor's hesitation strikes him as a traditional prejudice, which estranges them from one another. He asks himself: " What would the pastor say if I began to tell him of the painful details of my sexual disturbances ? " He rightly suspects that the pastor's moral prejudice is even stronger than his dogmatic bias. In this connection there is a good story about the American president, " silent Cal " Coolidge. When he returned after an absence one Sunday morning his wife asked him where he had been. " To church ", he replied. " What did the minister say ? " " He talked about sin." " And what did he say about sin ? " " He was against it."

It might be supposed that it is easy for the doctor to show understanding in this respect. But people forget that even doctors have moral scruples, and that certain patients' confessions are hard even for a doctor to swallow. Yet the patient does not feel himself accepted unless the very worst in him is accepted too. No one can bring this about by mere words ; it comes only through the doctor's sincerity and through his attitude towards himself and his own evil side. If the doctor wants to offer guidance to another, or even to accompany him a step of the way, he must be in touch with this other person's psychic life. He is never in touch when he passes judgement. Whether he puts his judgements into words, or keeps them to himself, makes not the slightest difference. To take the opposite position, and to agree with the patient offhand, is also of no use, but estranges him as much as condemnation. We can get in touch with another person only by an attitude of unprejudiced objectivity. This may sound like a scientific precept, and may be confused with a purely intellectual and detached attitude of mind. But what I mean to convey is something quite different. It is a human quality—a kind of deep respect for facts and events and for the person who suffers from them—a respect for the secret of such a human life. The truly religious person has this attitude. He knows that God has brought all sorts of strange and inconceivable things to pass, and seeks in the most curious ways to enter a man's heart. He therefore senses in everything the unseen presence of the divine will. This is what I mean by " unprejudiced objectivity." It is a moral achievement on the part of the doctor, who ought not to let himself be repelled by illness and corruption. We cannot change anything unless we accept it. Condemnation does not liberate, it oppresses. I am the oppressor of the person I condemn, not his friend and fellow-sufferer. I do not in the least mean to say that we must never pass judgement in the cases of persons whom we desire to help and improve. But if the doctor wishes to help a human being he must be able to accept him as he is. And he can do this in reality only when he has already seen and accepted himself as he is.

Perhaps this sounds very simple, but simple things are always the most difficult. In actual life it requires the greatest discipline to be simple, and the acceptance of oneself is the essence of the moral problem and the epitome of a whole outlook upon life. That I feed the hungry, that I forgive an insult, that I love my enemy in the name of Christ—all these are undoubtedly great virtues. What I do unto the least of my brethren, that I do unto Christ. But what if I should discover that the least amongst them all, the poorest of all the beggars, the most impudent of all the offenders, the very enemy himself—that these are within me, and that I myself stand in need of the alms of my own kindness—that I myself am the enemy who must be loved—what then ? As a rule, the Christian's attitude is then reversed ; there is no longer any question of love or long-suffering ; we say to the brother within us " Raca ", and condemn and rage against ourselves. We hide it from the world ; we refuse to admit ever having met this least among the lowly in ourselves. Had it been God himself who drew near to us in this despicable form, we should have denied him a thousand times before a single cock had crowed.

The man who uses modern psychology to look behind the scenes not only of his patients' lives but more especially of his own—and the modern psychotherapist must do this if he is not to be merely an unconscious fraud—will admit that to accept himself in all his wretchedness is the hardest of tasks, and one which it is almost impossible to fulfil. The very thought can make us livid with fear. We therefore do not hesitate, but lightheartedly choose the complicated course of remaining in ignorance about ourselves while busying ourselves with other people and their troubles and sins. This activity lends us an air of virtue, and we thus deceive ourselves and those around us. In this way, thank God, we can escape from ourselves. There are countless people who can do this with impunity, but not everyone can, and these few break down on the road to Damascus and succumb to a neurosis. How can I help these persons if I am myself a fugitive, and perhaps also suffer from the *morbus sacer* of a neurosis ? Only he who has fully accepted himself has " unprejudiced objectivity ". But no one is justified in boasting that he has fully accepted himself. We can point to Christ, who offered his traditional bias as a sacrifice to the god in himself, and so lived his life as it was to the bitter end without regard for conventions or for the moral standards of the Pharisees.

We Protestants must sooner or later face this question : Are we to understand the " imitation of Christ " in the sense that we should copy his life and, if I may use the expression, ape his stigmata ; or in the deeper sense that we are to live our own proper lives as truly as he lived his in all its implications ? It is no easy matter to live a life that is modelled on Christ's, but it is unspeakably harder to live one's own life as truly as Christ lived his. Anyone who did this would run counter to the forces of the past, and though he might thus be fulfilling his destiny, would none the less be misjudged, derided, tortured and crucified. He would be a kind of mad Bolshevist who deserved the cross. We therefore prefer the historically sanctioned imitation of Christ which is transfigured by holiness. I should never disturb a monk in his practice of identifying himself with Christ, for he deserves our respect. But neither I nor my patients are monks, and it is my duty as a physician to show my patients how they can live their lives without becoming neurotic. Neurosis is an inner cleavage—the state of being at war with oneself. Everything that accentuates this cleavage makes the patient worse, and everything that mitigates it tends to heal the patient. What drives people to war with themselves is the intuition or the knowledge that they consist of two persons in opposition to one another. The conflict may be between the sensual and the spiritual man, or between the ego and the shadow. It is what Faust means when he says : " Two souls, alas, dwell in my breast apart ". A neurosis is a dissociation of personality.

Healing may be called a religious problem. In the sphere of social or national relations, the state of suffering may be

civil war, and this state is to be cured by the Christian virtue
of forgiveness for those who hate us. That which we try
with the conviction of good Christians to apply to external
situations, we must also apply to the inner state in the
treatment of neurosis. This is why modern man has heard
enough about guilt and sin. He is sorely enough beset by
his own bad conscience, and wants rather to learn how he
is to reconcile himself with his own nature—how he is to
love the enemy in his own heart and call the wolf his
brother.

The modern man, moreover, is not eager to know in what
way he can imitate Christ, but in what way he can live his
own individual life, however meagre and uninteresting it
may be. It is because every form of imitation seems to him
deadening and sterile that he rebels against the force of
tradition that would hold him to well-trodden ways. All
such roads, for him, lead in the wrong direction. He may
not know it, but he behaves as if his own individual life were
instinct with the will of God which must at all costs be
fulfilled. This is the source of his egoism, which is one of
the most tangible evils of the neurotic state. But the person
who tells him he is too egoistic has lost his confidence, and
rightly so, for that person has driven him still further into
his neurosis.

If I wish to effect a cure for my patients I am forced to
acknowledge the deep significance of their egoism. I should
be blind, indeed, if I did not recognize in it the true will of
God. I must even help the patient to prevail in his egoism ;
if he succeeds in this, he estranges himself from other people.
He drives them away, and they come to themselves—as
they should, for they were seeking to rob him of his " sacred "
egoism. This must be left to him, for it is his strongest and

healthiest power ; it is, as I have said, a true will of God, which sometimes drives him into complete isolation. However wretched this state may be, it also stands him in good stead, for in this way alone can he take his own measure and learn what an invaluable treasure is the love of his fellow-beings. It is, moreover, only in the state of complete abandonment and loneliness that we experience the helpful powers of our own natures.

When one has several times seen this development take place one can no longer deny that what was evil has turned to good, and that what seemed good has kept alive the forces of evil. The archdemon of egoism leads us along the royal road to that ingathering which religious experience demands. What we observe here is a fundamental law of life—*enantiodromia*—the reversal into the opposite ; and this it is that makes possible the reunion of the warring halves of the personality and thereby brings the civil war to an end.

I have taken the neurotic's egoism as an example because it is one of his most common symptoms. I might equally well have taken any other characteristic symptom to show what attitude the physician must adopt towards the shortcomings of his patients, and how he must deal with the problem of evil.

No doubt this also sounds very simple. In reality, however, the acceptance of the shadow-side of human nature verges on the impossible. Consider for a moment what it means to grant the right of existence to what is unreasonable, senseless and evil ! Yet it is just this that the modern man insists upon. He wants to live with every side of himself—to know what he is. That is why he casts history aside. He wants to break with tradition so that he can experiment with his life and determine what value and meaning things have in themselves, apart from traditional presuppositions. Modern youth gives us astonishing examples of this attitude. To show how far this tendency may go, I will instance a question addressed to me by a German society. I was asked if incest is to be reprobated, and what facts can be adduced against it !

Granted such tendencies, the conflicts into which people may fall are not hard to imagine. I can well understand that one would like to leave nothing untried to protect one's fellow-beings from such adventures. But curiously enough we find ourselves without means to do this. All the old arguments against unreasonableness, self-deception and immorality, once so potent, have lost their effectiveness. We are now reaping the fruit of nineteenth-century education. Throughout that period the Church preached to young people the merit of blind faith, while the universities inculcated an intellectual rationalism, with the result that today we plead in vain whether for faith or reason. Tired of this warfare of opinions, the modern man wishes to find out for himself how things are. And though this desire opens bar and bolt to the most dangerous possibilities, we cannot help seeing it as a courageous enterprise and giving it some measure of sympathy. It is no reckless adventure, but an effort inspired by deep spiritual distress to bring meaning once more into life on the basis of fresh and unprejudiced experience. Caution has its place, no doubt, but we cannot refuse our support to a serious venture which calls the whole of the personality into the field of action. If we oppose it, we are trying to suppress what is best in man—his daring and his aspiration. And should we succeed, we should only have stood in the way of that invaluable experience which might have given a meaning to life. What would have happened if Paul had allowed himself to be talked out of his journey to Damascus ?

The psychotherapist who takes his work seriously must come to grips with this question. He must decide in every single case whether or not he is willing to stand by a human being with counsel and help upon what may be a daring misadventure. He must have no fixed ideas as to what is right, nor must he pretend to know what is right and what not—otherwise he takes something from the richness of the experience. He must keep in view what actually happens —and only that which acts, is actual. If something which seems to me an error shows itself to be more effective than a truth, then I must first follow up the error, for in it lie power and life which I lose if I hold to what seems to me true. Light has need of darkness—otherwise how could it appear as light ?

It is well known that Freudian psychoanalysis is limited to the task of making conscious the shadow-side and the evil within us. It simply brings into action the civil war that was latent, and lets it go at that. The patient must deal with it as best he can. Freud has unfortunately over-looked the fact that man has never yet been able single-handed to hold his own against the powers of darkness— that is, of the unconscious. Man has always stood in need of the spiritual help which each individual's own religion held out to him. The opening up of the unconscious always means the outbreak of intense spiritual suffering ; it is as when a flourishing civilization is abandoned to invading hordes of barbarians, or when fertile fields are exposed by the bursting of a dam to a raging torrent. The World War was such an irruption which showed, as nothing else could, how thin are the walls which separate a well-ordered world from lurking chaos. But it is the same with every single human being and his reasonably ordered world. His reason has done violence to natural forces which seek their revenge and only await the moment when the partition falls to overwhelm the conscious life with destruction. Man has been aware of this danger since the earliest times, even in the most primitive stages of culture. It was to arm himself against this threat and to heal the damage done, that he developed religious and magical practices. This is why the medicine-man is also the priest; he is the saviour of the body as well as of the soul, and religions are systems of healing for psychic illness. This is especially true of the two greatest religions of man, Christianity and Buddhism. Man is never helped in his suffering by what he thinks for himself, but only by revelations of a wisdom greater than his own. It is this which lifts him out of his distress.

Today this eruption of destructive forces has already taken place, and man suffers from it in spirit. That is why patients force the psychotherapist into the rôle of a priest, and expect and demand of him that he shall free them from their distress. That is why we psychotherapists must occupy ourselves with problems which, strictly speaking, belong to the theologian. But we cannot leave these questions for theology to answer; the urgent, psychic needs of suffering people confront us with them day after day. Since, as a rule, every concept and viewpoint handed down from the past fails us, we must first tread with the patient the path of his illness—the path of his mistake that sharpens his conflicts and increases his loneliness till it grows unbearable—hoping that from the psychic depths which cast up the powers of destruction the rescuing forces will come also.

When first I took this direction I did not know where it

would lead. I did not know what lay hid in the depths of the psyche—that region which I have since called the " collective unconscious ", and whose contents I designate as " archetypes ". Since time immemorial, eruptions of the unconscious have taken place, and ever and again they have repeated themselves. Consciousness did not exist from the beginning, and in every child it has to be built up anew in the first years of life. Consciousness is very weak in this formative period, and history shows us that the same is true of mankind—the unconscious easily seizes power. These struggles have left their marks. To put it in scientific terms : instinctive defence-mechanisms have been developed which automatically intervene when the danger is greatest, and their coming into action is represented in fantasy by helpful images which are ineradicably fixed in the human psyche. These mechanisms come into play whenever the need is great. Science can only establish the existence of these psychic factors and attempt a rational explanation by offering an hypothesis as to their sources. This, however, only thrusts the problem a stage back and in no way answers the riddle. We thus come to those ultimate questions : Whence does consciousness come ? What is the psyche ? And at this point all science ends.

It is as though, at the culmination of the illness, the destructive powers were converted into healing forces. This is brought about by the fact that the archetypes come to independent life and serve as spiritual guides for the personality, thus supplanting the inadequate ego with its futile willing and striving. As the religious-minded person would say : guidance has come from God. With most of my patients I have to avoid this formulation, for it reminds them too much of what they have to reject. I must express myself in more modest terms, and say that the psyche has awakened to spontaneous life. And indeed this formula more closely fits the observable facts. The transformation takes place at that moment when in dreams or fantasies themes appear whose source in consciousness cannot be shown. To the patient it is nothing less than a revelation when, from the hidden depths of the psyche, something arises to confront him—something strange that is not the " I " and is therefore beyond the reach of personal caprice. He has gained access to the sources of psychic life, and this marks the beginning of the cure.

This process, if it is to be made clear, should undoubtedly be discussed with the help of suitable examples. But it is almost impossible to find one or more convincing illustrations, for it is usually a most subtle and complicated matter. That which is so effective is often simply the deep impression made on the patient by the independent way in which his dreams treat of his difficulties. Or it may be that his fantasy points to something for which his conscious mind was quite unprepared. Most often it is contents of an archetypal nature, connected in a certain way, that exert a strong influence of their own whether or not they are understood by the conscious mind. This spontaneous activity of the psyche often becomes so intense that visionary pictures are seen or inner voices heard. These are manifestations of the spirit directly experienced today as they have been from time immemorial.

Such experiences reward the sufferer for the pains of the labyrinthine way. From this point forward a light shines through his confusion ; he can reconcile himself with the warfare within and so come to bridge the morbid split in his nature upon a higher level.

The fundamental problems of modern psychotherapy are so important and far-reaching that their discussion in an essay precludes any presentation of details, however desirable this might be for clarity's sake. My main purpose was to set forth the attitude of the psychotherapist in his work. A proper understanding of this is after all more rewarding than to cull a few precepts and pointers as to methods of treatment, for these are in any case not effective unless they are applied with the right understanding. The attitude of the psychotherapist is infinitely more important than the theories and methods of psychotherapy, and that is why I have been concerned to make this attitude known. I believe that I have given a trustworthy account. As for the questions in what way and how far the clergyman can join the psychotherapist in his efforts and endeavours, I can only impart information which will allow others to decide. I also believe that the picture I have drawn of the spiritual outlook of modern man corresponds to the actual state of affairs—though, of course, I make no claim to infallibility. In any case, what I have had to say about the cure of the neuroses, and the problems involved, is the unvarnished truth. We doctors would naturally welcome the sympathetic understanding of the clergy in our endeavours to heal psychic suffering, but we are also fully aware of the fundamental difficulties which stand in the way of a full cooperation. My own position is on the extreme left wing of the congress of Protestant opinion, yet I would be the first to warn people against generalizing from their own experience in an injudicious way. As a Swiss, I am an inveterate democrat, yet I recognize that nature is aristocratic and, what is even more, esoteric. *Quod licet Jovi, non licet bovi* is an unpleasant but an eternal truth. Who are forgiven their many sins ? Those who have loved much. But as to those who love little, their few sins are held against them. I am firmly convinced that a vast number of people belong to the fold of the Catholic Church and nowhere else, because they are most suitably housed there. I am as much persuaded of this as of the fact, which I have myself observed, that a primitive religion is better suited to primitive people than Christianity, which is so incomprehensible to them and so foreign to their blood that they can only ape it in a disgusting way. I believe, too, that there must be protestants against the Catholic Church, and also protestants against Protestantism—for the manifestations of the spirit are truly wondrous, and as varied as Creation itself.

The living spirit grows and even outgrows its earlier forms of expression ; it freely chooses the men in whom it lives and who proclaim it. This living spirit is eternally renewed and pursues its goal in manifold and inconceivable ways throughout the history of mankind. Measured against it, the names and forms which men have given it mean little enough ; they are only the changing leaves and blossoms on the stem of the eternal tree.

THE END